C000125085

MISSION TO CHINA

MISSION TO CHINA

HOW AN ENGLISHMAN BROUGHT THE WEST TO THE ORIENT

JOHN HOLLIDAY

AMBERLEY

This book is dedicated to the descendants of Walter and Betty Medhurst

First published 2016

Amberley Publishing
The Hill, Stroud
Gloucestershire, GL5 4EP

www.amberley-books.com

Copyright © John Holliday, 2016

The right of John Holliday to be identified as the Author of this work has been asserted in accordance with the Copyrights, Designs and Patents Act 1988.

ISBN 978 1 4456 6134 6 (hardback)
ISBN 978 1 4456 6135 3 (ebook)

British Library Cataloguing in Publication Data. A catalogue record for this book is available from the British Library.

Typesetting and Origination by Amberley Publishing.
Printed in the UK.

CONTENTS

FOREWORD

'When China wakes up, the world will shake,' Napoleon prophesied. Two hundred years later the world is coming to terms with China's growing economic and military dominance, and is only just starting to recognize its diplomatic and cultural influence.

In the front rank of those who wakened the Sleeping Giant was Walter Medhurst. By the time he left China in 1856 he had spent twenty-six years among the Chinese Diaspora of South-East Asia and, following the Treaty of Nanking, another fourteen years among the mainland Chinese. In so doing he became the Grand Old Man of the early foreign community in Shanghai, not just because of his achievements in publishing but because of his influence on that whole generation of British and American Protestant missionaries who introduced modern education, medicine and social reform to China. Their energy reflected the vitality and confidence of the English-speaking world of the time. In 1800 Britain had a population of ten million and the USA five million. By contrast, there were three hundred million Chinese. This tiny handful of first-generation British and American missionaries had an amazing impact in terms of fighting the opium trade their fellow countryman had inflicted on the Chinese. The publication of the Bible in Chinese and its revolutionary message of selfless love and the dignity and equality of all people, and the introduction of Western medicine and education, in particular education for females, also had a huge impact. Any honest assessment also needs to include the Taiping Rebellion as an unforeseen consequence, yet this epochal upheaval also played a part in the making of modern China.

Medhurst's effect on those remarkable men and women pioneers of Protestant Christianity in China was through strength of character, blending vision, faith, perseverance, scholarship, courage and humility. Here it must be said that one cannot imagine Walter's longevity and influence on China and its people without the partnership of his remarkable wife, Betty, who more than matched her husband in strength of character.

Walter Medhurst had become a personal hero and inspiration when I was vicar of the church in Jakarta that he had built and pastored for twenty years. The more I learned about him the more his faith and vision encouraged me in ministering to the expatriate community through the tumultuous years of Suharto's overthrow and the subsequent security crises. As I researched the origins of All Saints Jakarta and the Parapattan Orphanage, I was surprised and dismayed that this remarkable man had no biographer. Therefore I was excited when, on my return to Australia, John Holliday contacted me and told me of his project. But I am even more enthusiastic now that I have read the completed work.

John Holliday has done a great service by writing this excellent biography of his great-great-grandparents. Biographies of missionaries range from hagiographic tributes by fawning descendants to dubious psychosexual exposés by sneering iconoclasts. John Holliday has risen above this. The reader will relish the memorable scenes of Medhurst's life, ranging from carefree boyhood coach rides through the Cotswolds to the tense months of living under siege in Shanghai. Best of all the author lets his subject's actions speak for themselves. The chapters on his two epic journeys, distributing literature to the coastal ports in the *Huron* and reconnoitring the interior incognito, are graphic and unique portrayals of China at the dawn of its modernisation. Chapter 17, the account of Medhurst's bold but wise dealings with mandarins and their minions during the *Huron* expedition, just on its own makes this book worth reading. For the casual reader this chapter is entertaining, but for anyone seeking to understand the mind of Chinese officialdom it is salutary.

Of all the features of modern China no doubt what would most warm Walter's and Betty's hearts is the phenomenal growth of Christianity to the extent that on any Sunday there are now more worshippers in China than in all of Europe. It would vindicate the enormous sacrifices they made for the love of God and for the love of the Chinese people.

Revd Dr Andrew Lake
One-time vicar of All Saints church, Jakarta (1996–2004)

ACKNOWLEDGEMENTS

Firstly, I am grateful to my editor at Amberley, Aaron Meek, for his support and cheerful patience in helping a first-time author bring this book to fruition.

For help in providing me with introductions to sources in Jakarta and in admiration of their work as modern-day missionaries, I am very grateful to Thomas and Katrina Bergstrom of Family Care Indonesia. They introduced me to the directors and managers of the Parapattan Orphanage, who were most accommodating and helpful in providing me with historical information about the orphanage. Through Thomas I was able to meet the Vicar of All Saints Jakarta and make contact with Andrew Lake who wrote the history of All Saints. In turn, Andrew was extremely helpful to me in researching the early days of the mission in Batavia. I am also grateful for the assistance of John and Kalyani Selvaraj of the Church of South India, who hosted me at the former Madras Mission in Chennai and gave me a window into Betty's early life.

A large part of my research can be attributed to the archives and special collections of the SOAS Library. During the period of my research the staff members changed a few times, so lacking any specific names, let me say I am grateful to them all. Another descendent of the Medhursts, Andrew Hillier, was most helpful in supplying material from the Hillier family archives and his support and assistance was very much appreciated.

During the course of my research of the book I corresponded with a number of academics and other authors who were helpful in their comments. I am grateful to Daniel Bays, David Jupp, Hugh Mead, Emily Manktelow, Jane Kate Leonard, Paul Cohen, Robert Bickers, Scott Merrillees, Tom Oey and Ian Welch. I would also like to acknowledge the support and tolerance of my wife and family, who had to put up with several years of hearing me speak about long-deceased relatives.

The author and publisher would like to thank the following people/organisations for permission to use copyright and other material from their collections in this book:

1. Museum of London. Image of the Post Office, St Paul's Cathedral and Bull & Mouth Inn, London.
2. SOAS Archives and Special Collections. Correspondence, minutes, diaries, reports and illustrations collected by the London Missionary Society.
3. National Portrait Gallery. Image of Robert Morrison DD by Robert Wildman, engraved 1824.
4. Scott Merrillees, author of *Batavia in the Nineteenth Century: Photographs of Batavia*. Photographer: Woodbury & Page.
5. Victoria and Albert Museum. Image of Hackney in 1840.
6. Andrew Hillier. Correspondence from the Hillier family archives.
7. Gloucestershire Archives. Correspondence of Walter Medhurst.
8. David Jupp. Research papers re: the origins of the Chinese name for Australia.
9. The Kelton Foundation. Edward Duncan engraving after William J. Huggins of Pulo Penang (Prince of Wales Island), Malacca Straits. c. 1838

I

CHINA

It was 8 October 1835, and the American brig *Huron*, under the command of Captain Thomas Winsor, edged its way between the sandbanks along the Yangtze River towards Wusong, the gateway to Shanghai. The ship's situation was critical: the land was obscured by the swirling fog and in such shallow water they were in great danger of grounding at any moment. Sweeping along towards the sea, the Yangtze carried vast quantities of silt, which formed mud banks, rendering navigation dangerous and difficult. The channel between the banks was less than a mile wide and the depth on each side restricted to one or two fathoms. Had it not been for the vigilance of Captain Winsor and his crew they would most likely have gone aground and been at the mercy of the weather.

The gloomy weather obscured the vessel until it reached the mouth of the Huangpu River where the Chinese who were manning the forts spotted the ship. The *Huron*'s crew ducked for cover when the Chinese fired from either side of the river. The captain called out, 'Don't worry lads, they'll do us no harm.' He had recognised the report of the cannon as blank cartridges no louder than most muskets, most likely due to the use of badly mixed powder. The forts themselves were in a bad state of repair, and some of the walls had fallen in, an indication of the weakening economic state of the Qing dynasty. Rather than serving as a warning, the sound of the guns merely heralded the arrival of foreign devils in the forbidden empire.

A tall, slim man dressed in a long, black coat, light trousers and black boots stood with top hat in hand on the poop deck, staring into the mist, willing it to part and give him a glimpse of the land he had waited nineteen years to see. At age thirty-nine, with slightly receding light-brown hair and curly side-whiskers, Walter Medhurst looked a fit man in spite of having spent all those years living in the tropics. The way he stood with fixed stare hinted at his determination to influence, and be influenced by, the country that lay before him. The cannon fire from the forts did not augur well for any kind of welcome from the Chinese, but Walter was confident that this was only a reflection of the edicts issued by the imperial rulers in Peking and that ordinary people would welcome his peaceful visit. The next few days would show how correct his opinion was.

The London Missionary Society (LMS) had chartered the *Huron* for the Revd Walter Henry Medhurst and his American colleague, Edwin Stevens, to undertake a voyage up the east coast of China to distribute books and scriptures as part of their mission to spread the word of God. They had set sail from Canton, the only place in China where foreigners were permitted. They sailed on 26 August after experiencing great difficulty in securing a vessel suitable for their purposes. Few trading vessels travelled along the coast of China and most were involved in carrying opium, the illicit trade to which the missionaries strongly objected. This was just before the First Opium War between Britain and China, which itself resulted from the trafficking of opium by the East India Company from India to China. The missionaries were very keen to be seen by the Chinese as strongly opposed to the trade.

A month had passed with no success when a 210-ton brig, the *Huron,* arrived in Canton. The house of Oliphant and Co. had chartered it for $600 dollars monthly. A cargo not being ready, the charterers generously offered the use of the brig for several months for a voyage up the coast if the missionaries could reach an agreement with the captain for his trouble and for the additional cost of the expedition. A cautious character unfamiliar with China, Captain Winsor was reluctant to undertake the voyage. The coast had not been surveyed and navigation was dangerous. He also complained that his brig was too lightly manned and deficient in the necessary equipment for a coastal voyage, and that his copper was very much out of repair. If the missionaries insisted on the proposed expedition, they must ship six extra hands, provide another anchor, secure their own provisions, and pay him, in addition to the sum specified, $400 monthly for the additional wear and tear on the vessel and for the extra trouble and care necessary in navigating an unknown coast. With insurance, the total would be $600 monthly.

It was not easy to convince the captain to undertake the journey, even after the terms had been settled. Walter arranged a meeting between the captain and Mr Charles Gutzlaff who, as translator to Mr Hugh Lindsay of the East India Company, had made a similar trip some two years previously. He indicated the expedition could easily be made. Gutzlaff produced a copy of Hugh Lindsay's journals from that earlier trip and showed the captain copies of the old Dutch and French charts, and the maps and sketches made long before by Portuguese missionaries. Finally, a bargain was struck, stores were laid in, new hands were hired, and the travellers prepared to embark on the voyage – very much a journey into the unknown.

By the beginning of October they had travelled north to reach Shandong province and on their return wished to visit Shanghai, one of the largest commercial centres in China. Medhurst had nineteen years' experience as a missionary in Malacca, Penang and Batavia (now known as Jakarta), understood written Chinese, and was proficient in the colloquial use of more than one of its dialects. Recently arrived from America, Stevens was a younger missionary. Unlike Medhurst, he did not speak Chinese. Few foreign visitors had made this journey before them, mainly because ferocious Chinese laws forbade all trade with the West outside of a small area of Canton. Moreover, it was a crime punishable by death for a Chinese person to teach a European to speak Chinese.

The accuracy of Lindsay's journal proved invaluable in manoeuvring the ship to an anchorage upriver from Wusong, off which there were around 100 junks lying at anchor.

That evening, a junk anchored close by the *Huron* to watch what the visitors were up to. Captain Winsor ordered his men to keep a close watch on the vessel throughout the night. Over dinner, Walter reaffirmed the fundamental principle of the LMS, which was to bring the millions of China under the influence of Christianity, without promoting any single denomination over another. 'Tomorrow may be one of the greatest steps forward in our endeavour,' he said. 'Let us pray for God's blessing that our feeble attempt will be instrumental in awakening an interest on behalf of China and in promoting the spread of the Gospel in this populous and interesting empire.'

Early the next morning, the longboat was launched and four sailors were assigned to take the missionaries into Shanghai. The day was stormy and there was concern about undertaking such a long journey in dark and rainy weather. Medhurst was adamant that they should proceed as soon as possible; he wanted them to reach the city before any opposition could be organised against them.

The vicinity of Shanghai was marked by a forest of more than 1,000 junks that lay off the city. As visibility was poor, the approach of the longboat was not observed until it passed among the junks. Suddenly, an outcry erupted. A foreign boat had arrived and immediately every door and window was crowded and the sides of the junks were lined with spectators. All the onlookers were smiling and none was alarmed or displeased at their sudden appearance.

Medhurst observed the Tianhou temple, the temple of the Queen of Heaven, as described in Lindsay's journal, and he directed the sailors to land close by. Having never seen foreigners, the people pressed forward to get a good look at these strange visitors.

As the two missionaries were collecting their bag of books to commence distributing them, they heard a clattering noise on the granite pavement, which was produced by the thumping of long bamboos. They saw the people give way, right and left, to two officers, who greeted them in a friendly manner and invited them to the nearby temple. Happy to comply, Medhurst ordered a sailor to follow them with a bag of books and they made their way through the immense crowd towards the temple. The officers opened a path before them with their bamboo sticks, crying out, 'The visitors are come!'

In the temple, the visitors were invited to sit down opposite the two officers, one of whom was Wang-Laou-yay, a lieutenant colonel in the army. After a short conversation, cakes and tea were served and the missionaries presented their books to the mandarins and their attendants. With the rain continuing to fall, the officer requested the missionaries to delay giving out the books to the people until the weather cleared up. Perceiving that the officers' intention was to hinder their work and put it off indefinitely, Medhurst thought it best to divide their forces: while he continued to engage the officers in conversation, Stevens would return to the boat and distribute the books.

Back at the boat, Stevens dealt out the contents of the first box of booklets to a dense crowd of eager and anxious applicants. Police runners followed and endeavoured to restrain the crowd with their staves. Some of the runners were overcome and thrown to the ground. Stevens stood in the boat and attempted to hand out the books one at a time, but it soon became apparent that he could not meet the demands of the crowd, so he resorted to throwing the books over the heads of the people and letting them fall into outstretched arms. In no time at all, hundreds of volumes had been distributed among the people of Shanghai, in spite of the police who, with upraised hands, implored him to stop.

In the meantime, Walter Medhurst was engaged in a conference with the mandarins, an account of which described an unproductive conversation with a mandarin from the custom house department who tried to make light of Walter's offer to administer medicine to those in need of it.

This unproductive conversation with Chin ended when officers came in and announced the arrival of the chief magistrate of Shanghai, who requested to meet the visitor. He was seated in the central hall of the temple attended by a group of officers. As Medhurst approached, he paid the magistrate the usual compliments. Seeing a chair placed opposite, which seemed intended for him, he took a seat accordingly. The magistrate expressed indignation at seeing a barbarian seated before him and the officers around called out, 'Rise! Rise!' Medhurst rose as requested and asked why he could not be seated at the conference, and when told that he could not, he bowed and left the room.

Chin and Wang soon followed Medhurst and tried to persuade him to return to the meeting with the magistrate. Medhurst's response was that while subjects of the empire should be expected to comply with government regulations, a stranger and a guest should be treated with respect. 'I come as a friendly stranger and I am invited by you to a public conference. I have committed no offence, nor broken any laws and therefore will not stand as a culprit before any mandarin in the empire,' he said. 'But,' Wang stammered, 'our chief magistrate is the greatest Chinese in Shanghai.' 'Well then,' Medhurst replied, 'the individual who now addresses you is the greatest Englishman in Shanghai and I do not choose to compromise the honour of my country by submitting to be treated as a barbarian or offender. I have no favour to ask of the magistrate and if he does not wish to see me in the proper manner, then he need not see me at all.'

Finding that he would not be persuaded, the officers left to inform the magistrate of their discussions, but they soon returned saying that the chief magistrate was resolved not to swerve in a single instance from the regulations of the celestial empire. He further indicated that they were at liberty to return to their vessel. Medhurst replied that it was his intention to return when the wind and tide were favourable, but as they came in a friendly and not a hostile manner, they were not to be driven away as an enemy or an evildoer.

The position taken by Walter Medhurst may at first seem single-minded and uncooperative. He was not taking that position without a great deal of consideration about the best way to achieve his goals in the long term. His experience of negotiating with the Chinese went back over nineteen years and had taught him to be wary of acceding too readily to their demands. Every subsequent negotiation with that person or others of his nation would hinge on the first reception.

At the conclusion of this exchange of positions, Medhurst was joined by Edwin Stevens and they conversed informally with, and delivered books to, the officers and their attendants, as well as to some strangers present, until all the books were gone. The officers had already been given a list of fresh provisions needed on the ship, the intention being that the supplies would be paid for. When the articles were brought in, Wang offered them as a gift. Seeing as there was no other way to settle the question, they accepted the articles and resolved to send the Chinese some consideration in return.

As the rain had eased, they returned to the boat where the sailors were busy eating their dinner while thousands eagerly stretched forward to 'see the lions fed'. One man who had pressed through the crowd began rubbing his eyes and then took a second look, to be certain it was not a dream.

On the foreshore, close to the boat, the missionaries observed a basket nearly full of straw on top of which were around a half dozen books that were torn in pieces and about to be burnt. Medhurst immediately recollected having heard Chin giving directions to his servants to keep one or two of the books and to do something with the rest, which he failed to understand fully at the time. It now occurred to him that Chin had directed them to be burnt in the presence of the foreigners to antagonise and degrade them in the eyes of the people. As the torch was applied to the basket, Medhurst took the Chinese provisions lying nearby and placed them on the fire, to show them that if the Chinese despised the presents of the books, then he also disregarded theirs. Finally, the basket of burnt books was thrown into the river and the visitors departed, much displeased with the conduct of the mandarins. The destroyed books were only the few that had fallen into the hands of the mandarins; a thousand other volumes had been distributed among the people, which the authorities could neither discover nor destroy.

Their return to the *Huron* was difficult. With the wind against them, they wasted an hour tacking back and forth across the river without losing sight of the town. When night came on and the rain started again, all the passengers were extremely uncomfortable. Medhurst called out to the masters of several junks requesting shelter, but the Chinese were so alarmed by the sudden appearance of barbarians that their requests were in vain.

Through perseverance, they eventually arrived at the vessel at around 9 o'clock at night, wet, cold and tired. They were thankful to have arrived safely and pleased to have distributed over 1,000 volumes among nearly a million people.

2

ROSS-ON-WYE

The 'King of Good Neighbours' is how the St Mary's parish magazine referred to John Kyrle, the Man of Ross, in an issue published during the nineteenth century. You could not live in Ross-on-Wye at that time without appreciating the contribution this man had made to the town, from the Prospect public gardens, to the Ross church bell, to the walks he had laid out with shady trees and comfortable seats that would attract tourists to the banks of the Wye for 200 years after his death. John Kyrle's title and charitable works were immortalised by Alexander Pope, with which the children of Ross were quite familiar.

John Kyrle lived for most of his life in the timber-framed Jacobean house overlooking the Ross Market Hall, which after his death became the Kings Arms Hotel. In 1794, while staying as a guest at the Kings Arms, Samuel Coleridge was inspired to write another verse about the Man of Ross, part of which follows:

> Richer than Miser o'er his countless hoards,
> Nobler than Kings, or king-polluted Lords,
> Here dwelt the Man of Ross! O Traveller, hear!

Nine years after Coleridge penned those words, a young London family arrived at the Kings Arms to make Ross-on-Wye their new home. William Medhurst had been appointed landlord of the Kings Arms Inn with the objective of merging the business into the larger Swan Inn to create the town's largest coaching inn. Together with his wife Sarah, their sons William and Walter and their daughters Martha, Mary and Clara, they arrived in the town on a crisp winter's morning after almost thirty hours of travel by stagecoach. Five children erupted from the coach and ran up and down the High Street before disappearing into the inn to explore their new home. William embraced Sarah and she nestled into him as they looked approvingly at the scene.

Ross-on-Wye was a pretty town in comparison to the London they had just left. Situated in gently undulating landscapes along the banks of the River Wye, surrounded by woodlands and rolling hills, it was a prosperous community. The rich Herefordshire soil supported a vigorous farming industry, and the county was famous for its wheat, oats, barley and wool. The waterways that flowed over the surrounding hills provided the power for the woollen, milling, tanning, rope making, papermaking and brewing industries. The nearby Forest of Dean provided plentiful timber, with much of the produce being sold at auction in the town.

In 1804, the year after they arrived in Ross-on-Wye, this announcement appeared in the *Hereford Journal* and the Medhursts moved up the road to the Swan:

Swan and King's Arms Inns United
MEDHURST
Medhurst most respectfully informs the Nobility, Gentry, Gentlemen, Travellers and the Public in general, that in consequence of arrangements concluded between the Proprietors of the above Houses, The King's Arms Inn is now shut up and will not, in future, be occupied as an Inn. The business of both houses will therefore be carried on at The Swan Inn...[1]

England at this time was at the height of the coaching era. Travel by the middle classes was becoming more commonplace, with the railways yet to come. Stagecoaches depended on a chain of coaching inns where horses and drivers could be changed as necessary. The inns and the coaches were often under the same ownership, forming an important vested interest, and it was with a group like this that William Medhurst had established his position. The main coaching inns of each town were equivalent to the railway stations and airports of the twenty-first century, full of the hustle and bustle of travellers.

After merging with the Kings Arms, the Swan Inn became the biggest coaching inn in Ross-on-Wye, serving the town with daily coach services from Hereford and South Wales to London. The Swan was a busy place with a staff of hostlers (stablemen), yard boys, waiters, cooks, and chambermaids, supported by all the trades required to keep the coaches running, including wheelwrights, carpenters, farriers, saddlers, and harness makers. In their living quarters, the Medhursts employed a housekeeper and a housemaid who assisted Sarah Medhurst with the children.

Winter came early that year to Herefordshire, a bleak wind blowing down from the Brecon Beacons as a chilling warning of the frigid months to come. One by one, the children became sick and Sarah Medhurst confined them to bed. After a few days, they each broke out in a red spotty rash and it was apparent they had the measles. Most children recover from measles after around a week and this was the case with Walter, Mary and Clara. For Martha, however, the illness turned to pneumonia and the fever got worse. On 10 December 1804, she died. Although childhood diseases often turned fatal, it was a tragedy for the close-knit family and it was only their ability to support one another that provided comfort as they laid Martha to rest in St Mary's churchyard.

For the next three years, it was a delightful place for Walter to grow up. The Swan was situated at the high end of the town, just five minutes' walk from Walter's school alongside the churchyard. In the other direction, he could be down on the riverbank in the same time. Walter and his dog Nelson would go to the river, he to catch fish and Nelson to chase birds. With 2,500 inhabitants, the town was small enough that almost all the tradespeople knew Walter; all the shops were within easy reach of the Swan.

The summer of 1807 was a busy time at the Swan. Among the guests were the poet Robert Bloomfield and his friends who were touring the River Wye.[2] After this visit, Bloomfield would later publish *The Banks of Wye*, his journal of the walking tour in the footsteps of Wordsworth.

Walter's older brother William was home for the summer holidays and Walter would return with him to London to start at St Paul's at the end of July. The boys would leave Ross-on-Wye on the new post coach, the Royal Nelson, which came through Ross from Hereford. It left Ross at 7.30 a.m. every Monday, Wednesday and Friday and arrived in London at the Bull & Mouth Inn on St Martin's le Grand around twenty-four hours later. Passengers had the choice of inside or outside seats on the coach. However, because inside seats cost £1 10*s* – double those outside – Walter and William would sit on top of the coach, behind the driver. That would have been the first choice of any boy their age in any case, and since it was July and the weather was fine, what better seat could they have for such a great adventure?

Walter rose early on Friday 24 July 1807, the morning of his departure, taking Nelson out for a quick run down to the Prospect. Walter soaked up the familiar sights of his childhood to remember every detail while he was away. He looked down on to the River Wye where he had fished and, in summer, swum in the cool, clear water. He returned to the High Street and looked down towards Market Place, where he sometimes bought boiled sweets or roasted chestnuts. A couple of locals called out to him and wished him good luck. His pace slowed as he walked back home with Nelson by his side. Ross-on-Wye had been his whole world.

The activity back at the inn quickly returned his mood to excitement as his mother and Mrs Padstow, the housekeeper, fussed over what he should take and what he should look out for on the journey. Sarah held Walter at arm's length, taking a good look at him before pulling him close and giving him a hug. She was comforted in the knowledge that this was the right thing for Walter's future and that his education at St Paul's would lead to Oxford or Cambridge and a bright future for her son.

At 7.20 a.m., the Royal Nelson approached Ross from Hereford across the River Wye at Wilton Bridge and then made a steep climb up Dock Street, today known as Wye Street. In those days, the top half of Dock Street was known as Dock Pitch, indicating how steep that part of the road was. As the coach came across Wilton Bridge, the driver let out a long blast on the coaching horn. This was the signal to the hostlers at the Swan to provide a cockhorse, usually a draft animal, to help pull the coach up the hill. It was always an impressive sight to see a coach arrive from that direction with the horses in a steaming cloud of perspiration. As they entered Edde Cross Street, the sounds of twenty clattering hooves and four iron-rimmed wheels on the cobblestones, the multiple blasts on the coaching horn and the panting of four stressed horses added to the spectacle. Activity at the Swan was hectic as hostlers brought out fresh horses, their hooves adding to the cacophony, ready to take the coach on to the next stage. Crack teams of hostlers prided themselves on changing mail coach teams in as little as three minutes and the hostlers at the Swan were as competitive as any others.

As soon as the coach stopped, Walter was ready to climb aboard and take his seat, but with horses to change, luggage to load and passengers looking for refreshments, he had to be patient and wait his turn. This would not be a long stop, however, as the Royal Nelson was only two and a half hours out from Hereford and there was a long road ahead of them.

Walter's father knew the driver and explained to him that he would be taking two special passengers today. He requested that young Walter be given a seat in the centre with his brother on one side and another passenger on the other side. 'We don't want Walter nodding off and toppling off the side of the coach.' 'Don't concern yourself at all, Mr Medhurst sir. I'll take great care of them both,' replied the driver. 'I'll be taking the coach as far as Oxford and I will ensure that Mr Purley, the driver who takes over from me, knows of your concerns.'

A blast on the coach horn sounded as a warning for the passengers to climb aboard. Sarah Medhurst gave her sons one last hug and their father shook their hands before William and Walter clambered up the side of the coach and sat behind the driver. Moments later, the driver shouted a command and the four fresh horses started the coach moving. The driver pulled them around into High Street, down through Market Place to Copse Cross Street and then out on to the Gloucester Road. From their vantage point atop the coach, William and Walter had a panoramic view of the town. Some of the town boys waved when they saw Walter and ran alongside the coach until they could no longer keep up. With that, eleven-year-old Walter Medhurst moved on, leaving his parents and his childhood behind him.

It was 125 miles to London from Ross-on-Wye, a journey that took around twenty-four hours and required a further nine changes of horses at stages of between 10 and 15 miles, a total of forty horses for the complete journey. The first two stops were at Huntley and Gloucester, just long enough to change the horses and for passengers to stretch their legs briefly before they continued to Cheltenham, where a longer break enabled passengers to enjoy a quick lunch. By the time they pulled into Cheltenham, the passengers from Hereford had been travelling for over six hours. William and Walter had their own food with them so they sat outside the inn and ate some bread and cheese. Being in a new town triggered their curiosity and they wandered a short distance in each direction from the inn, but Walter kept on glancing back at the coach fearing it might leave.

The next stage of the journey took the coach through some of the most beautiful parts of England – across the southern Cotswolds. This was before the influence of the Industrial Revolution and the country was a mix of small agricultural pastures, heavy woodlands and small villages. On this day in July 1807, the boys were blessed by perfect weather to enjoy the scenery. The roads were dry and passable and in some places had recently been resurfaced. However, it would be several years before John Macadam revolutionised road building and cut many hours off this journey. This was a memorable experience for Walter, one that ignited his lifelong love of travel.

There were two kinds of coaches operating from Ross to London: the Mail Coach and the stagecoach. The Mail Coach was contracted to the Royal Mail and carried fewer passengers, made shorter stops and therefore made quicker time. Passengers could only sit inside or in two rows of seats by the driver. The rear seat was reserved for the guard, employed by the Royal Mail, who was armed with a blunderbuss and pistols as a defence against highwaymen. The Royal Nelson was a stagecoach and hence did not have a guard and carried a few more passengers. This raised the possibility that they might fall prey to highwaymen and this of course became a fearful fascination to the Medhurst boys. The more experienced passengers on board recounted tales of being held at gunpoint by fearsome-looking rogues to see what reaction they could summon up in the boys. Being older and more worldly wise, William laughed this off, but young Walter imagined a huge robber, as big and dark as the New Street blacksmith, pointing at him and shouting that he needed a boy as a hostage.

The Royal Nelson pulled into Oxford at around 7.00 p.m. and as it was midsummer, the passengers had a good view of the city as they crossed the Osney Bridge over the Thames. 'Observe your future, Walter. Mother says that this is where you will be going when you finish at St Paul's,' said William. 'We stop at the Bear Inn, which is close by the university so if you want to pick your future home, you will have lots of colleges to choose from.' Walter had heard many times the plans that his mother had for him but he already regarded the next four years at St Paul's as challenging enough for the present. He had to take his mother's predictions seriously, however, for just last week she had secured a promise from an acquaintance to get his brother William accepted into the Royal Navy as a midshipman when he finished at St Paul's. In William's mind, he was already there and ready to follow in Horatio Nelson's footsteps.

The next stage of the journey started and finished in daylight but once it got dark and the coach continued to bump and roll along the road, it became increasingly difficult to maintain a comfortable position on the bench. The boys were tired but there was no opportunity to catch any sleep for fear of falling from the coach. As promised, the coach drivers had ensured that Walter always sat between his brother and another passenger.

The sun rose at around 5.20 a.m. in London that July, so dawn broke well before the coach made its last stop for a change of horses in Uxbridge, Middlesex. The boys' relief at being near the end of the journey, and their excitement at the almost continuous villages and towns that they passed through, helped them to feel relatively fresh once more. William was going home but Walter could hardly remember what London was like, and he stared in wonder and anticipation, sometimes calling out for William to look at this or that.

The coach arrived into London via Oxford Street, which in those days was very different from its present-day appearance.

It had been one of London's main thoroughfares for 2,000 years, having followed the route of the old Roman road, the Via Trinobantina. In 1807, it had a mixture of businesses, including grocers, goldsmiths, hatters, brewers, distillers, ironmongers, cabinetmakers, stables, blacksmiths, saddlers, a tinplate works, and even an ostrich feather dealer, although the preponderance of drapers was indicative of Oxford Street's future as a centre of retailing. William and Walter's uncle, George Medhurst, had a weighing machine business at No. 465 Oxford Street and an iron foundry just two streets away on Little Denmark Street.

Saturday morning was a normal working day in London and the city had already come to life as the Royal Nelson made its way down Oxford Street towards Holborn. The street was filled with horse-drawn carriages and carts of all kinds, as well as handcarts and sedan chairs and more people than Walter could ever remember seeing before. Smoke rose from the barrows and stalls of street vendors selling hot food such as tea, pies and muffins. There were fishmongers selling eels and oysters, flower sellers and milkmaids. The street vendors called out and rang their bells to attract customers from the passing throng. The clattering of hooves on the cobblestones, the background hammering from nearby blacksmiths and factories, and the smoke and smells of this urban jungle created a wondrous spectacle for any first-time visitor. Young Walter's early memories of the sounds, sights and smells of London came rushing back.

The final effort for the horses pulling the Royal Nelson was to descend Holborn Hill and climb up Skinner Street, as this was before the Holborn viaduct was built. They passed Newgate Prison and the Old Bailey, then coasted down Newgate Street with St Paul's Cathedral on their right, turned left into St Martins le Grand and drove right into the yard of the Bull & Mouth coaching inn.

Their Uncle George, with whom William had been living for the last three years, met them at the Bull & Mouth. There was insufficient room for Walter to live with Uncle George and so he would live in the residence at St Paul's School. For the weekend, however, both boys would stay at George's home in Clerkenwell; Walter would move to St Paul's the following Monday.

George Medhurst was an engineer and clockmaker who had founded a weighing machine business in 1800. He was an inveterate inventor who had filed various patents, some very successful, especially those related to his weighing machines. He became famous for an engine he invented that created motive power from compressed air.[3] He proposed manufacturing coaches powered by his engine, to be operated by pumping stations along the route. William knew about this invention and he told Walter that in the future their coach ride from Ross to London would be made without horses, powered instead by Uncle George's invention.

For now, George Medhurst had to rely on horses and after collecting the boys, they walked across St Martins le Grand to hire a hackney carriage to take them the short distance to Clerkenwell.

3

ST PAUL'S SCHOOL

Founded in 1509 by John Colet, St Paul's School was established to educate boys in faith and letters and was set up with a City of London company as trustees, the Mercers' Company, established 700 years before, originally as a trade association for mercers (merchants such as drapers). By the sixteenth century, it had lost its connection with the original trade. In 1807, the Mercers' Company operated as a charitable institution, supporting various causes funded mainly from property investments in Westminster and the City of London. Consistent with the edict of the founder of the school, the number of boys to be educated at St Paul's at that time was limited to 153, the number associated with the miraculous catch of fishes in the Gospel of St John.

Most of the boys were Londoners who lived at home, but Walter was to board in the house of the High Master, Richard Roberts. Roberts was seventy-eight years old when Walter started at St Paul's and one can hardly imagine a close relationship developing between the young boy and the school principal. The other masters, Sleath, Durham (known as Whack) and Bean were hard disciplinarians. William Ballantine, a former student who went on to become Serjeant at Law (one of the most senior legal appointments in nineteenth-century England), recalled the three masters as cruel, cold-blooded, unsympathetic tyrants. Ballantine's first day at St Paul's was 'the blackest and most odious day of my existence'.[1] Reminiscences like this of painful school days are not uncommon but they are generally balanced by happy memories of students who learned to accept the system and avoid the disapproval of the masters. Walter found his own way of living and studying at the school without attracting too much retribution from his teachers.

Around and about St Paul's existed an education of another kind: the streets of London were full of fascinating and harrowing sights for a young boy from a country town. Just three streets away stood the notorious Newgate Prison, outside of which public executions regularly took place. Crowds gathered to watch as criminals were put to death on the gallows, onlookers yelling insults at the condemned as they took their last steps. One of the most popular publications of the time was the *Newgate Calendar*, a monthly bulletin of executions put out by the keeper of Newgate Prison. Along with the Bible and *Pilgrim's Progress*, the *Newgate Calendar* was famously in the top three works likely to be found in the average home. Encouraging young children to read the calendar and taking them to see public executions was considered a way to teach children to avoid a similar fate. The boys of St Paul's were discouraged from joining the crowds at Newgate. Most hangings were carried out at 8.00 a.m., by which time school had already started. Just three months before Walter started at St Paul's, twenty-seven people had been trampled to death in a crowd at Newgate, serving as a warning for the boys to keep away.

These were changing times in England and there was considerable debate about public executions, resulting in attitudes moving towards reform and rehabilitation. This was the age of Humanism. Debates included slavery, workers' rights and the right of all men to a vote. The Slave Trade Act was passed by Parliament just three months before Walter started school at St Paul's. In the same month, the United States moved to ban the import of slaves, although not its internal slave trade. A former student at St Paul's, Thomas Clarkson, was a leading campaigner against the slave trade and a member of the Clapham Sect, a group of activist evangelical Christians. The masters at St Paul's School and the parents of most of the boys were generally sympathetic towards these changing attitudes. Without painting them as revolutionaries, they influenced Walter's generation.

Another sphere of influence was found in the opposite direction to that of Newgate Prison, in the City of London, the world's centre for trade and commerce. For a young boy it was the source of all things exotic and adventurous. The Company of Adventurers of England Trading into Hudson's Bay was the full name for the Hudson's Bay Company whose head office was located nearby on Fenchurch Street. One street away was Leadenhall Street, the site of India House and the Honourable East India Company, the rulers of large areas of India and the Far East. Closer to St Paul's, running off Cheapside, was Old Jewry and the head office of the LMS, which already had missionaries in India and the South Seas. The fathers of some of Walter's close friends at school worked for these organisations so he heard numerous tales of exciting exploits.

Britain's military exploits also influenced Walter's generation but the war with France had been dragging on for several years, which dampened any enthusiasm he had for a military career. The patriotism and adulation elicited by Nelson's victory at Trafalgar in 1805 had a much bigger influence on Walter's older brother than it did on him.

Religion played an important part in Walter's upbringing during his school years but it was not dominated by any one view of Christianity. He was required to go to services in St Paul's Cathedral on Sundays, except when he was excused to visit his uncle's family, and on those Sundays he hardly ever attended church.

Walter returned only once to his home at the Swan Inn at Ross, in 1807 for Christmas. William Medhurst had taken on an ambitious project as landlord of the town's largest coaching inn when the war with France was having a negative effect on Britain's economy. Added to this challenge was the propensity of the Medhursts to reach beyond their capacity to support business activities that did not fully go to plan. William had been aware he was in some financial difficulty early in 1808 and he was actively trying to reduce the trouble he was in. He had some support from a benefactor in the coaching industry and managed to persuade the owners to allow him to transfer from the Swan Inn to a smaller public house in nearby Gloucester. The Maidenhead Inn on Northgate Street in Gloucester would be the new home for Walter Medhurst when he was not in school.

Downsizing his business did not solve William Medhurst's problems and later that year, a Commission of Bankrupt was awarded and issued against him. So began the proceedings to distribute the property of the Medhursts to their various creditors. It was two years before he was issued with a certificate releasing him from that situation. He was fortunate to be considered a person engaged in business or trade; otherwise he would have suffered the fate of other insolvent persons who ended up in a debtor's prison.

Unaffected by his father's financial problems, young William was accepted into the Royal Navy to be trained as a midshipman. It was necessary to have some family connection or benefactor to gain such a position. Often the trainee started as a senior officer's servant and was promoted to midshipman after two years at sea.

Even though he was not a fee-paying student, Walter had to discontinue his studies at St Paul's because of his father's financial problems, ending his mother's hopes that he would continue his education at Oxford University. She had to trim her ambitions for her youngest son to something less costly and, as she did at Ross-on-Wye, Sarah continued to seek out the most influential members of the community in an attempt to find a vocation for him before he completed his studies at St Paul's.

4

SOUTH INDIA

A little girl was playing in a hot and dusty yard in South India, chatting away to her friends in Tamil as fluently as she spoke to her father in English. Elizabeth was the daughter of Lieutenant George Martin of the Madras Native Infantry and she had only ever lived in India.

'Mama? Why can't I go to Madurai with Aaniya's family? I know all about the Lord Rama,' young Betty (as she was more commonly called) asked her mother. 'Oh, dear Betty. You are an English girl, the daughter of an English officer and you are different to your Tamil friends. You know that we are Christians and we follow the teachings of Jesus and not the Hindu gods. Aaniya's family would not want a little English girl to come along with them anyway.' 'But Jesus doesn't have any festivals, Mama, like the Lord Rama has,' said Betty. 'Why not?' Betty Martin was just nine years old and her best friend Aaniya was about to leave for a trip with her family for the Chittirai Festival at Madurai. The whole family had been talking about it and Betty had sensed their excitement and wished that she could go too. Although her mother tried to explain that Christians celebrate Christmas and Easter, it was of no comfort to young Betty. The Martins were not active Christians and her mother was a Tamil herself, but she was determined that her daughter should be raised as an English lady.

Betty Martin was born in Tanjore (Thanjavur), south India, on 23 October 1794. Her father served with the armies of the British East India Company in the Madras Native Infantry. She and her younger sister Sophia had moved with their parents to various regimental bases, living in tents and army barracks, and in August 1803 her father was promoted to major and sent to the fort in Trichinopoly. Like her mother, she spoke Tamil fluently, some Telugu, the other major language of south India, and her father's English.

Mixed marriages were actively encouraged by the East India Company, which paid a family allowance of 15 silver rupees for each child born to an Indian mother and an English father, a deliberate act of self-preservation by the English. The occupying British ethnically engineered this unique hybrid individual such that the Anglo-Indians were the only micro-minority community ever defined in a Constitution. Article 366 of the Indian Constitution stated, 'An Anglo-Indian means a person whose father or any of whose male ancestors in the male line is or was of European descent but who is domiciled within the territory of India and is or was born within such territory of parents habitually resident there-in and not established there for temporary purposes only.' In 1830, the British Parliament described the Anglo-Indian as those who had been English educated, and were entirely European in their habits and feelings, dress and language. They were more 'Anglo' than 'Indian'. Their mother tongue was English, they were Catholic or Protestant and their customs and traditions were English. While most of them married within their own circle, many continued to marry expatriate Englishmen. Without Anglo-Indian support British rule would have collapsed.

The Martins were a happy family despite the rugged lifestyle. Whenever Betty thought back to those years, she remembered the laughter most. Her parents loved each other dearly but they were also the greatest of friends and they were always making each other laugh. Betty and Sophia would get the giggles and join in, although mostly they had no idea what they were laughing at. She remembered also that people around them were happy, as if the joyful atmosphere were infectious. Even the servants seemed more cheerful than at other houses, always smiling and sharing the humorous mood of Major Martin's home.

The Martins entertained a lot – mostly George's fellow officers and their wives but also visiting government dignitaries. Often the visitors were accompanied by other children, so Betty and Sophia did not lack for English friends. Betty's best friend, however, was Aaniya, the daughter of one of the family's servants.

We can only imagine the early life of Betty Martin, but it seems plausible that she had a special friend like Aaniya and that her friendship with children of another culture and of much lower prosperity influenced her character. To understand better the life she led and the tragedies that were to befall her as a young woman, it is necessary to review her father's life and career.

George Martin was born in Trowbridge, Wiltshire, in December 1760. Like many young men from the shires, he was recruited by the East India Company (EIC) at age nineteen to enter officer training as a cadet. On graduation, he joined the army of the Madras Presidency, one of the three zones in India governed by the EIC. On 14 September 1780, he graduated as a second lieutenant and soon after sailed for Madras to join the Madras Native Infantry in a regiment mostly comprising Indian soldiers.

George Martin arrived in India during the Second Mysore War, 1780–83, when British dominion over India faced one of its gravest threats. Triggered by the entry of France into the American Revolutionary War, the underlying hostilities had been brewing for some time. Hyder Ali and his son Tippoo Sultan, the Tiger of Mysore, were long-term allies of the French. They employed foreign officers in their armies and were sophisticated in the use of European weapons. In many ways, the armies of the Mysoris were on a par with the Madras Native Infantry. By the time George Martin arrived, the British had suffered their worst defeat ever in India when Tippoo Sultan surrounded and annihilated a British detachment of over 3,000 men. The war continued badly for Britain until July of the following year when a force of 8,500 British stormed the Mysore camp and forced Hyder into retreat. The British lost 306 men against an estimated 10,000 of the Mysoris. Ten significant battles involving thousands of men in hand-to-hand combat were documented during this war, so George Martin would almost certainly have experienced some of this action. In April 1786, he was promoted to lieutenant. Eventually the war ended with a treaty in 1784, no side having gained any advantage. The more decisive Third and Fourth Mysore Wars of 1789–99 were to follow.

The mists of time obscure our view of the life of George Martin in India and the various actions and campaigns that would have had George leave his family at times. We do know that on 23 December 1795, in Tanjore, Colonel John Haliburton signed a certificate entitling Lieutenant George Martin to a share in the proceeds of a bond payable by the Rajah of Tanjore.[1] Martin's share amounted to 2,539 star pagodas in the currency of the East India Company. This was around £1,015, a tidy sum in those days. Whether this was a reward from the Rajah, an ally of Britain, or prize money from a battle or campaign, we do not know. It only became known in a document resolving the estate of the Rajah after all the parties were deceased.

On 2 July 1796, George Martin was promoted to captain and the following year he was given his first command of a battalion. The 2nd Extra Battalion was raised at Vellore under Captain George Martin. In 1798, it was restructured as the 2nd Battalion, the 14th Regiment of the Madras Native Infantry. With the aid of one British lieutenant, Captain Martin would command a native force of 660 privates and 118 NCOs.[2] The family and all their servants moved with the new commander to Vellore approximately 140 km west of Madras. Shortly after the move, Betty's sister Sophia was born.

This was an active time for Betty's father, whose regiment was maintaining the peace after the war with the Kingdom of Mysore. These wars had been raging on and off since 1766, culminating in the Siege of Seringapatam in 1799, which was won decisively by the British and their Hyderabadi allies.

In April 1803, Captain George Martin from the 5th Regiment was placed in charge of the 1st Extra Battalion at Trichinopoly with Lieutenant Trewman as Adjutant.[3]

Led by the now Lieutenant Colonel Martin, the battalion moved up to Chitaldrug around 1806. Chitaldrug is the site of an old fort belonging to the Rajah of Mysore. The Rajah was restored to the throne after the British and their allies defeated the Mysore Army at Seringapatam. Located over 300 miles from Madras, the fort, one of the strongest in India, was surrounded by rocky, bare hills. The plain of Chitaldrug consisted of black soil but owing to a deficiency of water, the area suitable for rice growing was small. Deep wells had to be dug to access the irrigation water, and that was of poor quality, partly attributed to the common practice of washing clothes, bodies and goats in the same tanks and wells from where the people drew their own water.

The biggest threat to the British and their families in India came not from the battles they fought but from the diseases rampant throughout the subcontinent, and the lack of treatment and prevention that in the twenty-first century we take for granted. Smallpox, malaria, cholera, dysentery, and tuberculosis were all prevalent. Between 1736 and 1834 only around 10 per cent of the East India Company's officers survived to take the final voyage home.

5

TROUBLE IN MADRAS

The spirit of revolt prevailing in Europe since 1789 also generated problems in Madras. By 1807, the newly appointed governor, Sir George Barlow, found himself pitted against a vociferous army faction led by its commander-in-chief, Lieutenant-General Hay Macdowall. The army had several grievances, some legitimate, some not, but the dispute crystallised when the governor decided that the commander-in-chief would no longer have a seat on the governor's council. Macdowall took this as a personal affront. An impetuous and hot-headed man, he openly voiced his dislike for the governor.

Taking up his lead, officers began circulating a memorandum recording their dissatisfaction with various measures the company's directors had taken. One of these concerned the Tent Contract system by which officers received an allowance to meet the expenses of supplying tents, equipment and personnel necessary for the movement of the regiment in the field. As the allowance became increasingly generous and abuses crept in, the system fell into disrepute. At the Government's request, a report was drawn up by a Lieutenant-Colonel Munro, which recommended ending the generous allowances. His report drew attention to some of the abuses. Although it was confidential, its contents became public knowledge and the army objected to the implicit allegations of fraudulent practices.

Macdowall received letters from officers complaining that the report 'unequivocally conveyed a most cruel and wanton insult, as well as an injurious aspersion' to officers. These complaints culminated in a charge against Munro, alleging that in writing the memorandum, Munro had been guilty of conduct unbecoming an officer and a gentleman. The charge could only properly be determined by court martial. The joint requisition was signed by twenty-eight officers in command of regiments and sent to Macdowall under cover of a letter dated 25 September 1808. This letter was signed by three lieutenant-colonels – St Leger, Rumley and George Martin. Martin had helped to draft the letter, which was a highly seditious document since it demanded the removal of the governor and implied a threat of mutiny if the demands were rejected. Copies of the letter and the joint requisition soon circulated among the regiments and the mood became menacing. There were, however, many officers loyal to the governor who wanted no part in the affair. Colleagues of George Martin who favoured loyalty to the government were quick to warn him that if things turned bad, he could face a court martial with the most severe penalties.

The response by General Macdowall was to support his senior officers. He ordered that Lieutenant-Colonel Munro be tried by court martial. George Martin was appointed to conduct the prosecution. Realising the danger he was in, Munro appealed to the governor to halt the proceedings. The governor received the clearest legal advice that the intended prosecution would be unlawful and that Munro should be released, but Macdowall refused to implement the advice. With the last fleet of Indiamen (East India Company ships) about to leave for England, General Macdowall departed on board the *Lady Jane Dundas*, leaving the court martial to his successor and submitting his resignation in writing from a port down the coast. As a last act of compliance, Macdowall issued an order for Munro's release, but then in a final act of defiance he issued a general order to be distributed the following day, in which he made a personal attack on Sir George Barlow for implied censure, which he believed 'compromised the honour of the whole army'. Without having received Macdowall's resignation, Barlow tried in vain to halt the sailing of the fleet. He denounced Macdowall for 'acts of outrage' against the government and dismissed him from his position as commander-in-chief.

Amid the crisis, during which time George Martin had been in Madras, word came that his wife was gravely ill with a fever back in Chitaldrug and he should return home as fast as possible for it was unlikely that she would recover. It normally took three or four days to travel to Chitaldrug and although he made the return journey in less than two days, by the time he arrived she had passed away. His daughters were distraught. Having little capacity to console them, he was reduced to the verge of physical and mental collapse. He had lost the love of his life and he had not been with her when she finally needed him. Adding to the utter despair he felt was the sense of desertion created by his commander-in-chief resigning and sailing back to England, leaving him and his fellow officers to sort out matters with the government. How was he going to support his daughters, especially if the army crisis turned against him and he was brought before a court martial and imprisoned or even executed?

His solution was to arrange for Betty, now just fourteen years old, to marry a fellow army officer, his adjutant, twenty-seven-year-old Lieutenant George Henry Braune. The couple were married at Chitaldrug on 14 October 1808. George Martin entrusted Betty's younger sister Sophia to their care and left Betty the family's furniture, a complete set of silver plate and her mother's jewellery and pearls. He then returned to Madras for further orders regarding the developing crisis.

Back in Madras, tensions were mounting. The governor realised that Macdowall would make representations against him to East India House in London and that it would be important to have someone to put forward his own case against the army. To this end, he decided to send one of his trusted aides, George Buchan. Since all the Indiamen had already set sail that year from Madras, he cajoled the captain of the recently arrived *Sir Stephen Lushington* into changing his plans and making an immediate return to Europe. On board would be Buchan carrying Barlow's despatches for London.

However, as soon as the army got wind of Buchan's mission, it sent its own envoy. Who better than the man responsible for the prosecution of Munro? Lieutenant-Colonel George Martin was to proceed to England and make further representations to the directors. 'So intriguing a prospect did this ménage present that the *Lushington* was nick-named Pandora's box.'[1] With both Buchan and Martin on board, she set sail on 2 March 1809, a month behind the Madras Indiamen but with orders to proceed home without stopping. After a few days of variable weather, the ship picked up a fresh trade wind blowing south-east by south and began to make around 200 miles per day. She managed to avoid the terrible hurricanes causing havoc among the East Indiamen, including the loss of Macdowall's ship.[2] The *Lushington* caught up with the fleet at St Helena, and from there sailed under the protection of Admiral Pellew and his flagship, the *Culloden*. The convoy reached England by mid-July and Buchan proceeded to East India House. Having heard him out, the directors wholeheartedly endorsed Sir George Barlow's dismissal of Macdowall for 'conduct highly reprehensible and having a distinct tendency to encourage a spirit of discontent and insubordination'.[3]

Whether Martin also tried to make representations on behalf of the army is not clear. If he did so, they were obviously not well received given the directors' lack of sympathy for Macdowall. The news that reached England in December 1809 of a threatened uprising by the Madras Army would have further undermined Martin's position.

Barlow, having tried and failed a conciliatory approach, moved to suppress the incipient revolt. It was decided to punish all the officers who were known to be the leaders. On the governor's advice, an order was drawn up dated 1 May 1809 that set out the penalties. The most senior officers were suspended from the service and others removed from their staff appointments.

But far from abating after the punishment of the ringleaders, the antagonism between the army and the governor intensified further. Throughout the Madras Presidency, there was resentment at the penalties imposed. This soon developed into open rebellion in what later became known as the White Mutiny. Barlow held firm, supported as he was by Lord Minto, the Governor-General. The British Army regiments would not support their Company army colleagues and the Madras sepoys had nothing to gain from what they saw as a private squabble between their commanding officers and the Company, their ultimate paymaster.

Eventually, after several sepoy regiments had come under fire from the British Army units and been cruelly deserted by their officers, the ringleaders realised that matters were out of hand and they could not win. The mutiny fizzled out and the leaders were punished, although they all escaped the normal penalty for such an offence, namely, capital punishment.

Martin, safely in England, was spared the temptation of involving himself in the events, as no doubt he would have done. It may be, however, that these events rather than the loss of his wife caused him to lie low and remain in England for the next four years. An indication of the haste with which George Martin left India is shown in the history of the Madras Army, where it is recorded that he was recommended for dismissal for leaving to return to England. He must have sorted this out with his superiors, however, as he was appointed commanding officer of the 13th Madras Infantry when he returned from England. George Martin found himself a new wife back in his home county of Wiltshire and married Mary Thring on 9 January 1813 in Warminster.

George Martin and Mary arrived in Madras on the *Metcalfe* on 6 July 1813. He was appointed full colonel of the 13th Madras Infantry. Soon after, he and his wife moved to Bellary, over 300 miles east of Madras, where he commanded the battalion. Here, Mary gave birth to her first child, a son named Francis Pitney Martin. Their life together was to be short, however. Tragedy struck again when George Martin fell ill with the fever. The regimental history reports that he died on 17 June 1815 in Bellary, India. Poor Mary had only spent two years with George before she was left a widow with a young son. To make matters worse, she soon discovered that she was pregnant and their daughter was born in Madras in February 1816.

Meanwhile, Betty and Sophia had returned to life with the army, this time with Betty as an officer's wife. By the time George Martin returned to India, George Braune had been promoted to captain and they had moved 300 miles north of Madras to Masulipatam, so Betty was unable to meet her father when he returned through Madras. This was not a happy time for Betty, but her stoic nature gave her the strength to make the most of it. She devoted herself to being the wife she had seen her mother be and took on the role of mother to her young sister, Sophia. George Braune tried his best to be a caring husband but the age difference and his penchant for gambling with his fellow officers worked against his efforts. It was an arranged marriage that should never have taken place. One can imagine him coming home drunk after losing at cards and taking out his frustrations on his young wife and sister-in-law. Marooned in a remote part of India, with no friend or relative to turn to, Betty had no choice but to accept her predicament.

She had two sons, the first at age sixteen. He was born in Masulipatam on 10 May 1810 and baptised George Martin Braune. Three years later, a second son, Henry, was born. Tragedy struck in 1815 when the younger son died on the day that Betty was to celebrate her twenty-first birthday. As if that was not bad enough, her husband was away on a campaign in Kurnool.

When Alif Khan died in September 1815, the younger son Mozuffer Khan took over against the wishes of the East India Company and the army was again mobilised to march to Kurnool and lay siege to the fort. Captain George Braune was part of that military action, and whether he died of wounds sustained during the action or from some other cause was not recorded. We know that he died on 26 November not far from Kurnool at Gooty, just six months after Colonel George Martin died in Bellary.

George Braune would have died not knowing that one of his sons had passed away after he left the coastal fort at Masulipatam, and Betty would not learn of the death of her husband for several weeks later, meaning she received that news as a dreadful Christmas present.

So in the year that Betty turned twenty-one she became an orphan and a widow, and she lost one of her children. Compounding her situation, she had no family other than her son and her younger sister. She had to sell her furniture, silver plate and all her jewellery to pay her husband's debts and she placed her sister Sophia in an orphanage in Madras. Betty moved to Madras with her son George to live with Mr and Mrs Loveless, missionaries with the LMS. Betty had no religious upbringing but she taught and looked after the children of the Loveless family in exchange for board and lodging for herself and her son. It must have been a wretched time for the young woman, but the way she handled the situation and got on with her life says a lot about her strength of character.

6

THE MISSION CHAPEL, BLACKTOWN

Life at the mission was a big change for Betty. Around fifteen years older than Betty, William Loveless and his wife Sarah had been in charge there since 1805. He was from England and she from Long Island, New York.

In order to get a footing in Madras, William Loveless secured the position of superintendent of the Military Orphan Male Asylum, where he imparted religious instruction to 350 boys. He held this position for six years, during which he also commenced preaching in other parts of the city and suburbs, concentrating on the Anglo-Indian children – the children of Europeans on the father's side.

In 1810, William Loveless commenced building the mission chapel on Davidson Street in Blacktown. Sarah Loveless took a very active part in this endeavour, and the business habits she learned in America proved to be of great advantage. The expense of the building was around £3,000 and not a penny came from Europe. Sarah Loveless practically managed the entire building fund. The mission chapel is as vibrant today as it was then, now operating as the William Charles Memorial Church.

By the time Betty went to live in Madras, the mission chapel stood in a garden of more than an acre, with a free school for boys to its right. It was a busy and exciting environment for Betty to move into and she and George soon considered this home. Having spent her whole life moving from one rural army base to another, she would have found Madras an exciting and cosmopolitan place and where her son George was able to attend school for the first time.

The Loveless family was the epitome of a Christian missionary family; the couple was known for their hospitality to friends and strangers alike. People frequently came to stay, with the overflow of visitors residing at the boarding school next door. This offered Betty the opportunity to meet people from all walks of life beyond the limited group of military people she was used to. She was an attractive young woman and no doubt receiving the attentions of single young men would have been new to her. Her marriage to Lieutenant Braune at such an early age precluded any experience of meeting and developing relationships with the opposite sex.

Betty had been at the mission only a few months when Richard Knill arrived in Madras on 26 August 1816 aboard the *Earl of Moira*. Richard was a new missionary sent out to assist the Loveless family in their work. He took up residency in the school next to the chapel. Richard was drawn to Betty. In his memoir, one of the first things he wrote was, 'We landed on a Tuesday, and the next evening I preached my first sermon, from these words, "Behold the Lamb of God, which taketh away the sin of the world" and God blessed it to the conversion of a young widow, Mrs Elizabeth Braune.'[1] Richard may have been a superb preacher but I doubt that anyone could convert someone to Christianity with a first sermon on a first meeting. There was wishful thinking in what he wrote and it was the first thing that betrayed the attraction he felt for Betty.

Mr and Mrs Loveless welcomed Richard Knill and he immediately became involved in raising funds for a girls' school to be built on the other side of the chapel from the boys' school. Richard Knill went on to write a book entitled *The Missionary's Wife, or a Brief Account of Mrs Loveless of Madras* in which he praises

Mrs Loveless as his affectionate and generous-hearted friend. He coined the phrase for the Blacktown Mission as 'the Saint's Rest'.

Unfortunately, no personal letters have survived from this period so we only have the letters and reports sent to the LMS, as well as the family memoir of one of Betty's descendants regarding the feelings and emotions developing at the mission. From what information we have, it is reasonable to assume that a relationship was developing between Richard Knill and Betty Braune. As a young and attractive woman, vastly more experienced in life than Richard Knill, almost totally comfortable with the local population and customs, she might have been a challenge for a farming lad from Devon. By all accounts, Richard was a very personable and affectionate man and he must have raised some interest as a possible partner in Betty's mind. For the time being, however, he was the only prospect around. The growing friendship eventually led Betty to having to make a very difficult choice following the arrival of Walter Medhurst in Madras. For now, Richard Knill had a five-month lead on Walter Medhurst.

7

GLOUCESTER

Walter's schooling ended prematurely at St Paul's in 1810 and he returned to live with his parents in Gloucester. Sarah had arranged for Walter to meet with Joseph Wood, the proprietor of the *Gloucester Herald,* who was prepared to take Walter on as an apprentice printer. Walter was a fast learner and his classical education gave him the ability to contribute articles and editorial in addition to learning how to design and print the newspaper. The sprightly character of the youth was developing. His face was open, frank, lively; his manners were brisk, quick, winning; his speech ready, off-hand, sometimes blunt and often racy with humour.[1] What he did, he did from the heart, promptly and without delay, and what he enjoyed, he enjoyed to the very core. These words from a memorial of the day describe the character that would show throughout his life. His youthful vivacity would never leave him and Joseph Wood must have been pleased to have him as his new apprentice.

Walter became known in Gloucester as an interesting youth without the fear of God. He was fond of the theatre and dancing, and was the life of the parties he attended, hardly the behaviour expected of a potential missionary. What was it that turned his attention towards Christianity with such enthusiasm? He did not come from a strong religious family background and his parents were not known as regular churchgoers of any particular Christian denomination. To cap it off, the information we have about his early days in Gloucester are that he had no interest in the church.

Sometime after he moved to Gloucester, his older brother William, now a midshipman, returned to London on sick leave, having fallen from the topmast and broken his leg. William had a reputation for being a wild and fun-loving fellow. One Sunday evening, as he hobbled along near London Bridge, he sighted the old Weighhouse Chapel, at that time under the care of the Revd John Clayton. Partly weary, partly curious, he walked in to take a seat. The straggler's attention was caught. A message from God fell on the youth's ear and softened his heart. Immediately on his conversion, William felt intense anxiety about the spiritual state of his brother Walter and wrote to him, affectionately urging him to attend to his concerns about religion. Using information from the Revd Clayton, William extracted a promise from Walter that he would go to the Independent Chapel in Southgate Street, Gloucester, and hear the Revd William Bishop preach.

Walter made good on the promise and visited the chapel, slinking in and taking a pew nearest the door, not daring to hold up his head. He felt awkward, a stranger in a strange place. Mr Bishop had already commenced his sermon but repeated himself on seeing the wandering youth enter. Walter remembered the words 'a firebrand plucked out of the burning' and they struck a chord in his heart. He felt that he was being addressed personally and left the chapel convinced that Mr Bishop must have known all about his wayward life and disregard for religion.[2] Judging by the reputation of Bishop and his chapel, we can understand why the reverend had such a powerful effect on him. Ralph Bigland Esq., the author of *An Original History of the City of Gloucester*, refers to 'the Revd Bishop, Minister, with all the leading charities of the City that this gentleman's name is connected'. The Revd

Bishop soon arranged for Walter to become involved in some of the charities he supported.

The immediate effect of Walter's visit to the independent chapel was not all due to the Revd Bishop's influence, however; it was as much attributable to Walter's character and his preponderance to make a commitment to something once he had made up his mind. His first step was to try and invite his friends to join him, even distributing tracts among his former drinking partners in the public houses to the extent that one landlord had him forcibly expelled. One of his first actions was to walk into the Sunday school rooms and ask, 'Have you anything for me to do here? I want to teach some children.'

His decision was also a reflection of the times. The late eighteenth and early nineteenth centuries had seen the emergence of the Evangelical movement led by early leaders like John and Charles Wesley, George Whitfield and many others. Evangelical Christians were a diverse group. Some were at the forefront of movements such as the abolition of slavery, prison reform, orphanage establishment, hospital building, and the founding of educational institutions; others were reaching out to the world through organisations like the Church Missionary Society and the LMS, which sent missionaries to the far corners of the earth. The campaigners of the Evangelical movement spread out to every town and city in England and held meetings to promote their activities among Christians of all denominations. Very few educated young people would not have had the experience of attending one of these meetings, most leaving with their interests aroused and willing to get involved.

It is difficult for a modern-day secular person to imagine what it was like to become so enthused with the ideas put forward by the Evangelical movement because it required a person to undertake obligations much greater than we typically associate with modern-day Christianity. It was more than a religious movement providing its followers with spiritual guidance and a chance to communicate with God. It was also a movement for social reform, presenting an opportunity to help create a better world and to learn about, and even explore, remote and uncharted parts of far-flung continents. Involvement provided adventure, a sense of achievement, spiritual comfort, moral satisfaction, and the chance for an individual to earn a community's respect.

Britain was building a great empire, where young people could exercise their influence by taking careers in trade, in the military and in colonial governance. There was a strong belief that Britons should also shape the world by spreading Christianity and instituting the social reforms that were rapidly being implemented at home. Walter must have read the reports of the pioneer missionaries to China like Morrison and Milne and could not help but want to become involved. Perhaps young people felt that there was a time limit on this opportunity, that it was an exclusive chance for their generation to make a difference, because for future generations the job would be done. How exciting it must have been to get caught up in this enthusiasm.

Walter recounted various moments of divine inspiration that led him to become a missionary. His daughter Augusta reported that it was at a missionary meeting in Bristol when 'he became fired with zeal to become a missionary and determined then that he would go to China whenever an opportunity occurred'. One meeting of this kind was reported in the *Royal Cornwall Gazette* on Saturday 24 October 1812, held in Bristol to form an Auxiliary Missionary Society in aid of the LMS. Not only was it very respectably attended, but also so numerously that in addition to the morning services, two places of worship were opened in the evening and the financial contributions exceeded the highest expectation.

Towards the end of 1815, Walter's brother William returned to Gloucester with a sickness that rendered him a shell of his former self. We don't know what his ailment was but the cold winter of

1815–16 would not have helped his condition. The years 1815–17 were known as the years without a summer in the northern hemisphere, and were believed to have resulted from a succession of volcanic eruptions culminating in the eruption of Mount Tambora in Indonesia on April 1815, the largest volcanic eruption in over 1,300 years. Thousands perished in England during that winter and William succumbed and died on 6 February 1816, aged just twenty-three. Many years later it was reported in a memorial, 'The seed that was cast in Weighhouse Chapel, almost fifty years ago, fell on good soil; was carried by a brother's hand into a brother's heart and through that brother has been sown in China.'[3]

An indication that all was not well with the Medhurst family in Gloucester was that the announcement of William's death in the local newspaper referred to his father William Medhurst as the late landlord of the Maidenhead Inn.[4] This revealed that his movement to a smaller establishment had not been successful and his position as landlord was over. The family appeared to be domiciled in Gloucester at the time of William's death, but within a year their whereabouts was unknown. Walter was addressing letters to them for pick-up at a London hotel.

8

LONDON MISSIONARY SOCIETY

Whatever difficulties the Medhursts faced in Gloucester, Walter was determined to follow his ambition and become a missionary to China. His opportunity came when he spotted an advertisement in *The Evangelical Magazine* for a printer to join the mission in South Africa. His was one of six applications. Although not selected, he was offered a similar position for Malacca (Malaysia). His application was strongly supported by the Revd Bishop, and his employer, Joseph Wood, assured the directors that they could not find a young man better qualified in every respect. He was rushed through a three-month course at Hackney Theological Seminary in London under the charge of Dr George Collison.

Although the intent of the LMS was to hire a printer for Malacca, Walter Medhurst was determined to become a missionary to China. No doubt, the LMS saw in Walter the makings of a missionary but there was no time for him to study to be ordained; a printer was needed urgently. The directors wrote to Medhurst:

At a period of life, unusually early, it hath pleased our Lord to enlist you, as we trust, into his service to fight under his banner in the Heathen world, and to engage you under the direction of the Missionary Society to assist in spreading abroad, by the means of printing, the saving knowledge of the Son of God. That great invention has been a principal instrument in his hand to diffuse in the Western part of the world, in Europe and in America, the light of the Reformation. Now, the great Lord of all is imploring it in the East for the same purpose.[1]

Walter was described as being of wiry frame, good health and unfailing cheerfulness, so it was not surprising that the LMS sent word to William Milne at the Malacca Mission to expect 'a very superior youth who can not only print well, but has a taste for languages and an ability to attain them with ease'.[2] However, it was ten months until he arrived. Before leaving London, the LMS commissioned a portrait of Walter Medhurst by W. T. Strutt, a well-known miniaturist, showing him as an elegant young man dressed in the Regency style.

Along with fellow missionary John David Pearson, bound for Calcutta, Walter Medhurst left London on 30 August 1816 on board the *General Graham* under Captain Weatherhead. The voyage had a slow start. After arriving off Deal in Kent on 2 September, the *General Graham* reportedly sailed down the Channel even though the cross-Channel packet boats had been cancelled because of bad weather. Three days later, the *Morning Post* reported that the *General Graham* had put back to the Roads, an anchorage just north of Deal – it was common for sailing ships to wait there for favourable winds to carry them down the English Channel. According to the Deal Maritime Museum and other sources, there are records of as many as 800 sailing ships at anchor at one time.

Apart from that initial storm, it appears that the ship had an uneventful, if long, journey to Madras. It was scheduled to take in and discharge goods at Madeira, and stopped at St Helena and Cape Town to replenish water and provisions. Medhurst wrote back to the mission headquarters from Madeira confessing that he was largely unimpressed with the place, at the same time also revealing his anti-papist views.[3]

A stop at St Helena would have been especially interesting, as Napoleon had been imprisoned and held in exile there since the previous year after his defeat at the Battle of Waterloo. We have no further reports from the passengers en route, however.

Arriving at Madras was unlike arriving at any other port city. There was no natural harbour and ships came to anchor several hundred feet offshore from a surf beach. Passengers were transferred to local surfboats called masulas for the dash through the surf, usually coming ashore a little wet. A masula was a flat-bottomed, high-sided vessel built in pliable sections of mango wood sewn together with coconut fibre.

Madras was the first major British settlement in India, based around Fort St George, which by the late eighteenth century had become the administrative capital of the East India Company's Madras Presidency. Walter stayed with Mr and Mrs Loveless, the missionaries at the Blacktown chapel where he would find a bed at the boarding school next door. Walter wrote the same day to the LMS headquarters in London:[4]

Dear Sir

By God's good blessing we are arrived safe here far better in health than when we left our native land. The Lord has been very good to us – not an accident or a storm the whole passage...I am in hopes of obtaining a Chinese to teach me the rudiments of the language while I stay here which will probably be three months on account of the monsoon; it was a great neglect that I brought no Chinese books with me. The vessel by which we send this sails tomorrow for England and in half an hour the packet closes. Excuse therefore the hurry, inconsistency and confusion of my letter.

Be so kind as to inform my parents Mr Medhurst, Thomas's Hotel, Berkeley Square of my arrival and you will lastingly oblige your willing servant in the Lord.

W.H. Medhurst

It seems from Walter's last statement in the letter that he was aware his parents had left Gloucester and had probably taken temporary accommodation, with instructions to send mail to a London hotel.

Walter settled in for a three-month wait for a ship to take him on to Malacca, partly because of the East India Company's reluctance to transport missionaries but largely because it was the monsoon season. He had hoped to begin his Chinese studies during his wait but was unable to find a suitable teacher. His hosts were more than hospitable. Before he left Madras, he wrote a letter to London dated 12 May 1817:

No language of mine can describe the deep obligation I feel myself to Mr & Mrs Loveless for the kindness, hospitality, friendship and affection with which I have been received and entertained for these three months – I shall always think it my duty to remember them, for as parents towards a beloved child so has been their conduct been towards me.

It seemed that he still had heard nothing from his parents:

Should my parents apply at the Missionary Rooms for any letters from me, be as good as to inform them that there is a letter by this vessel directed to be left at Thomas's Hotel, Berkeley Square.

He informed London that he had obtained a Chinese grammar from Calcutta and commenced studies. Such was his enthusiasm for language studies that he said he had filled the time by teaching himself Hebrew and was able to read a great part of the Book of Genesis.

His love of languages and his keen desire to master them must initially have been a major factor in his attraction to Betty Braune; he would have been fascinated by her fluency in Tamil and her ability to converse in Telugu. Aged twenty-one, he would have been physically attracted to a girl just a year older but he had an ideal cover story to gain her initial interest. He was genuinely interested in her language abilities and her knowledge of local customs and religious beliefs. She could not help but be impressed by how interested he was in her intellectually. Furthermore, her life as an officer's daughter in the Madras Army would have supplied many stories, increasing Walter's attraction to her. What an exciting, interesting and capable woman this lady must have seemed, not to mention that she was something of an Anglo-Indian beauty.

In return, she would probably have found his background and life experiences to have a certain fascination. She would have wanted to know all about life in England and London, especially as one of London's foremost social events of that decade took place just before Walter's departure, namely the marriage of Princess Charlotte of Wales, daughter of George the Prince Regent (later to become King George IV), to Prince Leopold of Belgium in May 1816. Huge crowds filled London, as the princess was extremely popular and was likely to become Queen Charlotte once her unpopular father and grandfather had passed away. Walter had lived close to where Betty's father came from during his years in Ross and Gloucester, and she would have loved to hear his views and stories of the places he had seen. With his frank and lively manner, he would have quickly won over anyone he wanted to impress.

Time was on his side. Betty may have felt less pressured initially by any developing relationship because Walter Medhurst was in Madras only a few weeks. Her friendship with Richard Knill had been developing slowly and he would still be in Madras after Walter left. By the time Walter was to leave for Malacca, the relationship had developed further. He made his intentions clear and Betty had to make a decision. Walter was leaving on a great adventure and she and her son could join him or she could stay and become an assistant missionary's wife in the country in which she had grown up, where she had seen such sorrow. She possibly considered a position as assistant missionary at Blacktown considerably below her mother's position as the colonel's wife. Added to this were the unknown complexities of Betty's feelings about being an Anglo-Indian woman. Walter Medhurst was heading to Malacca as a printer but his enthusiasm, determination and persistence would have been good signs of greater things to come. Perhaps she had fallen in love with Walter but was upset that she may have led Richard Knill to think he had a chance at winning her hand.

Walter knew that he would benefit greatly from continuing life's journey as a married man and the chances of meeting any prospects after Madras were slim. He had fallen in love with Betty and she had the attributes of the ideal partner in his future missionary activities. On 20 May 1817, he wrote to the LMS headquarters:[5]

My dear Sir

I have written already to you by this packet, but as the vessel is detained a few days longer, I embrace the opportunity of informing you of a circumstance of the greatest importance which has occurred respecting myself. Yesterday I entered into the Holy State of Matrimony with Mrs Elizabeth Braune, widow of the late Captain Braune of the 15th Madras Infantry – who has resided in the house of our brother Loveless for these nine months and during that time given every indication of fervent piety and zeal in the good work of our Redeemer in which we are engaged. I feel great pleasure in the union I have thus formed and am happy to say it meets the approval of the brethren, particularly Brother and Sister Loveless, whom I made it my business previously to consult. She has no money but has been blessed with a good education, which has brought forth into existence the powers of a good understanding although the character of the Indian ladies is in general sloth, luxury and inactivity yet I hope my dear wife is an exception to this. Should you however doubt in relation I feel persuaded Brother Loveless will on application confirm it. I trust she will be a good servant to the Missionary cause by studying the Chinese language and otherwise assisting her husband in the important duties of his station. She speaks Tamil as fluently as English and can also talk in Gentoo. Born in India and having travelled over the greater part of the peninsula, living in tents under a scorching sun she is more likely to endure the terrors of an Eastern climate than one of our English ladies. It is true she is not a member of any Church but is a candidate for admission and if our departure had not taken place so soon would have been admitted a Member of the Missionary Chapel, Blacktown.

Before I made any proposals to her she displayed much love for the heathen and zeal for their good on one occasion at our Missionary Meeting she was animated by what was brought forward as to take the golden earrings from her ears and consecrate them to the service of God.

You are aware that my increase of family will require an increased salary as well as swelling my travelling expenses to a greater height than might be otherwise expected. However I believe I shall not exceed what I have previously drawn of our agents – viz. 100 pagodas for my passage, 30 pagodas for incidental expenses and a letter of credit for 100 in case I shall want it at Penang, We embark at 1 o-clock this afternoon on board the Fair Trial, the other vessel having taken a different course.

I remain yours and the Society's devoted servant
WH Medhurst

My dear Mrs M has a little boy by her former husband to whom I have thought it but justice to present 260 pagodas as the whole is late of my wife's previous to our marriage.

It is vested in the hands of trustees till he comes of age when he will possess both principal and interest but if he should previously die the money will return to my wife.

So, the decision was made, albeit at the last moment. Now it would be Mr and Mrs Medhurst who left the next day to sail aboard the *Fair Trial* to Malacca and a future together, which would also include Penang, Batavia and maybe even China itself. Betty had to say goodbye temporarily to her sister Sophia with a promise that she would be able to follow them later when they became settled.

Left behind in Madras was a sad and lonely Richard Knill. On the same day that Walter wrote to report his good news to London, Richard Knill sent the same news but with a rather depressing postscript, betraying the fact that he had probably wished for the hand of Betty himself.

My Dear Sir
…Having thus briefly stated the circumstance of Brother M, which he will communicate more fully, furnish me now dear Sir to hint at something intimately connected with the subject. I mean the propriety or impropriety of the Directors wishing or permitting young men to go out as missionaries in an unmarried state. I am not married myself and it is very likely I never shall but I enter on this subject for the following reasons.

A young person in this country is in a great measure banished from society except that which would be injurious, no domestic happiness to cheer his heart amidst his arduous work and he must wander in solitude and sink into melancholy gloom.

More dreadful still. There is no remedy; or at least, not the remedy which God has ordained if he wishes to change his state who can he marry?!!! It is not every pious young woman in England that has half the knowledge, prudence and energy which a missionary's wife requires but alas! it may be after he leaves his native shores he never sees a pious devoted young female as long as he lives.

Missionaries are sent to seek the conversion of the people and not to marry with them. A very devoted female is one of the dearest things in the Peninsula – perhaps our Brother Medhurst has the best that Madras would afford to him.

Home in Britain say 'O let the missionaries send home if they want a suitable partner' is very pretty to talk about but very different to act upon. Two years the mind would be in a state of anxiety and suspense – very suitable this for a missionary who certainly wants nothing to retard him, the burning sun and almost constant lassitude are hindrances, bad enough without having any mental ones.

I entrust you my dear sir and the other Fathers of the Society if you wish the happiness and success of your missionaries and the honour of the Society let them all leave their native land with pious, zealous, sensible and devoted wives whom life and conversation will strengthen and refresh the soul of their husbands who are bearing the burden and heat of the day.
I cheerfully unburden myself most devotedly
Richard Knill[6]

Two things were revealed in this letter. First, it showed that Betty Braune left her decision to the very last moment. Had the captain of the *Lion* not changed the arrangements, the wedding might not have taken place. Second, of course, it showed that poor Richard Knill was heartbroken and despondent as a result of the apparent loss of someone he had hoped would become his partner.

Richard Knill went on to spend only three years in India. Having suffered from cholera, he returned to England where doctors recommended relocation to a cold climate. The society sent him to St Petersburg with intentions of having him proceed to Siberia. He later returned to London, where we shall meet him again.

9

JOURNEY TO MALACCA

The couple's honeymoon consisted of what Walter somewhat unromantically referred to in a letter back to London as 'a tedious two months' journey' to Malacca. We don't know what his real feelings were because we only have the letters that he wrote to the LMS headquarters, letters in which he reports on matters strictly limited to his missionary activities. It would be completely out of character to report that he was enjoying himself or to show feelings of earthly love towards his new bride. Indeed, in his first letter from Malacca he says that 'seriousness, humility, watchfulness and prudence' should be the chief features of his conduct.

Walter and Betty's journey to Malacca would have been filled with the experiences of getting to know each other and with Walter in the role of stepfather to Betty's seven-year-old son George. Travelling on a sailing ship was the biggest adventure of George's life so far and there would have been a thousand things to gain his attention. The questions for his new stepfather would have poured out. What are all the different sails called? What are all these ropes for? What is the name of that bird? Why does he follow the ship? Where are we now and when will we get there? What will our new house be like?

From what we know about Walter Medhurst, he would have spent much of that time sharing his plans for the future and gaining the support of his wife towards the accomplishment of his dreams. There was much to teach Betty about the plans the LMS had for the lands beyond India, which they referred to as the Ultra Ganges Mission, and for the role he and his wife would play. She would have had considerable doubts about her decision but we know from her subsequent support and involvement in the missionary activities that she had made the commitment to Walter's dream during the voyage to Malacca, even if not in Walter's over-zealous manner.

Let us imagine the story that Walter unfolded to Betty. The activities of the Ultra Ganges Mission had started ten years previously when the LMS sent the Revd Robert Morrison to live and work in Macao and Canton (today Guangzhou) as the first Protestant missionary to China. Hitherto, India had been the main objective for Protestant missionary work in Asia, despite the official East India Company's discouragement of missionary activities in their territories.

The objectives of Morrison's assignment were significantly different to those of a traditional missionary, which were primarily of teaching and preaching the Gospel. Morrison's instructions were to acquire knowledge of the language, create a Chinese dictionary and translate the scriptures. Nothing about preaching or related activities was mentioned.

Morrison met with a predictably cool reception from both the Portuguese government in Macao and from the officials of the East India Company in Canton. The Chinese authorities imposed tight controls on the conditions of foreign trade and Canton was the only place where foreigners could conduct business. No contact was established between the Chinese and European governments. The only contact allowed was between registered merchants like the East India Company and merchants appointed by the Chinese Government, known as Cohongs. Foreign traders were to comply with ferocious Chinese laws and only men were allowed to visit

Canton, many of whom had to leave the country at the end of each trading season. A strict prohibition, punishable by death, was enforced against the teaching of Chinese to foreigners.

The steady growth of Britain's China trade during the eighteenth century had been developed on the back of the tea trade when tea became Britain's national drink. In addition, silk, exotic plants and handcrafted articles were other Chinese items that fetched high prices in European cities. Britain traded cotton textiles and payments in silver in return, but the Chinese were reluctant to take advantage of the manufactured goods produced by Britain's industrial revolution. Consequently, Britain developed a growing trade in Indian-grown opium as a means of paying for Britain's increasing demand for tea. Both Chinese and foreign merchants made mounting profits in the opium trade, despite the Chinese Government's attempts to make the trade illegal.

This was hardly the best place to start a Christian mission and Morrison was largely ineffective in gaining converts to his cause, although he had great success in studying the Mandarin and Cantonese dialects. From the start, he was accepted by the American merchants and allowed accommodation in their factory, which he gladly accepted. During his first years in Canton, he dressed in Cantonese style, wearing a queue (plait of hair) and allowing his fingernails to grow long like those of a Chinese scholar. This must have helped him become close with the locals for, by the end of 1808, he had already translated parts of the New Testament, completed a Chinese grammar and was well into a project for a Chinese–English dictionary. In 1809, he married Miss Mary Morton, the daughter of an Irish doctor who was visiting Macao. Around the same time, the East India Company recruited him as a Chinese translator for the company's Canton factory at a salary of £500 per year.

All through this period, Morrison was communicating with the society's headquarters in London and providing the advice that the next missionary they sent should explore Penang, Java or Malacca as a base to serve as a stepping-stone to China. He imagined that the society might think his serving the company as translator might be incompatible with his being a missionary, in which case a separation should take place, and he raised the possibility of removing to Malacca or Java.[1] The society could see distinct advantages in the relationship that Morrison had established with the company and they decided not to end it. They concurred with Morrison about the possibilities of setting up the mission in South East Asia and in 1812, they sent another young missionary out for service in the Ultra Ganges Mission.

William Milne was born in Aberdeenshire in 1785. He was accepted by the LMS at twenty-five and sent for training at the Gosport Academy in Hampshire in 1810, where he was ordained in July 1812. He married Rachel Cowie of Aberdeen and they sailed from England on 4 September 1812. During the ten-month passage to Macao, with a stopover in Malacca, Milne made good use of his time studying Chinese characters and learning to read. His short visit to Malacca proved positive, with the English military commandant, Major William Farquhar, assuring Milne that should he and Morrison need to withdraw from Canton, the society's mission would be made very welcome in Malacca.[2] The Milnes arrived in Macao in July 1813 and, although welcomed warmly by Morrison, the Portuguese civil and religious authorities were not so keen to have two Protestant missionaries resident in Macao and issued an order that Milne must leave within ten days. The solution was for Milne to move up to Canton to find accommodation and begin an intensive study of the Chinese language. Of course, under the rules imposed on foreigners in Canton, Mrs Milne could not join him and had to stay in Macao.

Anything but a short-term residence in Canton also looked problematic for Milne. The East India officials refused to accept Milne as Morrison's assistant and the Portuguese authorities stood firm on their decision to prohibit his residence in Macao. After some months, Morrison and Milne agreed that the mission should be established at Java or Malacca, and Milne sailed for Java on 14 February 1814. With Milne were his Chinese tutor, Liang Fa, a printer who understood printing in Chinese and English, and a servant. One of Milne's objectives was to distribute copies of Morrison's recently completed translation of the New Testament and other literature in Chinese and to assess the printing facilities at each location in order to print Morrison's new Chinese-English phrase book.

Milne arrived in Batavia (Jakarta) on 10 March 1814, when the Indonesian islands were under the control of the East India Company. He stayed as the guest of the Lieutenant Governor of Java, Stamford Raffles. It is worth reviewing a brief history of Batavia because the paths of Raffles and the LMS missionaries, including Walter Medhurst, will cross again. In 1806, Holland was absorbed into the French empire and since Britain and France were at war then, the presence of the Dutch colonies in the East Indies was considered a threat by the neighbouring British possessions then under control of the East India Company. By 1810, the Governor General, Lord Minto, based in Calcutta, began to consider how the French could be cleared out of Java. He appointed a junior member of the Penang Presidency, Thomas Stamford Raffles, to the post of Agent to the Governor General in Malaya to prepare a plan for the invasion of Batavia. Raffles spoke Malay fluently. He had made acquaintances with several Malay rulers on whom he believed the British could rely for support. His plan for the invasion, led by Lord Minto himself, was carried out in August 1811. It resulted in the British successfully defeating the combined French and Dutch forces in two weeks. Lord Minto rewarded Raffles by appointing him Lieutenant Governor of Java, and in 1817 Raffles was knighted by the Prince Regent in London.

The cousin of Stamford Raffles was the Revd Thomas Raffles, a congregational minister from Liverpool and a director of the

LMS, and the two of them communicated regularly, which meant that Stamford Raffles would be well informed and supportive of the society's operations. Raffles invited Milne to investigate the possibility of setting up the mission in Batavia. He considered Milne 'a liberal, well-informed, excellent man'.³ Milne remained in Java from March to August 1814, collecting information about the country and its inhabitants, especially the Chinese, and he travelled extensively with the assistance of transportation and introductions arranged by Stamford Raffles. He gained an audience with the Javanese Emperor of Mataram and stayed at the palace of the Sultan of Madura. Overall, Milne was very impressed with Java, writing back to the society that it was an island in which 'the botanist, the mineralogist, the antiquary, the linguist, the historian and the missionary have each an immense field'.⁴

In August 1814, Milne took to the sea again for the week's crossing to Malacca. As in the year before, Major William Farquhar, the resident military commandant, welcomed him. Malacca was a cosmopolitan settlement with a long history of foreign control under successive Malay, Portuguese, Dutch, and English regimes, although the Chinese had almost always wielded commercial control. Milne reported that the main Chinese population seemed to be concentrated in the town and appeared to adhere more to their native language than did the Chinese in Java. He observed that the Malaccan Chinese enjoyed prestige among their countrymen, so for this and other reasons, Malacca would be a good site for the mission. However, as Milne was feeling oppressed by the heat and humidity of the climate, he decided that to continue to Penang would be too much for his health and so decided to return to Macao to discuss what he had learned with Morrison.

On his return in September, he was pleased to discover that the Portuguese raised no objection to his presence in Macao. Whether Morrison had already decided on a plan before Milne's return or whether they worked out a plan together, by the end of 1814 they had chosen Malacca as the location of their new mission and developed the idea of an educational institution as its centrepiece. Elementary education, religious instruction, printing, and publishing would be major priorities of the station, mostly aimed at the Chinese community but not exclusively. It would become the headquarters of the Ultra Ganges Mission, supporting a network of missionaries serving other communities in the region. It was an ambitious plan for two men who were over 6,000 miles from home, living in a foreign culture, and planning to teach a philosophy that was hardly known among the native people.

Morrison wrote to the society justifying their decision and explaining that preaching the Gospel from Canton was impracticable due to the hostility of the Chinese Government. He informed them that Milne had left for Malacca, confident in the belief that the directors would agree with their decision. Morrison concluded by reminding the society of his earlier suggestion of a training college: 'Let Malacca be the seat of your missionary college for training both natives and Europeans to the work of the ministry in the countries beyond the Ganges.'[5]

Milne left Macao for Malacca in March 1815 with his pregnant wife and daughter, his tutor-assistant and the printer Liang Fa. Five days later, on a ship without a medical doctor, Rachel Milne gave birth prematurely to twin boys. A month later, they arrived in Malacca. Just imagine the challenges that Milne faced after landing to find a home for his family, including three children under two years of age, accommodation for his assistants, premises for a school and a printing works, and all this in a foreign culture some 6,000 miles from home, this, when the man was reportedly in poor health and easily debilitated by the heat and humidity of the tropical climate. The fact that he went on to achieve everything he and Morrison had discussed in Canton is a testament to his hard work and determination.

During the first year at Malacca, Milne set up a school in the grounds of his home. By the end of the year, a Chinese master taught reading, writing and arithmetic to eighty students, some being taught in Hokkien, others in Cantonese. He was issuing a monthly publication called *The Chinese Magazine,* distributing 500 copies monthly throughout the Chinese community, mostly containing articles he had written. He was also occupied in language study, writing and translating Chinese literature.

In January 1816, Milne visited Penang to appeal to the governor for a grant of land in Malacca as a base for their growing mission centre. The governor provisionally agreed to Milne's request subject to the agreement of the new Dutch administration, which was scheduled to take control of Malacca under the Congress of Vienna at the end of the Napoleonic wars, and a plot of land was offered. Milne exchanged this land for a smaller but more definite commitment of land with a local Indian merchant. The new land was located on the seafront just outside the town's western gate and included an old building that could be modified as living quarters for Milne and any new missionaries who arrived from London.

Throughout 1816 and into the beginning of 1817, Milne organised the construction of outbuildings to house the English, Chinese and Malay presses that he had frequently requested the society to supply. At the same time, Morrison suggested that Milne should try to source printers and presses from Bengal. He did so, only to face coping with an onrush of printers and presses that he had to set up before the arrival of his promised master printer. To keep the Bengal printers busy, he set them to work on a new project of his own, a quarterly periodical in English, *The Indo-Chinese Gleaner*, which first appeared in 1817.

Well before their ship reached its destination, Walter made sure Betty was apprised of the Ultra Ganges Mission, a life that they were shortly to join. When the *Fair Trial* stopped briefly in Penang, the Medhursts went ashore and were entertained by Captain Gilbert Cooper, Brigade Major of the troop at the Penang garrison, to whom Walter had been given an introduction. Mrs Cooper would have been good company for Betty, sharing her experiences of family life within the Madras Army and motherhood with a six-month-old daughter.

10

MALACCA

On the morning of 12 July 1817, Walter, Betty and George were up on deck as the *Fair Trial* moved slowly along the coast of the land that would be their new home. Around two hours before reaching their destination, they passed Cape Rachado, named by the Portuguese colonials who built the lighthouse in 1528, marking the last hazard that the captain would have to navigate before reaching port. As the ship approached the city from the west, they looked out for the mission property just outside the walled city on the seafront. Seven-year-old George Braune provided his own commentary in bursts of excitement as he spotted anything he associated with their new house. After spending seven weeks cooped up in a small space, he was wound up like a clockwork toy. Apart from a short stop in Penang, they had been out of sight of land since leaving Madras.

We have the recollection of William Milne when he first saw Malacca from the deck of a ship four years earlier. The city had retained something of the atmosphere of an international trading port, yet it also had an air of quiet dignity and charm, with its central hill topped by the ruins of an ancient church, its neat colourful houses, its tree-shaded seafront, and the pleasant surrounding countryside of Malay villages, coconut plantations and green rice fields. 'A town much the appearance of a country village in England,' Milne noted.[1] Located on the west coast of what is now Malaysia, midway down the Malacca Strait, Malacca was a river port city through which all maritime traffic passed between India and China. Founded by the Malays in 1400, the city was invaded in 1511 by the Portuguese who built the A'Famosa fortress on a hill above the east bank of the Malacca River where the river meets the sea. The Portuguese held Malacca until 1641 when it fell to the Dutch, and in 1795 the city was occupied by the British as a temporary colonial prize during the Napoleonic wars. The British initially began demolishing the fortress and made plans to evacuate the population to Penang but in 1808, Stamford Raffles arrived and on his recommendation, the city was saved from destruction and the plan to evacuate was abandoned.

When the ship docked in the Malacca River, the Medhurst family stepped ashore with a mixture of excitement and trepidation, receiving a welcome from William Milne that immediately reassured them. As Milne reported at the time, he 'hailed with unspeakable pleasure the arrival of a colleague, Walter Henry Medhurst, who landed, with his family at Malacca on the 12th July'.[2] Milne had been struggling under a heavy load and his health was suffering badly. Rachel Milne had given birth to a daughter in April, but sadly the child died after a few days, leaving the mother in the grip of a fever. She had recovered sufficiently the week before the Medhursts arrived in Malacca to travel back to Macao where he hoped the change in climate would benefit her. In addition, the only assistant that Milne had, the Revd Claudius Thomsen, had returned to England the previous September due to ill health.

The group travelled through the town and out to the mission house with its recently constructed outbuildings housing the English, Chinese and Malay printing presses, storage facilities and living quarters for the printers. The Medhursts were moving into the living quarters in the main mission house, previously occupied by the Thomsens. There was now a regular mission staff of around twenty people whose work needed to be organised and supervised – printers, translators, language assistants, teachers in the junior schools outside. Milne had been in sole charge since Thomsen's departure. He had been planning to visit Morrison in China the previous year but the sickness and departure of Thomsen had made that impossible. Now, if the young printer looked capable of taking charge of the mission, then perhaps Milne could follow his wife and children to China after all. The picture was quickly forming in Walter Medhurst's mind that he would be taking on a lot more responsibility than simply superintending the printing operations. Nine days after arriving in Malacca, Walter wrote to the society in London:

Malacca July 21st 1817
Dear Sir
In my letter dated May the 20th I wrote informing you of my marriage, which I hope has come safe to hand. I have now the pleasure of informing you that we arrived here safe on the 12th inst. after a tedious passage of nearly two months from Madras.

As you expected Mr Milne received us with the greatest kindness – we consider him as our father – he takes every opportunity of instructing me – pressing on my mind the importance of my office, that I may be able to carry on the affairs of the Mission during his absence in China, with prudence and cautious consideration. There is more doing in the Mission Garden at Malacca than I expected – it seems almost too much to lie on the head and heart of one man.

My dear Mrs Medhurst is well and is studying the Malay. I am fagging hard at the Chinese though yet I have not gone far enough to know my difficulties. Pray for me my dear Sir, that I may have perseverance and above all maintain spirituality of mind in the face of such dry studies. Assuring

you of every wish to be the devoted servant of the Church as long as I live, I remain yours affectionately
W H Medhurst

Please to inform my Parents there is a letter for them by this vessel.

We see from Walter's letter that despite her workload supporting her husband, Betty was already learning Malay. This showed she was immersed in missionary activities, soon to be put to good use in the Malay school.

Just four weeks after Walter and Betty arrived in Malacca, William Milne left for Macao, leaving the whole care of the mission including preaching, schools, printing, and tract distribution to his newly arrived assistant. Walter wrote, 'This, together with the acquisition of the language, became a heavy burden for a young beginner, but by God's help, the machine kept in motion; while the demands on ingenuity, to render himself intelligible, soon forced the inexperienced labourer into a tolerable acquaintance with the vernacular tongue.'[3] It must have been quite a challenge because for the remainder of that year, for five months, the whole mission was left in sole charge of the twenty-two-year-old printer. During this time, Betty discovered that she was pregnant with their first child, due sometime in March. Fortunately, on 29 December, fresh assistants arrived from England. The Revd Claudius Thomsen returned from fifteen months' sick leave, accompanied by the Revd John Slater and Mrs Slater. Thomsen returned to his work in the Malay department of the mission and soon reopened the English and Malay schools, where Betty assisted with the teaching. Slater came out to help in the Chinese Mission and employed himself in the study of Chinese. When Mrs Jemima Slater arrived, she was eight months pregnant. Although relieved to have new female company, Betty was soon recruited to help in the care of Jemima and her new daughter.

Mr and Mrs Milne's health, considerably improved by the change of climate and the many attentions of kind friends, allowed them to return to Malacca on 17 February 1818. Young Walter, anxious to get on with his Chinese language studies, gladly handed charge of the mission back to Milne. The Chinese written language used the same characters throughout China but there were several different dialects. The most common among the Chinese population around Malacca was Hokkien, followed by Fujian, but ultimately any missionary serious about China had to learn Cantonese and Mandarin. Walter's responsibilities as a printer meant that he had to master thousands of Chinese characters.

Walter and Betty's first child was born on 27 March 1818, a son named William Henry. Mother and child appeared initially to be doing well and some weeks passed before they realised that the boy was not growing as he should. The standards of medical care in 1818 would have been very basic, even in a city like London, but in far-off Malacca, the poor parents would have been almost totally on their own. They would have consulted a variety of medical opinions from Europeans and Chinese but all to no avail. The child became weaker and weaker and on 14 May, at the age of eight weeks, he died. Milne wrote that, 'This heavy stroke was felt by the fond parents, but they were enabled, by divine grace, to bear it with submission to the will of him who cannot err and who makes all things, even those most adverse in their own nature.'[4] An autopsy carried out on the infant gave the immediate cause of death as an inflammatory obstruction of the bowel, but childbirth and infancy were such risky periods of life then that we cannot know for sure what went wrong. Betty felt the loss in the extreme for this was her second child to die in infancy. The loss tested her new-found Christian faith but in the end, Walter's support and rock-solid faith in God allowed them to overcome the tragedy and keep going.

Walter found solace in his faith but his work in managing the printing operations kept his mind and body fully occupied.

By the middle of 1818, eighteen people were employed in the printing works, which turned out publications in Chinese, English and Malay, including a regular Chinese magazine, a print run of the New Testament, the Book of Psalms, and various tracts. Two apprentice boys were employed, one a Chinese for the Chinese printing press and the other a freed slave for the English and Malay printing office. Printing in different languages was complicated further by the operation of different printing methods. Xylography, or block printing, was the traditional method used for printing in Chinese, whereas typography was used for English and Malay printing. A further method of lithography was used experimentally for Chinese and Malay. The Malacca Mission press was already working towards the introduction of Western typography for Chinese printing, which would later revolutionise printing throughout China. The objective of the missionaries' endeavours was religion, but a significant by-product was a technical revolution in Chinese printing.

Printing was an important activity of all the Ultra Ganges missions, but the vision of both Morrison and Milne was firmly focused on developing the college. While in Macao and Canton, William Milne had extensive discussions with Robert Morrison about the future of the Malacca Mission. They determined that Malacca should be the launching site for the great eventual mission to China itself, and Morrison wrote to the society, 'We must use every means to raise up native missionaries. I therefore beg to press again on your attention the *Anglo-Chinese College*.'[5] Preparations for starting the college went ahead at Malacca. The *Indo-Chinese Gleaner* formally announced the scheme in its February 1818 issue, anticipating not only the approval and support of the LMS but also the incoming Dutch government's approval of the Malacca Mission itself and its tenure of the mission premises. Milne's approach to Major Farquhar paid off. The Major wrote to the Dutch commissioners requesting that they favour and protect

Revd Milne of the Chinese Protestant Mission and confirm the conditional grant of land made by the British Government.

The Dutch authorities responded favourably to these approaches and preparations were soon underway for the ceremony of laying the foundation stone of the new college. To mark the occasion, a three-page prospectus entitled *General Plan of the Anglo-Chinese College at Malacca* was prepared and printed for general distribution. The whole tone of the document suggested the broad aim of an essentially liberal, secular institution with the twin objects of the cultivation of European and Chinese literature and the diffusion of Christianity – in that order. This commitment was printed and published at least two months before an approval or rejection could be received from London.

The other sections of the plan dealt with the facilities it proposed to offer, the make-up of the teaching staff and the broad categories of students that the college might admit. Finally, it was announced that the Revd W. Milne, Malacca, or the Revd Dr Morrison, China, would thankfully receive subscriptions. Morrison enclosed a copy of the general plan in a letter to the society's treasurer, W. A. Hankey, dated 28 October 1818, in which he wrote,

I now send you a Plan of the Anglo-Chinese College; I will thank you to lay the plan before the Missionary Society and advise such measures as appear to you right. I should be glad of your hearty concurrence and that you will be pleased to make it known to benevolent men in London or any other part of the British Empire.

The Missionary Society must furnish our European professors of Chinese. I hope they will see this to be perfectly in the way of their duty.

PS I trust that the Missionary Society not appearing in the Plan will be no objection. It wishes to do good, let who will take the honour.[6]

So here was a college that would be funded and supported by the LMS but not bear its name, whose missionaries would be the professors, and the diffusion of Christianity would only be a secondary goal.

During the summer of 1818, news reached William Milne that on 24 December 1817, the University of Glasgow had conferred on him the honorary degree of Doctor of Divinity in recognition of the philological works he had published.

Throughout 1818, Walter Medhurst continued to run the printing office and the Chinese schools but his activities now expanded outside of the mission centre, distributing pamphlets and preaching his Christian message to those on the Chinese river junks and to the villages and plantations surrounding Malacca. Like other recently arrived missionary colleagues, Walter was attracted to getting out among the people, rather than being confined to activities within the college.

II

ANGLO-CHINESE COLLEGE

The Anglo-Chinese College was launched before any approval, rejection or alternative could be received from London. This would have been unavoidable due to the slow turnaround of messages at the time – it would have taken ten months at best to get a response from London. This tyranny of distance was a constant factor limiting remote control by a central authority, whether that was a colonial official, company merchant or missionary. Such conditions required that a person be able to operate independently as what was known as 'the man on the spot'.

The Evangelical missionary was typically an independently minded individual who did not easily submit to authority. This is evident with Dr Morrison in the way he developed the Anglo-Chinese College, pushing through local government support and presenting it as a fait accompli to the society. His relationship with William Milne was a positive one and they worked well as a team to build the Malacca Mission Centre and start the operation of the college, but it was Morrison's idea and his plan that was implemented. It was also largely Morrison's money; he had donated £1,000 to the erection of the building and £500 for the instruction of one European and one Chinese student for the first five years.

The directors met in London to consider the resolutions passed by Morrison and Milne in Canton, including the general plan of the college. General concern was expressed on several points and the directors warned against the dangers of bringing together, in one institution, students with purely religious aims and those with primarily secular aims. However, they approved the general design of the college and the allocation of some of the land at Malacca for the proposed building. The irony was that this meeting took place on the very day that the foundation stone was laid in Malacca. Morrison wrote, 'I am glad that you approve generally of the College.' In reference to the directors warning about mixing religious and secular students, he said, 'If your missionaries cannot bear contact with secular students, alas, how do you think they will do to be sent into the wide world, surrounded by vicious heathens and profligate Europeans and spiritual enemies and in exile from Christian society?'

In September 1818, three new missionaries arrived from London – Thomas Beighton, John Ince and Samuel Milton. They each began learning the rudiments of the different languages. Meanwhile, Walter Medhurst took charge of the three Chinese schools that the mission ran while at the same time continuing to superintend the English, Chinese and Malay printing operations. Thomsen continued to run the Malay schools while Slater had taken a spell in Canton, partly for his health but also to improve his language skills.

The Malaccan mission centre was now almost overloaded with keen, young, independently minded young missionaries, full of passion and zeal and ready to go out and spread the word of God wherever and whenever an opportunity arose. They had arrived at a place where a mild-mannered but authoritarian William Milne was trying to implement Robert Morrison's vision of an international educational institution to be staffed by these new arrivals. To Milne, the mission *was* the Anglo-Chinese College and he exercised authority over it as principal of the college. He saw the new missionaries as language students to be educated under college discipline and then become professors there. They saw themselves as trained missionaries sent to Malacca to learn the language before being sent out to perform their missionary labours preaching the word of God to the people. The root cause of the uncertainty surrounding the mission centre lay in the fact that Morrison had conceived the college plan in Canton and Milne had enacted it in Malacca, with almost no input or direction from the society in London. The mission centre had become the college and the relationship between the college and the society went unresolved. To some of these new missionaries, the college was not a missionary centre at all.

Once the new arrivals had reached some competency in Malay and the major Chinese dialects, it was time to plan the expansion of activities and establish other missions in the region. Having visited Penang three years earlier, and gained government support to establish the Malacca Mission, Dr Milne determined Penang as the first new mission to be established. Walter Medhurst was sent to meet with the governor of Penang for assistance with the grant of some suitable land. With Milne's wife still sick and expecting another child in early 1819, the possibility of going to Penang himself was ruled out. None of the newcomers was proficient enough in the local languages to make a good impression on the governor.

Walter took up the challenge enthusiastically, sailing from Malacca on 2 January 1819 in the brig *Brother*. The master Captain Eddis provided free passage, and they arrived on 6 January. Soon after his arrival, Walter was granted an audience with Colonel John Bannerman, the governor of Prince of Wales Island (Penang), along with two members of the governing council. He outlined the plans of the LMS. He went on to solicit the support of the government for funds to cover the salaries of one or two teachers as well rent for a suitable schoolhouse.

Walter made a very good impression on the governor. Three days later, he received a response from the government secretary at Fort Cornwallis advising him that the governor 'has determined to give patronage to the objects you have described and to support the contemplated instruction to a reasonable extent'.[1] Everything that Walter asked the governor for was granted. He took immediate steps to establish two schools, one for Fujian and the other for Canton children. Furthermore, he gained the support of the Chinese community who agreed to provide space for a schoolroom at the temple.

Dr Milne followed up Walter's meeting with the governor by writing a letter asking the government to consider assisting the society with a grant of land to build the Penang Mission. This resulted in Walter Medhurst being called back to another meeting with the governor, who supported Dr Milne's request subject to knowing which missionaries might be sent to Penang and whether they would be proficient in Chinese and Malay. The governor was aware that Mr Thomsen was moderately proficient in Malay and he had already been impressed by Medhurst's capability in Chinese, which left no doubt that if Medhurst and Thomsen were to be sent to Penang, then the government would accede to Milne's request. This was obviously beyond Medhurst's authority to discuss without further consultation with his associates back in Malacca, and so he indicated he should return immediately to update Mr Milne, who would respond to the governor with the names of those he proposed sending to Penang.

The good impression that Walter made on Governor Bannerman was all the more spectacular when you understand what historically significant activity was taking place in Penang at the same time. On 1 February, Sir Stamford Raffles concluded his long-held mission of establishing Singapore as a British outpost, having made alliances with local Malay sultans, the effect of which outwitted the neighbouring Dutch colonial rulers. After appointing Colonel

Farquhar as Resident and Commandant, Sir Stamford Raffles left Singapore for Penang on 7 February. He was acting with the full support of the governor general in Calcutta but his actions did not have the support of Colonel Bannerman. Raffles determined that he should gain that support to cement the success of the new settlement in Singapore. Raffles arrived in Penang on 13 February and stayed at Government House until 8 March. On 16 February, the Dutch official protest was received in Penang, which prompted Bannerman to advise Raffles to order Colonel Farquhar to evacuate Singapore for fear that the Dutch would attack. Raffles held firm, confident in the belief that Calcutta and London would support him. The matter took a decisive turn in Calcutta when the *Calcutta Journal* declared the founding of Singapore as an event of the greatest importance to the China trade and expressed the hope that the settlement would receive the support of the government. It also congratulated the governor general for his part in overcoming a Dutch monopoly on trade in the East Indies.

During this critical period in the founding of Singapore, Walter had his second meeting with Bannerman and gained the support of the government for the Penang Mission. Government House at Penang was a small place, with both Raffles and Medhurst meeting there over the same two weeks. Raffles had a special interest in missionary activities through his cousin, the director of the LMS. They would have met, but without being able to see the future for Singapore, Walter did not appreciate the importance of recording that meeting. Walter wrote to the directors in London on 28 February that he was on board a ship about to leave Penang for Malacca and added that there were now forty boys in the school he had established.

By the time Walter arrived back in Malacca, the mission was abuzz with talk about which missionaries would be settled in Penang. Arriving by the same ship was a letter from Colonel Bannerman to Dr Milne formally requesting that Mr Medhurst be assigned to establish the new mission, leaving the implication that the grant of land might well depend on Dr Milne acceding to his request. Thomas Beighton and John Ince were both adamant that it should be their opportunity, since it had been discussed before they left London. Compounding the problems for Milne in managing the mission centre was the fact that his wife had given birth to a son in February, leaving her dangerously ill. By mid-March, Rachel's health continued to deteriorate and a change of air was advised, but since there was no opportunity of a sea voyage, a move to the country was the only alternative. Three days later, on 20 March, 4 miles from Malacca at Clay-Bang, she died. Milne took the loss very heavily and for the remainder of his life his letters and articles were sprinkled with references about how much he missed his wife and how it was now a week, a month, three months, etc. since his dear Rachel departed this life.

The whole mission centre pulled together to support Milne in his loss and any dissension among the group was put aside temporarily. Betty Medhurst took on the responsibility of looking after the four Milne children: a five-year-old daughter, the four-year-old twin boys born on board ship, and the new six-week-old Farquhar. Rachel Milne was buried the following day in the Dutch burial grounds alongside her son and daughter who had both died in infancy. Rachel was just thirty-five years of age.

The tense situation developing over Penang could not be avoided however, and Dr Milne made his decision at the end of March. He wrote to Colonel Bannerman that he presently found it impossible to spare Mr Medhurst since he was the only one who could superintend the printing operation, manage the Chinese schools and take over Dr Milne's role if that became necessary. He reported, 'On maturely weighing all circumstances I find it impossible to part with Mr Medhurst at present.'[2] Walter Medhurst had made himself indispensable. The letter went on to introduce Thomas Beighton and John Ince as the new missionaries for Penang.

The question of whether the grant of land might still be made was not answered and in his letter, Dr Milne expressed fear that it might not. Milne's decision antagonised Thomsen and Medhurst. It gave them the impression that they had been passed over by these late arrivals. Walter felt a grave sense of injustice since it was he who had earlier prepared the ground for a mission in Penang by establishing the Chinese school at the specific request of Colonel Bannerman. Walter stewed over this perceived injustice for a while and even though his impetuous nature made him inclined to do something about it immediately, his rational side told him that his work managing the printing and the Chinese schools was important enough for him to remain tolerant to the situation. From then on, however, his relationship with Dr Milne cooled and Walter was rarely mentioned in Dr Milne's memoirs after this date.

Two more events took place that year of great significance to Walter and Betty. On 27 April 1819, two days before his twenty-third birthday, he was ordained. The service was performed privately at the Medhursts' home, expedited due to the imminent departure of some of the missionaries. He wrote to the society, 'I felt my own unfitness for entering on so weighty and important work at so early a period, but the expected departure of the brethren seemed to point out the necessity of performing the service without delay.' Dr William Milne led the service, assisted by the reverends John Slater, Samuel Milton and John Ince.

An indication of the cooling of Walter Medhurst's relationship with Dr Milne is shown by the fact that the ordination did not even rate a mention in Dr Milne's book, the only mention for that date referring to the Revd John Slater leaving that day for Batavia.[3]

The second significant event to take place that year occurred on 16 November, when Betty gave birth to a daughter, Sarah Sophia. After the loss of baby William the previous year, the parents were very nervous about their new child but there was no cause for worry as Sarah was born healthy and well. The hope that she would stay that way, however, was threatened by an outbreak of cholera spreading through Malacca at the time, the disease carrying off victims daily. Walter wrote to London with this news:[4]

Malacca, November 23rd 1819

My dear Sir

I received your kind letter of date 25th of February this morning and as there is a ship in the roads about to sail for Calcutta I shall sit down and answer it immediately. Accept my thanks my dear Sir, for your warm expressions of attachment and your kind and ready offer of assistance in any thing that regards my family affairs, or the disposal of our dear son George, who is by this time I dare say in England. We were in great hesitation about sending him, as we knew nothing of the circumstances or situation of Mr C, to whose care he was to be entrusted; but your letter has entirely removed our concerns and we can fully confide in your judgement, in conjunction with Mr C as to what seminary he should be sent. We should certainly have preferred Mill Hill as being a seminary of established reputation but if it is full, there is no recourse but to select one of the most eligible of those schools which are conducted on evangelical principles. It was expected that he would come under the care of Dr Chalmers and indeed he did proceed with that gentleman as far as Calcutta; but Dr C having resolved to remain in India a few years longer he resigned his charge to a Captain Simon, who sailed with George in the ship Christopher, Captain Lockerby in the month of March 1819. We are now anxious to hear of his arrival in England, being perfectly satisfied with respect to his disposal when he does arrive. May the blessing of the Lord attend him while removed from under a parents eye, guard him from all dangers, raise him up to be eminently useful in the world.

My last to you was dated from Penang in the month of February in which I requested that you would be kind enough to pay my mother or sister £1 5s monthly or £15 per annum, to commence from July 1819. I have from that period regularly paid that sum into your funds at Malacca and therefore hope that no objection will arise as to the transmission of it to my relatives.

Before the departure of our dear brethren to the several islands around, they judged it suitable that I should be ordained. The service was accordingly performed on the 27th April, privately in a room of our own house. Mr Slater introduced the service by an appropriate discourse. Mr Ince asked the usual questions. Mr Milton prayed the ordination prayer and Mr Milne gave the charge. The service was exceedingly solemn and impressive though our number was small yet I trust the presence of God was experienced among us. I felt my own unfitness for entering on so weighty and important a work at so early a period, but the expected departure of the brethren seemed to point out the necessity of performing the service without delay. I hope that no part of my conduct in future life will tend to belie the professions made on that evening and that no lapse of time will obliterate from my memory the solemn engagements then entered into. The Lord is my helper.

On the 16th inst. Mrs M presented me with a fine little girl; both the mother and child are now doing well and will I hope be spared to the long lived blessings to the circle in which we move. Mrs M gratefully acknowledges your affectionate enquiries and she most personally desires to present you her kind regards to all the friends of Zion.

I remain dear Sir, yours very affectionately, W. H. Medhurst

Walter's letter revealed that his mother and sister were now living apart from Walter's father, and that their son George had been sent back to school in England, a long lonely journey for a nine-year-old boy, away from his mother and stepfather to start a new life in a strange land. Within days of writing the letter and on the day that Sarah Sophia was baptised, Walter was struck down with cholera and confined to his sick bed. Fortunately for him and his young family, he was destined to be one of the lucky ones and after a week of Betty's care, he recovered and returned to his duties.

Immediately after the ordination, the missionaries began dispersing to their various stations. Beighton went to Penang, Samuel Milton to Singapore and John Slater to Batavia, leaving Dr Milne, Ince, Thomsen, and Medhurst in Malacca. Ince was destined for Penang but his Chinese language skills were not up to the level required to manage the Chinese schools in Penang. Walter probably wondered what use he could be as a newly ordained missionary when he was locked into running the printing works, managing the Chinese schools and teaching in the Anglo-Chinese College. There were no replacements on the horizon to take over his management duties in any of these areas and his deteriorating relationship with Dr Milne probably meant that he was unlikely to be considered as a replacement for Dr Milne should that opportunity arise. Milne himself appeared to be suffering from serious depression following the loss of his wife.

Claudius Thomsen was Walter's closest friend in Malacca, one who shared Walter's frustrations about the college. He worked with Betty at the Malay school. Thomsen was a Dane, originating from Holstein, and he had first come to Malacca with his wife to support Milne in 1815. Mrs Thomsen had fallen ill in Malacca and together they returned to England, but unfortunately she died at sea, after which Claudius Thomsen returned in 1817. Walter wrote in his book, 'Mr Thomsen's labours in the English and Malay school, were rewarded by the gratifying progress of the children and their willingness to instruct others. Mr T. succeeded also in rescuing a Malay family from slavery, whom he regularly instructed and was happy to see them renounce Mahomedanism and embrace Christianity.'[5]

It would be sixteen months before the gaps created by the departure of the four missionaries were partly filled by the arrival from London in September 1820 of Mr G. H. Huttman, a printer, to take over Walter's print office management duties, and Mr Robert Fleming, a missionary to work on the Chinese side. It was intended that Mr Huttman would learn Chinese, but Huttman refused to apply himself. Mr Fleming's position became a short-term one, as within a year, 'for acknowledged adultery and for derangement of mind,' Milne suspended him. The new arrivals did, however, relieve Walter Medhurst of the obligations he felt towards the college and the mission centre, as there would now be other hands to take over the printing, leaving Milne to manage the Chinese schools.

Walter had maintained communication with various members of the community in Penang after Beighton left Malacca. For a start, Beighton did not understand Chinese and his focus was on establishing the Malay schools, which left Walter to correspond with the teachers he had hired to run the Fujian and Cantonese schools. In addition, he maintained some of the connections made among the Europeans when he was in Penang the previous year, although Colonel Bannerman had died of cholera in August 1819. He and Thomsen regularly discussed the opportunity for another mission in Penang and convinced themselves that the community could support two missions. Betty would have supported her husband's decision anyway, but her working relationship with Thomsen in the Malay school convinced her that Walter and Claudius would make a good team.

By September 1820, the decision had been made. The Medhursts would leave for Penang and Thomsen would follow once they were established. Walter wrote to London to inform them of the reasons for his decision. It was one of the hardest decisions Walter had made since joining the society, and there was no going back. He would just have to get on with building a mission centre in the way he thought it should be done. Having made the decision, he had to make the decision right. He would let his results convince London that he had done the right thing.

In spite of Walter practically walking out on Milne and taking some of the printing equipment with him, Milne was reluctant to condemn the action in his letters to London. 'I have a great regard for him,' he said, even though Walter's leaving was an 'ill-advised, imprudent, precipitate step and one very badly executed'. He continued, 'I did not know of his intention until the Captain of the ship told me. I do not know why he left Malacca unless it was that he had been taught to call me arbitrary, reserved, stiff and fond of dominion.' It sounds like Milne's conclusion is that someone else had been involved in persuading Medhurst that he should leave, and the consensus was that it was Thomsen.

It must have been an emotional and difficult time for all parties. The relationships formed between the missionaries and their families at the mission centre had been very close. They had shared good times and bad. Walter and Betty, sometimes with Claudius, agonised over the decision to break away, compounded by Milne's recent bereavement. Most of the records of the day show that everything was normal before the break up. Walter and Thomsen were reported as taking part in a memorial service for Rachel Milne on the anniversary of her death. Milne wrote how pleased he was with a geographical catechism created by Walter in Chinese, and Walter made no criticism of Milne in his book. However, Morrison wrote from Canton, 'Milne was completely deserted by all the missionaries.'

Thomsen's intention to join Medhurst in Penang can be seen from a letter by Beighton, who wrote, 'I beg of you not to come here without the Society's approbation ... I left Malacca with hope of finding peace and quietude at my own station, but you and Medhurst seem determined to overturn all rules whatever. You know this island is too small for two distinct missions from one Society. Though you found fault with Mr Milne for aiming at power, yet you encouraged Medhurst to come here and act more the part of a Pope than anyone I ever met with.'[6] Thomsen may well have taken note of that letter for he abandoned his plans to join Medhurst in Penang and the following year he moved to Singapore, although not to join Samuel Milton – the two missionaries did not get along, and Thomsen set up a Singapore mission for the Malay population quite separate from Milton's mission for the Chinese.

The geographical catechism Milne referred to was the first of many Chinese publications that Walter produced during his life. It was an atlas designed for use in elementary schools and it was first published as a series of five articles in Dr Milne's Chinese magazine. The atlas comprised maps of the world's major regions, including information about population, religion and production of the principal countries of the world. It was one of many secular works that Walter created with the belief that spreading the knowledge of Western culture was as important as spreading the Christian message. Another interesting fact about this publication is that it was the first time that the four characters of the Chinese name for Australia were seen in print. At the time the publication was produced, the more common name for Australia was New Holland, for which Chinese characters already existed. The transition towards the continent becoming known as Australia was just starting and it was unlikely that anyone had bothered to invent Chinese characters for this previously unknown name. In a research paper by David L. B. Jupp,[7] the writer concluded beyond reasonable doubt that the creator of the Chinese characters for Australia was Walter Henry Medhurst. This was just one of Walter's many achievements and it remained unknown until the twenty-first century.

12

PENANG

In October 1820, Walter, Betty and Sarah sailed from Malacca for Penang, taking with them all the supplies needed to start a mission centre. On 6 November, he wrote in his journal, 'Arrived at our new residence in James Town to commence my labours among a people hitherto unacquainted with the Gospel. Lord! Smile upon the attempt & let thy spirit accompany thy word to the conversion of sinners. Commenced family prayer with my servants and dependants in the Malay language, but very imperfectly.'[1]

Once established in James Town, the Medhursts set up a Chinese school for twenty orphans who resided in their house, and he recruited a Chinese teacher to assist them. They held regular clinics for the sick, dispensing medicines they had brought with them from Malacca. Walter arranged for Mr Ramsey, one of the European surgeons, to examine the sick, advise on treatments and supply additional medicines. After the patients came in for their treatments, Walter took the opportunity to preach his message and offer up a prayer for their recovery. He wrote that he found 'unspeakable pleasure in contributing in a small degree to the relief of their pains'.

He often went to Kwan-yin, the Chinese Taoist temple in George Town, where he sat and talked with anyone willing to receive his message that there was only one God and that it was wrong to worship the idols in the temple. One would think that this could be taken as aggressively criticising their beliefs right there in the temple, but he had a way of communicating his ideas without raising the ire of his listeners. He often entered into philosophical conversations, which resulted in him learning as much, or more, about Taoist and Confucian beliefs as the Chinese learned about Christianity. Although he did not claim any conversions from these activities, he distributed books and pamphlets, which the recipients retained and read.

On 29 December, two Taoist priests called at their house to solicit subscriptions for the erection of a temple at a celebrated cave in China, supposedly the favourite residence of some deity. For Walter this was too good an opportunity to miss. He wrote, 'These being the first priests of Tao I had seen, I was more observant of their dress and manners – they wore long blue gowns, with very large sleeves and on each side of the head their hair was tied into a knot, resembling the horns of a young heifer.' He described how they communicated in Mandarin, discovered where they came from and learned what their beliefs were and what kind of life they led in the monastery. He compared elements of their beliefs to Buddhist, Confucian and Catholic beliefs and recorded his observations in the journal, which he sent to London, revealing much of this information for the first time.

Walter was not a person to stay at home and wait for opportunity to come to him. He travelled all over the island to preach, visiting the bazaar, the Chinese Poor Asylum and the junks in the port, and he went from house to house in the Chinese quarter. While he was away, Betty welcomed visitors, greeting them in Malay or Chinese. She oversaw the school activities and gave out books when the people heard they were available gratis. Having been born and raised in Asia, she was at ease meeting people from different cultural backgrounds and her own experiences inspired in her a desire to help others whenever she could. Sometimes the books they distributed were received with expressions of disappointment when they found that they were not Chinese but the production of foreigners. It was a trait of the Chinese to hold anything foreign with a measure of contempt. Walter recounted the meetings and conversations he had with people he met on his travels and recorded everything in his journal, displaying the difficulties of communication, not just in the language, but also in the sweeping differences in the culture and the abstract nature of the message. It required patience and persistence to be a missionary to the Chinese.

An example of the contrast between cultures was revealed in the entry for 18 January:[2]

A man came for medicine today with whom I conversed a while privately. I asked him how long he had left China & whether he ever thought upon his family there. He said he frequently thought of them & intended next year to return and visit them, for he had three sons and one daughter who was married. 'I had another daughter,' he added, 'but I did not bring her up'. 'Not bring her up?' I said, 'What did you do with her?' 'I smothered her,' said he. 'This year I heard by letter that another daughter was born. I sent word to have her smothered also, but the mother preserved it alive.' I was shocked at his speech & still more at the horrid indifference with which he uttered it. 'What,' said I, 'murder your own children? Do you not shudder at such an act?' 'Oh no!' said he, 'It is a very common thing in China. We put the female children out of the way to save the trouble of bringing them up. Some people smother five or six daughters.' I felt I had a murderer by my side, who must, without repentance, inevitably perish. I told him he was in danger of eternal wrath. Though I said this with the greatest seriousness &

earnestness at first he only laughed & it was some time before
he would acknowledge that he had done wrong. What an
awful view does this present of the 'Celestial Empire', loaded
with crime, deluged with blood & rife for destruction – surely
some heavy vengeance or some awful judgement are awaiting
that sinful nation.

The next evening he went into James Town, and since the evening
was leisure time for the Chinese, they could easily attend his
preaching in great numbers, but he said, 'They have no heart to
it. They refuse to listen. What shall I say in order to awaken their
attention and induce them to enquire the way to life? However it
is my duty to try by all means, in season or out of season, through
honour or dishonour, to bring converts to Christ.'

The next day was a Sunday and he relished the joy of preaching
to 'my little flock' (the children). He could not help wishing that
he had fifty such under his care and a temple in which to worship
God. 'This would be the summit of my wishes.' He was pleased
on catechising the children to find that most of them remembered
what they had heard. Perhaps this indicated that the conversion of
the Chinese would start with the children.

Not all his missionary work was around the towns in Penang.
On 23 January, he wrote about travelling to the other side of
Prince of Wales Island and the difficulties of returning after dark.

This day crossed the hills to the other side of the island where
I had an opportunity of administering a little medicine and
speaking a word to the people whom I met. On returning
home, we were by an accident detained till dark before we
commenced ascending the hill to return. The night was dark,
so that we could not discern our way. The path is narrow
and winding and in many places runs along the edge of a
steep precipice so that we were in the greatest danger of

losing ourselves or being dashed over the precipice into the vale below. Our horses instead of being a help, created an additional trouble first by staying out of the way & then by kicking violently when they came near to us or to each other. We were obliged to proceed slowly step by step, a native man going before to feel the way, this man having unwound his turban (about 10 yards long) by which we were led, not being able to see our hand before us. At length with some bruises and much fatigue we reached the foot of the hill, thankful for being preserved from the evils of the ways.[3]

Tragedy was to hit the Medhurst household one more during their time in Penang. Betty gave birth to another son on 21 September, whom they baptised Walter. Sadly, there were problems with the birth and baby Walter died and was buried the following day. Could anything be more heartbreaking than the loss of a tiny helpless child? Without the support of family or close friends, the Medhursts relied heavily on their faith to get them through this dreadful period.

The society considered that Walter was making a success of the mission centre in Penang, although Thomas Beighton continued to call for his removal elsewhere. The opportunity for Beighton's wish to come true arose from reports reaching the directors regarding John Slater's conduct in Batavia. The first that Walter knew of this was when he received a request from the directors in London to be transferred to Batavia as soon as possible. At the same time, Dr Milne received a similar request for someone from Malacca to be sent, in response to which he made it clear that no labourer could be spared from his operation. Dr Milne asked the missionaries of the Ultra Ganges whether it would be suitable for Medhurst to proceed to Batavia. Those of his brethren with whom Medhurst had time to consult agreed that it was a providential opening and one he ought not to neglect.

Walter Medhurst wrote in January 1822 that the first he heard was, 'Towards the close of last year a letter arrived from the Directors addressed to the Brethren in Penang, respecting my removal thither and at the same time, another addressed to Dr Milne, recommending that a missionary be sent from Malacca to the assistance of Mr Slater in the Batavian Mission.'

In any case, the Medhursts quickly packed up in James Town and moved to Georgetown to wait the arrival of a ship. No further information was provided regarding the reports that the directors had received regarding Slater's behaviour. The Medhursts sailed in December to Batavia via Malacca and Singapore. Of the orphans that had been living with them in James Town, ten went with them on the ship. They left two in the care of Dr Milne, four stayed with Claudius Thomsen and the Medhursts took the remaining four to Java.

In Singapore, they observed how rapidly the new settlement had grown from a small fishing village to a town of over 10,000 inhabitants in just over two years. Numerous ships were in port, with lighters going to and fro, and the docksides were crowded with merchants and coolies with their carts and carriages. Behind the warehouses, the layout of the town was clearly visible, with new buildings completed or under construction as far as the Singapore Hill. Samuel Milton ran the Singapore Chinese Mission and Walter's old friend Claudius Thomsen ran the Malay Mission. This gave the missionaries and their families the opportunity to enjoy two days together, sharing ideas and information about their various activities. It was also opportune for Walter to discuss what might be happening in Batavia to warrant their urgent transfer. Walter was in effect going to Batavia as the junior member of the mission but his communication with Dr Milne indicated that Medhurst would be required to resolve certain unspecified problems at the mission. From what he knew of Slater's personality during their time together in Malacca, Walter had a challenging undertaking ahead of him.

13

ARRIVAL IN BATAVIA

Batavia had been a centre of activity for European traders for over 200 years by the time the Medhursts arrived in 1822. For most of those years, Batavia was under the control of the Dutch East Indies Company, the Vereenigde Oost-Indische Compagnie (VOC). In her prime, the city was known as the Queen of the Orient, but by the end of the eighteenth century the VOC was bankrupt and its possessions were taken over by the Dutch Republic.

The British invasion of 1811 and the appointment of Raffles as the lieutenant governor marked the beginning of five years of British occupation of Java and an enlightened period of government and reform. Among the changes that Raffles introduced were the suppression of slavery and piracy, encouragement of trade and the propagation and protection of Christianity. The opening of trade with Britain also brought new settlers to the city and their influence remained even after control reverted to the Dutch in 1816. Today Batavia is known as Jakarta, the capital of Indonesia, and has a population of ten million people.

In 1822 Batavia was the biggest city Walter and Betty had seen since leaving Madras and it may have rivalled Madras for the size and splendour of some of its public buildings. The population was approximately the same size as Madras, with the majority being

Javanese, but, significantly for the LMS Ultra Ganges Mission, Batavia had the largest overseas population of Chinese with the exception of Manila. The state of Christianity would have been at a low ebb following the collapse of the VOC, after which no more clergy were sent out from Holland. Among the small English-speaking community, there was some interest in spiritual matters and a group of residents had been raising funds to secure a chaplain at around the same time as Slater arrived in Batavia.

The Medhursts arrived in Batavia on 7 January 1822 with Captain Gray aboard the brig *Amity*. The *Amity* became a famous ship in Australia where she was used in several voyages of exploration and settlement. She was built in 1816 in New Brunswick, Canada, and in 1823 was sold to Robert Ralston of Scotland, who, with twenty family members and livestock, emigrated to settle in Van Diemen's Land (Tasmania). Ralston sold the *Amity* to the government of New South Wales in Sydney and the ship was used to transfer the first European settlers and convicts to Queensland, landing in what is now Brisbane. The northern tip of North Stradbroke Island near Brisbane is named Amity Point after the ship. The *Amity's* Australian role continued when she was used to transport the first European settlers to Western Australia and, in the City of Albany where the settlers landed, visitors today can view a full-scale replica of the ship. As with most ships of those times, she ended her days in a shipwreck when she went aground in Tasmania in 1845.

The Medhurst family of Walter, Betty and Sarah were embarking on a new venture as they sailed from Singapore across the Java Sea, to the city that would become their home for the next twenty years. The sea was calm but the weather changeable as tropical thunderstorms built up during the heat of the afternoons, forcing the crew to make numerous sail changes in order to handle the squalls. As they came into the Bay of Batavia, a magnificent scene lay before them – a long range of volcanic mountains inland and thickly forested jungles stretching down to the edge of the water. On one side, there were many small islands with beacons on them and in the middle distance was the broad plain between the shore and the high ground on which the City of Batavia stood. Here in the Batavia Roads they came to anchor along with around sixty other ships of many sizes and from many different countries. Besides these, the harbour was thronged with barges, boats and other small craft. Four huge Chinese junks were anchored nearby, indicating that Batavia was a city with a big Chinese influence.

Lacking any natural harbour, the only access to the City of Batavia was via the Haven Kanaal (Harbour Canal), the entrance of which extended between two sea walls through the marshy shoreline to the Batavia Roads where ships could anchor. The journey from the newly arrived ship to the safety of dry land could be a long and even traumatic experience for passengers. Having transferred to a small lighter, the Medhursts and their servants were rowed up the canal, from which unpleasant and pungent odours arose as it was the major drain of Batavia. Their terminus was the Kleine Boom (customs house) where they cleared their luggage before entering Batavia. They then joined the throng on the dockside, looking for the familiar face of John Slater.

Slater was there with two carriages to transport the Medhursts, their luggage, the servants, and four orphans to the mission centre, which he had established in the new European suburb of Weltevreden south of the old town of Batavia. Weltevreden was around 5 miles from the port, accessed along a straight tree-lined avenue and canal called the Molenvliet (Mill Way), one of the key topographical features of Batavia at that time. From the early 1730s when the walled City of Batavia was becoming a dangerously unhealthy place to live, it became fashionable for the wealthy to build large houses with spacious gardens along both sides of the Molenvliet. One of the grandest buildings there was the Hotel Des

Indes, rivalling anything Betty had seen before. This was the area that earned Batavia the title of 'The Queen of the Orient'.

The property Slater had purchased for the mission centre included two houses, one sufficient for two missionaries and their families and the other a smaller bamboo house. Slater had rented the larger house out and had moved into the bamboo house, which shortly afterwards was burnt to the ground, perhaps by some dishonest servant, and numerous New Testaments and pamphlets were lost. Fortunately for Slater, the British residents raised a subscription to rebuild the house and there was enough money left over to build a small bamboo chapel. Now, due to the shortage and high cost of housing in Batavia, the Medhursts initially moved in with the Slaters. At least Sarah would have Henrietta Slater to play with.

The Medhursts were unsure of the welcome they would receive from John Slater. The hurried way in which the transfer was arranged, and Milne's reference to possible problems at the Batavia Mission, had left a feeling of uncertainty. As it turned out, Slater's welcome was very warm and he told the Medhursts what a great blessing their arrival would be to the mission in Batavia. They were shown around the mission grounds and through the chapel where they reviewed plans for the addition of a vestry, a library and a schoolroom. Next door, Slater pointed out the ground on which they would build a house for the Medhursts as soon as the current rainy season ended. Slater's servants lived in various outbuildings, among which space was made to house the young orphan boys from Penang. First impressions were that Slater had achieved a great deal in establishing the mission and Walter enthusiastically told him so. From their first discussions, Slater was keen to criticise Dr Milne and he asked Walter to review a long letter he had written to the directors in which he responded to criticisms Milne had made of him. Walter did not then fully understand what the criticisms were about since it referred to letters Walter had not seen, but he advised Slater not to send the letter since no good could come from keeping up the contentions. Slater then wrote a shorter letter to the directors, on 16 January, saying that Milne had sent him letter after letter and resolved he would return any future letters from Milne unopened and communicate with the directors only. He said that Milne's letters 'had very much unsettled my mind'.

It wasn't long before the initial excitement of arrival waned as Walter evaluated the state of the mission and spoke with members of the British community. Slater had not been a good student of language when in Malacca and it was now obvious that his skills had deteriorated and he could no longer preach in Chinese or Malay. The only services conducted were in English and those were very poorly attended, as he seemed to be held in some disrepute among the English inhabitants.

A short time later, three of Slater's servants asked to speak with Walter and told him of the most horrendous treatment that they and others had received at the hands of the Revd Slater. They were regularly beaten and one of his female servants accused him of rape. 'Why did you not report this to the police and why did you stay in his employment?' was Walter's response. 'Sir,' replied the man who was the spokesperson, 'we are not servants. We are not free to leave. We are slaves.' Walter was astonished. He had heard the rumours but scarcely believed them. He had encountered slavery in Malacca and Penang and expected Batavia to be no different, but to discover that a fellow missionary had slaves in his own house was almost beyond belief. What kind of person had Slater become and what must this do to the reputation of the society? Walter assured the slaves that he and his family would treat them no differently from any other servant and that he would endeavour to resolve the matter of their freedom once he had determined the legal situation with slavery in Batavia. They were safe for the time being.

Walter immediately discussed the situation with Slater but the initial response he received was silence, followed by an angry outburst. He found John Slater to be extremely distant and reluctant to communicate any detail about his personal life or problems. He easily lost his temper, and because they lived nearby they heard Slater strike his wife several times. Soon after the Medhursts took up residence in Batavia, Slater avoided contact and went every day into town for other business, which he refused to discuss.

Once the matter was accepted as more than a mere rumour, it was as if a dam had burst and the reports of Slater's involvement with slavery rushed like a torrent from every source. It appeared that he had bought and sold slaves for profit in addition to having them for his own use. The English inhabitants all appeared aware of Slater's actions and many of them would not attend any service at which he was preaching. An American resident told Slater he degraded the role of a minister, to which Slater responded by quoting a passage from scripture to prove that slavery was allowable.

Being the persistent personality that he was, Walter continued to try to help Slater, whom he considered a troubled soul. Eventually, Slater put forward the suggestion that his health was the problem and the only solution was to take a sea voyage. As far as Walter could see, there was no apparent physical health problem but Slater's mental state was questionable. He determined that the best course of action was to support his plan to travel to Singapore for a few months to see if the change of climate benefited him. Meantime, Walter would be free to evaluate the mission centre and make his own decisions to remedy any problems.

With Slater out of the country, Walter's work now was to evaluate the damage done and develop a plan for regaining the population's respect for the mission. He also had to determine what he could do when Slater returned, for as the junior partner he had no authority to direct Slater to do anything. Under normal circumstances, he could send a message to Dr Milne in Malacca, less than a week's sailing time from Batavia, but in the midst of all this drama, word came that Dr Milne had taken ill and was staying with the missionaries Beighton and Ince up in Penang. There he was diagnosed with consumption (tuberculosis) and he returned to Malacca to settle his affairs before leaving for England. Unfortunately, his condition deteriorated on his return as he set about arranging the affairs of the Anglo-Chinese College. The relative newcomers Humphreys and Huttman tried to convince Milne to send for Medhurst, Milton or Beighton to take over, but Milne would not have any of the original missionaries back and he passed away at the college on 2 June 1822.

The next option for Walter would be to contact Dr Morrison in Canton. Unfortunately, Morrison's attention was completely absorbed by his beloved Anglo-Chinese College and finding someone to take over from Dr Milne. Morrison sailed from Canton in January 1823 heading for Malacca, on the way staying four days in Singapore where he met with Sir Stamford Raffles. Raffles suggested that the college be moved to Singapore and merged with his Malayan College. This seemed to be the solution to how the college would survive the loss of Milne and he vowed to explore the suggestion further after visiting Malacca, even though that option would terminate any relationship the college had with the London Missionary Society. Morrison threw himself into the task of managing the college in Malacca and communicated to Raffles that he intended to go through with the plan to move the college to Singapore. Later that year he returned to England on leave, and around that same time Raffles left Singapore for the last time. With neither Morrison nor Raffles present in Singapore to develop the project, the whole scheme fell apart.

Meanwhile, Walter Medhurst remained in Batavia, isolated from any support in the matter of removing a slave trading head of the Batavia LMS Mission Centre. He spent the time gathering information about Slater's activities with the society and communicated with Beighton, Ince, Milton, and Thomsen for any information they could add. He also examined the records of the land purchased for the society, which revealed that Slater had purchased the original property and partitioned off a part for himself, where he had built the house held in his name and rented it out.

Slater returned unannounced to Batavia towards the end of 1822 and told the Medhursts that he would not be moving back to the mission property as he had purchased another house nearby. His excuse for the ownership of slaves was that he was unable to hire staff or retain those he had hired. He stated his intention of continuing as a missionary with the society. Walter challenged Slater with the accusations of beatings and rape, but Slater merely resolved to treat them more humanely in future.

Within days, it was reported that the poor woman who had accused Slater of rape had been treated most cruelly. He had beaten, kicked and maimed her so much that she ran away to the police, who did nothing but return her to Slater. He made her walk behind his conveyance through the town to see if anyone would buy her, and afterwards attempted to sell her at a public auction. She complained to the resident of the hardship that would be caused by being separated from her daughter who was still a slave at Slater's house. As a result, the sale was forbidden. Disappointed in not selling her at auction, he disposed of her privately to a Chinaman for half the original value.

Slater had been up to Penang as well as Singapore and there he purchased two slave boys to bring back to Batavia. On returning via Singapore, he was observed beating one of the boys so severely that a Captain Dickey intervened and took the boys away from him. Claudius Thomsen got involved in rescuing the boys and they were sent back to Penang where Thomas Beighton gave them their freedom. Beighton wrote, 'Tears of pity were shed when the back of the poor boy beat on the hill was exposed.' Beighton's letter also referred to Slater's deception and cruelty before they left England, for which he hoped 'you have asked pardon to God and obtained forgiveness or I should fear the ashes of the dead would cry for vengeance'. It appeared that Slater's character had been known before he left England.

Thomsen also wrote about Slater in Singapore who, he said, 'Acknowledges to the fact of having beat his wife and resolved that he would separate from her company and never see her again.' Thomsen also said that Slater took a loaded gun to commit suicide. Others confirmed this from Singapore and said that he was seen running about the place with a loaded gun in his hand. Back in Batavia, Slater continued to abuse his slaves and ignore his responsibilities as a missionary. The house and ground that he had partitioned off for himself was sold for 4,700 rupees and the money used by Slater to fund his other activities.

By the beginning of 1823, Walter Medhurst decided to take action, demanding Slater's resignation and announcing that he was taking over the affairs of the mission pending a decision by the directors of the society. An angry Slater berated Medhurst as a meddlesome troublemaker whom he should have dealt with long ago, but by this time, the fight had gone out of him. He scribbled out in pencil an undated, unsigned piece of paper, which served as a resignation, threw it down in front of Medhurst and stormed out of the building.

On 23 August 1823, Walter wrote the following letter to the directors:[1]

Hon'd Fathers and Brethren
... It now becomes my painful duty to bring before the Directors a subject of the most distressing nature relative to the misconduct of Mr Slater. Perhaps I may be chargeable

with neglect for not having before informed you the state of things here but I was deterred from making too early an exposure of a brother's failings, out of regard to his character and his family & lest my interference should be imputed to any sinister motive of jealousy or ill will; however as Mr Slater has now left the service of the Society it becomes my inferiors duty to state the circumstances which led to his relinquishing the missionary work & to show that it originated in his own imprudence and misconduct. When I first came here I found that Mr Slater was in disrepute among the English inhabitants for having several slaves in his house & for frequently displaying much violence of temper; with respect to the slaves.

With respect to his violence of temper there are many instances of his beating the natives, & one of his knocking a Chinaman into the water. I have seen him likewise use dumb animals in a very unfeeling manner, such as knocking them on the head till they are stunned – once in particular on a Sabbath day, he knocked a horse down flat in the public road, with the pole of a cart, because he would not draw...

There are instances of his having deceived the Directors in his representations to them of his proceedings, saying that he could preach in Chinese & Malay in 1821, when in 1822 he could preach in neither; and particularly in his last letter to you dated in June, wherein he spoke of it as his greatest affliction, that he could not go about to the schools & among the natives as formerly, when at the same time he was well enough to go every day to town about other business & passed almost by the door of the school without going in; & for the greater part of last year when in good health, he was for months together without visiting the schools or conversing with the natives on religious subjects. His time has been principally employed in building houses & endeavouring to make money...

I am aware how much grieved the Directors will be to hear of these things, but perhaps more hurt than surprised as by the brethren's letter it will appear that his character was partly known before he left England. May we learn therefrom to be more watchful over our own hearts, live more near to God by prayer & let him that thinketh he strayeth take heed lest he fall. Oh I feel that I need a double portion of grace to sustain me in this trying time – it is to one as when a standard bearer fainteth – when I see one much older in years, prior in profession & who assisted at my own ordination to the Ministry, sadly declining in good things, I tremble for myself & see reason to cry out Lord, hold thou me up & I shall be safe...

I remain the Society's faithful and devoted servant

W.H. Medhurst

Throughout this troublesome time, there were many examples of progress and achievement taking place in the lives of the Medhurst family. Within six months of their arrival in Batavia, the Medhursts moved into their new house on the mission property and were settled in time for the arrival of a new baby. A son was born in November and named Walter Henry after his father, this time with both mother and child safe and well. Word came from England that his sisters Clara and Mary had married and that Clara now had a new daughter, also named Clara. Also at this time, Betty's sister Sophia was on her way from Madras and would soon join them in Batavia. Five years after leaving Madras, the family would again be reunited. Meanwhile, Betty's son George was doing well at Mill Hill School and was able to spend his school holidays with cousins in the Medhurst and Martin families.

During the year, Walter preached weekly in Chinese at four locations around Batavia, both in Fujian and Mandarin. He also held services in English and Malay at the English chapel on the mission property every Sunday. Two Chinese schools were being run, one in town and the other in the Chinese campong close to Weltevreden. The printing establishment at the mission centre was producing a Chinese magazine (1,000 copies a month) as well as books and pamphlets. He also ran a small dispensary from his home.

On 29 January 1823, a group of a dozen English inhabitants met in the vestry of the English chapel to consider ways of supporting the Revd Medhurst so that he could continue to provide his gratuitous church services. A subscription was raised to be collected quarterly, with amounts of up to 1,500 Spanish dollars per year made over to the reverend as long as he continued as the minister of the English chapel. The meeting concluded by saying that they had no intention of interfering with Medhurst's engagements with the society but only wished to render his situation as comfortable as possible among them. This was a sure sign that he had established the support of the community personally, despite John Slater's behaviour.

Walter Medhurst received two letters from the directors dated 29 September and 23 October 1823, which indicated that they had received reports of Slater's behaviour before they received his letter of 23 August. From Beighton's letter, we know that Dr Morrison knew of the allegations early in 1823 and he would have notified the directors then. Also, Beighton said that the Captain Dickey who rescued the slaves in Singapore was leaving for England at that time and he stated his intentions of reporting the matter to the society's directors. In his reply to the directors of May 1824, Medhurst reiterated the evidence of Slater buying and selling slaves and his cruel treatment of them. He informed the directors that he had sought the opinions of all six missionaries in the region and there was not one dissenting voice. They all thought that Slater should be silenced and suspended from the office of a missionary until the pleasure of the directors be known. The only update to the news about Slater in this letter was the fact that he had by then opened a shop and was engaged in trade, having no connection whatever with missionary affairs.

Walter's letter of May 1824 had some good news: he had been appointed a burgher with the freedom of the colony and full permission to print in the Chinese language. This approval was of special significance to Walter because two former applications by British Baptist missionaries for the same purpose had been rejected. Not only that, but the officials waived the normal fee of $50. In this and other instances, the distinctive treatment he received could only be attributed to the relationships he had built with Dutch officials, as well as those of the local British community. The approval to print in Chinese was subject to his submitting a copy to the censor before publication and to printing for the government on request. This second condition was easy for Walter to agree to because any printing performed for the government would be billed and paid for.

Walter wrote to London of his encouraging visit to a nearby village, Depok, inhabited by native Christians. He explained the interesting origins of this village. More than 100 years before, in the early 1700s, a Dutch gentleman named Chesterling, with an estate around 6 miles long by 2 miles wide, cultivated entirely by slaves, proposed to liberate them and leave his land to them. The only condition was that they consent to being instructed and baptised in the Christian faith. In compliance with his proposal, he built a church in the village, established a schoolmaster over them subject to the supervision of the Dutch clergy, and liberated his former serfs, leaving them and their families free. When Walter visited the village in 1824, there was a population of around 200 and he reports, 'there never was a more quiet village, or a more inoffensive people'.[2] Walter returned to preach in Depok monthly for several years.

Not far from Depok was the village of Buitenzorg, where the Muslim judge of the district expressed a concern about his eternal interests. Struck by his humble manner and the seriousness of the question, Walter conversed with him. The Muslim acknowledged he had no satisfactory answer to what happened after he died and he wished to hear how he might find peace with God. The discussions continued over several visits. Walter left him with a Malay Bible, various pamphlets and a prayer that he might be enabled to find the pathway to Heaven.

The Chinese captain of this same town was the opposite of the Malay judge, being taken up with the 'wind and water system' of his countrymen. They believed that the fortunes of the living were influenced by the position or 'feng shui' of important items. In one of the houses, a Chinese had set up a picture of Napoleon Bonaparte in a gilt frame over his altar, where he gave the customary offering of incense. Walter wrote, 'Probably in the height of his ambition, the French Emperor little dreamt of being worshipped as a God.'

In Walter's letter to the directors of the society of 3 June 1825, he wrote that John Slater had not changed or repented his misdemeanours, and that he had been charged and convicted in the public court of Batavia for smuggling contraband opium, and was fined 2,000 rupees. No Englishman had ever before been convicted of this crime in Batavia. Slater was reported to be in great poverty and distress, having had to sell his house.

It seems the directors had refused to pay some of the bills incurred by Slater in the society's name and Walter urged them to reconsider, since it would only bring more hardship on the other missionaries in the region. Further, he reasoned, if they sued Slater for the debt, of what use was it to throw a destitute man in jail and leave his family to survive on charity.

The final word on the Revd Slater came in Walter's letter dated 8 September 1825, reporting that he had died: 'For the last two months of his life he resided with our friend Mr Diering, expecting him to leave by the next ship for Calcutta when God had decided he would leave for another world.' Diering was a Baptist layman at the Baptist Missionary Society who had assisted Walter when he was trying to rebuild the mission after Slater's neglect. Mr Slater's estate being barely solvent, Mrs Slater and her children were left destitute, and she in an advanced state of pregnancy. On the very day of Mr Slater's death, while Walter was away from Batavia with a delegation from the society, Betty went to the Slaters' house and invited Mrs Slater and the children to live with the Medhursts and make it their home until circumstances allowed them to return to Europe. Jemima Slater hid her face for some time and wept before she could look on her long-estranged friend and be willing to accompany her back to the mission house. Walter returned to find Mrs Slater in considerable distress, but over the next few weeks she became more reconciled to her situation. Mr Diering had unfortunately been afflicted with the same fever as Slater and they died within a few days of each other. Walter rushed to Diering's bedside to spend his last moments with him. Diering was laid to rest on the evening he died, his funeral being well attended. Walter Medhurst gave a funeral address at the graveside, which was unusual for normally the Dutch of the East Indies interred the corpses of their friends in silence.

The community in Batavia and Semarang established a subscription and 5,000 rupees was raised, including 500 rupees from the visiting society deputation. With this sum, Mrs Slater had enough money to return to her native country where she hoped to engage in education, for which she was well qualified. It was necessary, however, to wait until her confinement was over before she could embark on so long a voyage. The birth took place on 30 September, but, as if to pile tragedy on misfortune, the infant closed her eyes as soon as she had opened them. Poor Jemima Slater was again thrown into grief and it was November before she had recuperated enough to proceed on her journey. The Medhursts finally bid farewell to Mrs Slater and her two children when they sailed with Captain Hyde of the *Palambang* on 10 December. Mrs Slater thanked Walter and Betty with tears in her eyes and they parted with prayers and best wishes for a safe journey, expecting not to meet again in this life, but God had planned otherwise. Scarcely a week had gone by before news came that the *Palambang* was dismasted and was returning to Batavia. On 20 December, the Slaters returned to live with the Medhursts. The disappointment of the voyage ending so soon and the delay while repairs were made to the ship weighed heavily on Jemima Slater. She spoke of being destined never to leave the place, complained of feeling unwell and became confined to her bed. Before long, it was apparent that she was displaying symptoms of the Batavia fever, the same ailment from which her husband and Diering had died. Walter and Betty were both highly alarmed.

She died on 8 January, the day before her expected embarkation on the *Palambang*. While the other passengers were boarding the ship, she was carried to her grave. The captain of the ship behaved very generously and immediately returned the whole of the passage money, offering to take the children home at no cost. The Medhursts could not consent to this, however, because it was the mother's dying request that the Medhursts should take care of the children – they knew of no one who could take that responsibility in England. Walter and Betty took charge of the two Slater children and wrote to Mrs Slater's sister in Edinburgh and her brother in the Royal Marines to ask what their wishes were regarding the children. If they declined to take care of them, the Medhursts determined that they had better adopt the children.

Walter informed the directors that it was Mrs Slater's dying request that the portraits of her husband and herself taken before they left England and now at the missionary rooms be preserved for their children, so that the little orphans would remember their departed parents.

14

TYERMAN AND BENNET

In July 1825, the mission played host to a deputation from the society's headquarters in London – Daniel Tyerman and George Bennet. They were circumnavigating the world, visiting the operations of the London Missionary Society to determine the opportunities for the further spread of Christianity.

The Medhursts had been running the mission in Batavia for almost three years by this time, three years of hard struggle without much progress towards the expectations they both had for the operation. Much of the problem lay in Slater's neglect of his missionary duties and being involved in illegal or immoral activities, counteracting the message the Medhursts were trying to spread. During this period, the Medhursts had operated in isolation without any visitors from the society. Dr Milne had died soon after they arrived in Batavia, after which Dr Morrison occupied himself completely for the first year with the Malacca College before leaving for England in 1823. They were alone, motivating each other and relying on the encouragement of friends to maintain their passion for their vocation. Now with visitors from the London society, here was an opportunity to revitalise their goals with kindred spirits. After showing the visitors around Batavia, they decided to take a tour of Java, visiting Semarang and Solo (Surakarta), a journey of over 900 miles. A visit to the governor of Java, Baron Van der Capellan, was arranged. Walter Medhurst had an excellent relationship with him and he gave his permission for the trip. The group obtained introductions to meet government officials, Javanese princes and other useful contacts on their journey.

Having procured ponies and a four-wheeled carriage, they set off for Semarang, around 400 miles east of Batavia. The government of Java maintained stages for regularly changing horses and in the mountainous regions, buffaloes were available to take the place of the horses. Most of the way they drove on well-constructed roads, but occasionally it was necessary to lower the carriage down steep ravines to be dragged across suspension bridges, following which buffaloes were required to haul the carriage up the other side. In some places, river crossings were accomplished on bamboo rafts hauled across by rattan cables. The route frequently lay through thick jungles, the home of man-eating tigers. From time to time, they were reminded of this danger by the cries of goat kids, used as live bait in the tiger traps set alongside the road. Just a few days previously, when a carriage was passing through the area, a tiger had sprung out from the jungle and attempted to take a passenger from the back of the carriage. The driver instinctively whipped the horses when he saw the tiger and the beast missed his target and got tangled up in the back wheel, causing it to squeal in pain and run back into the woods. Fortunately, the missionaries were spared any such event.

At each stage, the missionaries enquired about the safety of the road ahead. There was a rebellion against the Dutch Government and it was wise to be informed of the movement of the rebels. From Semarang to Solo (Surakarta), they were guarded by five Dutch horse soldiers and accompanied by five other travellers sharing the escort.

The population of Solo was estimated at 100,000, of which fewer than 500 were European, mostly Dutch. In the centre of town, the Dutch had built a large fort surrounded by a wet moat with four drawbridges and fifty cannon. Adjacent to this was the residence of the Javanese leader, who bore the title of emperor, even though the Dutch were the real masters of his empire. That evening the delegates were entertained by the resident governor and by General de Kock, along with a large party of civil and military personnel. All appeared interested in hearing about the affairs of the LMS. Walter expressed a desire to be introduced to the emperor and the governor arranged an audience for the following morning.

The governor led the visitation with General de Kock and various senior officers, all in carriages driven from the fort to the palace. Word had got around, as there were thousands of spectators, who were kept in line by native soldiers where the visitors alighted. The military presented arms and let fall their colours in honour of the general. As they entered the court, the emperor's officials were sitting bare chested and cross legged and the emperor himself, who was seated on a throne mounted on a stone platform, rose up and advanced to the edge of the platform where he took the hands of the governor and the general and bowed graciously to the other visitors. General de Kock was placed in a chair of state on the emperor's right hand and the local governor was seated to his left. Three rows of chairs were arranged in front of the platform to accommodate the Dutch officers, with the missionaries on the right and the native courtiers and nobility on his left.

The emperor was around eighteen. He wore a black vest, closed at the neck and reaching to the waist, and below a Javanese cloth, dark brown, spotted with white, which descended to the mid-leg. His stockings were light-coloured and his shoes were black with gold buckles. He wore a chocolate-coloured cone-shaped hat without a brim, encircled with gold bands. Three brilliant stars of jewellery adorned his chest. The throne was around 4 feet square, covered with yellow silk and fringed with gold. His Majesty sat upright with great dignity, a sword in a gold scabbard lying at his side. Once everyone was seated, the sovereign conversed affably with his distinguished visitors while tea, coffee, sweetmeats, and wine were served.

Dancing girls appeared and sat on a platform. They were flanked by a band of Javanese musicians and a choir on one side, and a second band with European instruments on the other. The girls were no more than sixteen, beautifully dressed. The exposed parts of their skin were stained a delicate yellow tint with sandalwood and perfume. When the musicians and singers began to perform, the girls rose slowly from the platform in perfect synchronisation and danced.

After half an hour, the entertainment ended. The emperor rose and the visitors were directed to follow. They were conducted to another open court where a vast range of tables, in a T shape, had been laid with all kinds of meats, delicacies and fruits set out in European style. The tables were so crowded with dishes that there was no room for any more and even the gaps between the dishes were filled with brilliant aromatic flowers. The emperor sat in the centre of the T arrangement, the general and resident governor on his right and left respectively and the rest of the guests in the remaining places. The meal was sumptuous and everything was conducted with as much order as it might have been with any European prince. Servants were in waiting, while the band played a selection of Javanese and European tunes. They concluded, as a compliment to the visiting delegation, with 'God Save the King'. The emperor honoured each of his guests with a toast of wine, followed by several more to all the company.

After this, the emperor rose and the company returned with him to the dancing hall. When they were all seated, another group joined the dancers, each carrying an anklung, an instrument resembling a bamboo frame lacquered in red and decorated in gold. The dancers rose and took up their colourful instruments. Each instrument was tuned to play a different note, enabling the group to perform beautiful music with each member taking up a different part. The music and songs represented traditional Javanese mythology, highlighting important stories in their history. At the completion of the anklung performance, the visitors rose and were permitted to shake the emperor's hand, wishing him a long and prosperous reign as they did so. This token of friendship he bestowed on them with hearty goodwill, and no European leader could have excelled him. Having spent around three hours at the palace, the curiosity of the missionaries was satisfied and they left with good feelings about their hosts. The group returned to Batavia on 12 August after a journey of almost three weeks.

During the next few weeks, Tyerman and Bennet visited the Chinese schools, the dispensary and the printing works, and attended services at the mission chapel, which were all part of the Batavia Mission. They accompanied Walter on his visits to the Chinese temple and the Malay village where he preached and handed out religious pamphlets. Although they could not understand either Chinese or Malay, they could not help but be impressed by the zeal and determination with which Walter Medhurst applied himself to the spreading of the society's message. Walter reported to the directors, 'The visit by these gentlemen has been the means of reviving and encouraging us to no small degree.'[1] He also recognised that the visitors observed the lack of any progress in Batavia and the failure in the conversion of believers. Tyerman's report said, 'In this island (Java) up to this time, it is doubtful whether any abiding religious impression has been made upon the heart of a Chinese or a Muslim.'[2] Tyerman and Bennet left Batavia on 6 September, bound for Singapore.

Around the time of their departure, word came to Batavia that the rebellion against the Dutch Government had taken a turn for the worse. The problems started when Prince Diponegoro from Yogyakarta revolted over Dutch rule and drew the support of many disaffected chiefs in various parts of the island. A battle was fought on 2 September in which 180 Dutch troops were routed, leaving few survivors and the rebels advancing on Semarang. Walter reported that several Englishmen he knew well were among those killed. The whole town was in a state of great alarm. If Semarang fell, Batavia would also be in danger and Walter discussed with Betty the prospect of evacuating the family to Singapore. Meanwhile all of the troops had left Batavia to confront the rebels and the local merchants and burghers of the town had been formed into a militia to mount guard like regular troops. The fear of Batavia falling to the rebels declined when word came that General de Kock had successfully taken Yogyakarta on 25 September, but it was to be five years before the rebellion was finally quelled.

15

JAVA, SIAM AND BORNEO

In 1826, the Medhursts received word that Dr Morrison was returning to China and that his ship was scheduled to call at Anjier in the Sunder Strait, 65 miles from Batavia. This would be the first and only time that Walter met the man whose letters in the *Evangelical Magazine* had inspired his ambition to become a missionary to the Chinese. Walter travelled to Anjier and met Morrison's ship. Morrison reported that Medhurst was in good health but somewhat depressed from the idea that he had laboured in vain without achieving converts. Morrison also said that he had approved of Medhurst taking a tour among the Chinese settlers of Borneo, Bangka and Siam during 1827. Morrison stated his priority in a letter back to London: 'We are very near our brethren at Java, Singapore and Malacca. I am not indifferent to the welfare of their Mission but I think it right to devote all my strength and resources to the Chinese.'[1] Morrison's brief stop in Java, without visiting Batavia, would almost certainly have reminded Medhurst that he was very much on his own.

The lack of success in converting the Chinese to Christianity was by no means limited to the mission in Batavia. Throughout the region during the nineteenth century, very few Chinese were converted. The big difference between Medhurst and his fellow missionaries in the region was his ability to communicate with the people. He was one of only a handful of early Protestant missionaries who acquired fluency in both spoken Chinese dialects and he was able to draw bystanders into discussion, explaining a section of the Bible in their own terms. He was in fact learning far more about Chinese culture and Confucianism from his flock than they learned Christianity from him. He often referred favourably to Confucian moral precepts in order to make a point about the correctness of Christian beliefs. Christianity was the hard rock on which his passion for China was built.

Notwithstanding his failure at conversion, Medhurst and the society would have been pleased with the progress of the Batavia Mission. In most of Walter's missionary activities, and especially during his many travels away from Batavia, he was supported extensively by his wife Betty and by her sister Sophia, who had recently arrived from Madras. Sophia Martin turned out to be another gifted linguist and quickly learned Chinese so that she could assist at the Chinese schools.

While Tyerman and Bennet were in Batavia, they visited the Governor General of Java, Baron Van der Capellan, who believed that the inhabitants of the Tengger Mountains in the far eastern part of the island might be the most receptive to missionary activities. They were an indigenous race who followed a form of Hinduism with a reverence for the volcano that dominated the region, and they had so far resisted any conversion to Islam. Time did not allow the deputation to travel so far during their visit but Walter determined that he should make the trip. He travelled on horseback with one of his servants and headed back through Semarang and along the coastline to Surabaya. Here he met Mr Van Emde, a watchmaker and leader of a small group of Dutch Christians who had formed themselves into a missionary society, holding regular prayer meetings to spread the Christian message among the heathen. They had composed evangelical pamphlets in

Malay and Javanese, translated the New Testament into low Malay and raised funds for printing it. Walter returned with copies of their manuscripts where he worked with Dirk Lenting, the local Dutch minister in Batavia, to revise the translation, and arranged for the government printing office to print copies of their work.

After Surabaya, Walter headed inland up into the Tengger Mountains, to 6,000 feet above sea level, made contact with the Tenggerese people and was invited into their village. The Tenggerese venerated fire, erecting altars to the rising sun and worshipping the volcano Mount Bromo. A small group of them ascended to the edge of the crater and Walter described the effect that the stillness, the absence of all animal and vegetable life, and the deep roaring of the volcano produced on the awestruck villagers. They prayed to the mountain, throwing offerings into the crater and calling for preservation from its fires. Around the peak of Bromo was an extensive flat of sand which the wind had formed into gentle undulations resembling a sheet of water but as hard as solid ground. The natives called it the 'sand sea'.

Walter concurred with Baron Van der Capellan, that the Tenggerese were an eligible field for missionary exertions. He wrote that they already possessed a simplicity of manners favourable to the introduction of the Gospel, while the extreme salubrity of the climate and the splendour of the surrounding scenery were sufficient to invite and reward the residence of a missionary. When he wrote this ten years later, he added, 'But alas! This fertile, peaceful, beauteous region is left, to this day, without a single effort to evangelise its inhabitants, beyond the distribution of a few pamphlets in the Javanese language and a transitory annunciation of the Gospel.'[2]

When Morrison passed through the Sunda Strait in August 1826 and stopped briefly at Anjier, he recounted a meeting in London with a young German who was expected to arrive in Java with the Netherlands Missionary Society (NZG) in the next few months.

The young man's name was Karl (Charles) Gutzlaff and Morrison asked Medhurst to give him a friendly welcome. Gutzlaff arrived in Batavia on 6 January 1827 aboard the *Helena Christina* and Walter was there to meet him. The NZG had assigned Gutzlaff to work in a mission among the Batak people in north-west Sumatra, but owing to the Dutch Government fighting a rebellion at that time, Gutzlaff could not proceed to his post. In the meantime, he was welcome to stay and assist the Medhursts in the Batavia Mission. Fellow Protestant missionaries were always welcome at the Medhursts'. After spending weeks or months among unresponsive 'heathens', missionaries derived comfort and support in the familiar company of fellow evangelists. Like Medhurst, Gutzlaff was as passionate about China as he was about Christianity and his desire to go and serve among the Bataks of Sumatra was a stepping-stone to China. His desire was also to work among the Chinese of South East Asia in preparation for when China opened up. Unlike the missionaries of the Ultra Ganges Mission, who were allowed to operate anywhere in Asia east of India, the Dutch missionaries were restricted to operate only within the Dutch colonies, and the Dutch Government did not like them preaching to the Muslim population, considering it disruptive to their rule. With a larger streak of independence than was usually found in most missionaries, Gutzlaff was not the kind of person to settle down in a small community, as the NVG expected of him. He wanted the kind of freedom the LMS gave its missionaries. The planned tour by Medhurst of the Chinese settlements of Borneo, Bangka and Siam, as approved by Morrison, was the topic for hours of conversation between the two men and Gutzlaff vowed to accompany Medhurst on that expedition. First, he had to learn the language and in this, he was reported to have made astonishing progress.

Gutzlaff was to stay with the Medhursts for four months, assisting Walter in his missionary duties and accompanying him when he went out preaching and distributing pamphlets. He was very impressed by Walter's methodology and determined to acquire similar skills as soon as possible. He wrote, 'Whenever Mr Medhurst spoke, I listened as attentively as possible, even though I was not capable of speaking either Malay or Chinese. As long as I am here, I shall apply myself to this purpose in order to contribute to God's grace.'[3]

After spending four months in Batavia, Gutzlaff reported to his Dutch superiors that it was still not safe to travel to his post in Sumatra and he left for Bintan in the Riau Islands, close to Singapore but still a part of the Dutch East Indies. Within a year, he wrote to Walter that he was organising a ship in Singapore so that he and Jacob Tomlin of the LMS could make the tour of Siam that they had spoken of in Batavia. He asked Walter to join them, which he agreed to, and the middle of 1828 was tentatively set for departure. By this time, Gutzlaff had broken his links with the NVG, although he had garnered the support of various other benefactors to support his travels. He had become, and was to remain, an independent missionary whose path would cross with that of the Medhursts on several occasions during their lives.

Meanwhile, Jacob Tomlin, who had joined the Ultra Ganges missions the previous year, was also headed to Batavia. It seemed that the LMS considered it a useful exercise to send new missionaries through Batavia to learn from someone who, at the age of thirty, was becoming something of an old hand. Jacob Tomlin was three years older than Walter, educated at St Johns College, Cambridge, and ordained before he was recruited to join the LMS in Malacca.

Like Gutzlaff, Tomlin was intrigued by the opportunities to travel throughout South East Asia, blazing a trail to new lands and spreading the Christian message. He recognised that Walter's command of languages was a necessary skill and the two months he spent in Batavia initiated that process. Just as with Gutzlaff, Walter spent hours discussing with Tomlin the places they should visit and reviewing the problems they might encounter and how they could make the journey. They discussed travelling east of Java to the island of Bali, a journey for which Tomlin would return some two years later.

The Medhurst family by this time was quite large, with daughter Sarah, son Walter, the two Slater children, and Betty's sister Sophia, not forgetting the four orphan boys who had come with them to Batavia from Penang. The mission centre was in a constant state of construction and expansion. The chapel had been expanded to include a vestry, a library and a schoolroom; a printing office had been constructed and several modifications had been made to the living quarters on the property. With frequent visitors like Tyerman, Bennet, Gutzlaff, Tomlin, and the occasional drop-in, the place was a hive of activity. It would have been a noisy household but one with a very positive feeling engendered by the shared ambitions to grow, learn, teach, and travel.

The Slater children stayed with the Medhursts for around a year after the death of their mother but eventually a passage back to England was organised and they said goodbye to their adoptive parents. Happier news for Walter and Betty at that time was to receive correspondence that young George Braune had performed so well at Mill Hill School that he had won a scholarship to attend Sidney Sussex College in Cambridge.

A new member of the Batavian Mission to be appointed as assistant in 1828 was William Young. Born to a Scottish father and a Malay mother, and raised as a member of the Baptist church, Young had recently moved to Batavia, where he struck up a friendship with the Medhursts. They soon realised that he would make an ideal deputy for Walter Medhurst when he was away on his planned tour to Siam. So began a religious calling that would last the rest of his life.

The mission press was becoming more and more important to the operation in Batavia. It already printed in English, Chinese and Malay using typographic, lithographic and block printing methods. That year, the expertise of the mission press was extended to include Japanese. Walter had been offered the loan of some Japanese books and he was given full permission to copy what he wanted in order to develop further skills in that language. Both Morrison and Milne had long desired to gain knowledge of Japanese but the task had been extremely difficult, compounded by the isolation of that nation. The most important of the works appeared to be a Dutch, Chinese and Japanese dictionary, drawn up by the Japanese themselves and arranged according to the Japanese alphabet, two or three Chinese and Japanese dictionaries, and a Japanese and Chinese encyclopaedia with plates, maps and charts. In addition, there was a copy of the 'Four Books of Confucius' in Chinese, with Japanese translation. After analysing these works, Walter was able to compile and print an English to Japanese vocabulary. He did not claim it to be anything more than a start in the study of Japanese and he admitted that it would be impossible to proceed further without the opportunity for conversation with the people. This was the first time that Japanese had been printed at any of the LMS mission stations.

The correspondence between Medhurst, Gutzlaff and Tomlin showed that they planned to travel up to Bangkok in Siam, departing from Singapore in the middle of 1828. There was only one problem with that plan: Betty was pregnant, with an expected birth date of July. With a medical history of losing two of her four babies over the previous nine years, the last thing that Walter could consider was a trip away at the time of the birth. It was two years since Morrison had approved the trip to Siam and Walter struggled to balance his impatience to be off on this new adventure against the reality of supporting Betty. He sent word to Gutzlaff and Tomlin that they could expect him to join them but that if he did not reach them before their ship departed, they should go on without him.

A daughter named Eliza Mary was born on 24 July 1828 and both she and the mother were healthy. With sister Sophia there to help with their care, Walter decided that he could safely leave Batavia for Singapore and meet up with Gutzlaff and Tomlin. William Young would be left to deputise for Walter in running the mission, while Sophia was already providing valuable assistance in the Chinese schools. He could leave Batavia confident that his family and his missionary operations would continue to flourish.

Walter secured a passage to Singapore in the brig *Alexander* and departed with a large stock of books on 2 August. They made good speed for Singapore and arrived there on 6 August, only to find that Gutzlaff and Tomlin had left for Siam only two days before. Without any hope of communicating with them or of catching up with their ship, Walter was faced with abandoning his plans and returning to Batavia or journeying to other places in the region, taking advantage of the supply of books he had with him. Once again, he discussed his situation with his old friend Claudius Thomsen who, knowing Walter's ambition and sense of adventure, urged him to double the success of the Gutzlaff tour to Siam by taking the message to other new lands.

Walter's first thought was to find a vessel to take him up to Cochin China (Vietnam) and Cambodia, but he was unsuccessful. He finally embarked on a Chinese proa, a multi-hull, open vessel with a junk sailing rig, bound for the east coast of the Malayan peninsula, heading initially for the state of Pahang and what today is the town of Pekan, around three days' sailing from Singapore. On the first day, they passed Tinggi Island, known for producing edible bird's nests and inhabited by a few people who gathered the nests for the Rajah of Pahang. It was reported, however, that pirates who infested the coast had murdered the local people, both men and women.

The shore along the east coast of the peninsula from Singapore to Pahang was mostly covered with thick impenetrable jungle, without any sign of habitation, except at the mouths of a few small rivers. They sailed close enough to the shore to observe sandy beaches forming a white border between the blue of the ocean and the dark green of the forest behind. Further on, they passed Pulau Tioman, a large island with high mountains covered in green forests slashed with the white of mountain streams and waterfalls. Paddy fields and other signs of population were evident in the foothills at one end of the island. The people lived in constant fear of pirates. The Rajah of Pahang, to whom the local islands belonged, was too weak to protect them or any other settlements along the coast.

The approach to Pekan was picturesque, through the estuary of the Pahang River, which was dotted with several small islands. However, until they reached the town no firm ground could be seen among the low and marshy riverbanks. Walter recorded his arrival by writing, 'The town has a miserable appearance, the houses merely covered with attap (palm fronds) and with the exception of a Chinese street, all scattered here and there, in as wild a state of confusion as the jungle in the midst of which they appear.'[4]

The Chinese houses stretched along the shore, partly built over the water and partly resting on land. Behind the Chinese campong were a few gardens planted with vegetables cultivated by the Chinese, who appeared to be the only labourers there. On the opposite side of the river stood the Malay campong with the rajah's residence in the middle. Walter recorded, 'The Malays strut around in silken breeches with their glazed sarongs folded over, in such a stiff and awkward manner as shows that they were never made for work.' This illustrated the typical relationship between Chinese and the Malays. The Chinese were allowed to settle and work there but the Malayan rulers imposed great restrictions and extorted as much as they could, insisting on their paying a fee in gold when they left for China.

The primary economic attraction for the Chinese were the gold and tin mines in the interior of the Pahang State, reached by a three-day journey upriver where approximately 800 Chinese resided, and the gold mines were a further twenty days upriver, making for a total population of around 5,000 Chinese miners. Many of the Chinese were addicted to smoking opium, which consumed most of their gains and in time undermined their health. Most of these miners were Cantonese people, and they were literate, so Walter decided that a distribution of books and religious pamphlets would be beneficial. It was Walter's intention to travel into the interior but the rajah forbade him travelling further so he had to limit his activities to learning about the country and finding ways to forward his books to the Chinese miners. Behind the gold mines was a range of mountains over which there was a road leading to Malacca, which meant that one of the missionaries from Malacca should be persuaded to make the journey.

The State of Pahang was free of any European power and the rajah acknowledged fealty to the sultans of Rhio and Lingin, to whom he paid an annual tribute. He expressed a great fear of the English, which Walter considered may have prevented any harm coming to him during his stay and also was the probable reason the rajah opposed Walter's journey into the midst of the interior, for fear that he would spy out the wealth and resources of the country. All of the Malay inhabitants were strictly Islamists and no doubt any attempt at conversion would be severely punished. This did not stop Walter from having long discussions with the Malays that he met in the Chinese campong where he felt he was on neutral ground, expressing himself far more plainly and pointedly than he could in the Malay campong or in the rajah's palace. The language spoken in Pekan was pure Malay, in which Walter was fluent, but another dialect prevailed in the interior with a group of indigenous people who had not yet converted to Islam.

The captain was eager to set sail for Terengganu, a further two days' sailing along a thickly forested coast. Between Pahang and Terengganu, two pirate ships attacked them. The pirates advanced during a calm, powered by double banks of oars, and each ship was equipped with a six-pounder gun, with which they kept up rapid fire. Walter's Chinese crew was very cool in the circumstances, handling their oars with precision while the captain and his mate returned the enemy fire. A desperate conflict was expected, the Chinese realising that no quarter would be given and that it was most probably a fight to the death. It appeared that the pirates were gaining ground. Just as all hope was slipping away, a breeze sprang up and the Chinese proa, having a superior sailing rig, lurched forward, picked up speed and was soon out of sight of their opponents. Walter gave thanks to a merciful providence for sparing the ship and its crew and they sailed happily on to Terengganu.

Kuala Terengganu was the capital of the State of Terengganu, a larger settlement than Pekan but with a smaller territory and no gold mines. Situated halfway between Siam and the Straits of Malacca, it became a convenient port and trading post but since the establishment of Singapore, this source of commerce was in decline. While Walter was in the town, two ships sailed for Siam with royal presents from the Rajah of Terengganu to the King of Siam, consisting of gold, tin and silk sarongs. The Terengganus were obliged to seek the favours of their more powerful neighbours in order to prevent an attack on their country. They were not afraid of an attack from the ocean side as the Siamese were not a seafaring people, but from the landward side they were very much exposed. If the Siamese made an attack by land, which they could easily do on elephants, they would easily swallow up Terengganu. Along with the annual gifts to the King of Siam, whenever a new rajah was appointed, they sent to Siam for confirmation of the appointment to guarantee his safety on the throne.

No written laws appeared to exist in Terengganu and there was no court of justice, which left causes to be settled at the will of the ruler or by the pride or passion of the royal judge. Murder, of all crimes, seemed to be dealt with most leniently and consequently, it seemed, daily assassinations occurred, which were mostly passed off as proof of the courage of the perpetrator or as the just desserts of the victim. The consequential insecurity of persons and property meant that every individual was obliged to carry half a dozen weapons and no man dared make known the extent of his property, for fear it should be taken from him. The Chinese especially were greatly oppressed by their Malay rulers who came into their houses and took away the best of their goods, or the fairest of their wives and daughters, without redress. The abject Chinese tamely submitted to all of this in the hope of making up by deceit what they lost by violence. The shops in Terengganu were provided with railings like prison bars through which the purchaser threw his money before receiving his goods. Every article was hastily removed to the inner apartments when a follower of the rajah appeared, because these bullies insisted on purchasing everything valuable without the slightest intention of paying for it.

The palace of the rajah was larger than the one at Pekan but the rajah himself did not make an impression on Walter, dressed in nothing more than an old sarong. His son, around fourteen years of age, was carried around like a child lest he should defile his royal feet by putting them on the ground. A few elephants were kept on which the great man sometimes rode, but the chief means of commanding respect was to make every individual crouch down in the presence of him and his family. This was required not only in the palace but in the streets and markets. Whenever a royal personage appeared the whole multitude immediately crouched down until the cavalcade passed.

Walter wrote in his journal:

What most disgusts and offends the eye of a stranger in Terengganu, is the multitude of deadly weapons which abound among the people. Every man has a creese (a dagger with a wavy blade), a sword and one or more spears. The men are all idlers and the women do all the work, both carrying goods to market and disposing of them when there. The people being so plentifully armed, quarrels are frequent among them and murders not uncommon; immediately a cross word is given, the creese is drawn; if a man tries to escape, the spear is thrown and if it misses another is ready and frequently a third to do the work effectually.[5]

The acceptance of murder and robbery, and the tyranny of the Terengganu leadership, made these shores a dreaded place to visit and a huge challenge for any missionary. Walter concluded that there were better and more productive places for his labours and he was pleased that the Chinese captain and crew were as eager to leave as he was.

The next state to the north was Kelantan, rich and populous owing to its extensive gold mines. North of Kelantan was Pattani, today a part of Thailand. It had formerly been a base of English and Dutch activities and carried on a significant trade between India and China. At the time of Walter's visit, the Europeans had long gone and the old town of Pattani was a ruin. Most of the stones and bricks had been collected to build the mosque, now the most prominent building they saw as they entered the bay. Although still officially a Malayan state, the Rajah of Pattani retained merely a shadow of royalty, being entirely subject to the Siamese authorities to the north. The visitors decided not to stay here and moved further up the coast to Songkhla, which was the first regular Siamese town, today a part of Thailand. The approach to Songkhla was picturesque. As they rounded the point, they observed Siamese pagodas on the hilltops surrounding the bay and junks lined up at the wharf. Walter was unfamiliar with the Siamese language spoken there but the current ruler was of Chinese extraction and much of the trade and commerce was carried out in a dialect with which he was familiar. He saw several Chinese temples around the town, as well as Siamese pagodas, and the adherents of the two religions seemed to get along well – not surprising since both were worshippers of Buddha. The town was full of Siamese priests and every morning the yellow-clad priests went about their business of begging for alms. Walter reported, 'They live in a state of idleness and that no business must occupy the attention of the holy brotherhood, not even the transcribing of their manuscript prayers, lest their attention should be taken from the repetition of the sacred name of Buddha.' Again, there appeared to be little opportunity for spreading the Christian message outside the Chinese community.

A regular caravan of elephants set off from Songkhla to cross the peninsula to Quidah, just north of Malacca, taking six or seven days to complete the journey. The Chinese were continually travelling between these two places and Walter would have taken the journey but for the fact that it would be twenty days before the next caravan set out and he hoped to be back in Singapore in that time to start his planned visit to Borneo. Walter therefore returned to Singapore.

They arrived back in Singapore on 1 October 1828, having spent almost two months travelling to Songkhla and back. His journal records a 'complaint of the bowels' but he recovered quickly enough to fulfil his ambition of visiting West Borneo. He soon discovered that an English schooner was about to sail for the west coast of Borneo and after twelve days they arrived in the port of Pontianak, on 25 October. An Arab pirate named Seyed Abdoor Rachman, who set himself up as an independent prince, first established this settlement around 1750. Pontianak lay at the junction of two important rivers, one coming from the diamond mines at Landak and the other from the gold mines at Sangow. Here he built a mosque and a fort and took the title of Sultan of Pontianak. As the new sultan of the surrounding territory, he soon attracted traders from all parts and his command of the entrance to the Landak and Kapuas rivers raised the concerns of the neighbouring territories. The sovereign of Landak, the former titleholder to the land that Pontianak was built on, transferred his right to the Dutch, who took possession of the land on the right side of the river, close to the settlement of the sultan.

Here the Dutch remained, although they had to abandon the coast during the French war and they struggled to subject the numerous hordes of Chinese attracted by the gold mines at Landak, Mandoor and Monterado. The government was in the hands of the Europeans in cooperation with the sultan and his Malay chiefs. Walter met with the Dutch Resident, Mr Gronovius, who explained that the river stretched an immense distance into the interior and was one of the largest in Borneo. He told Walter of his travels in 1823 up the Kapuas River without arriving at its source, and that he had reached the famous lake in the middle of Borneo but found that it was not as large as generally represented. The river was studded with native settlements, inhabited chiefly by Dayaks and governed by Islamic rulers.

The population of Pontianak was around 25,000 Malays and 2,000 Chinese. Outside of the town the country was populated almost totally by Dayaks, a race of cannibals. Walter wrote, 'These people are a wild race, wearing no clothes and utterly destitute of civilisation. No young man may marry unless he brings two or three human heads as a dowry, which are received by the women with triumph, who suck the blood that may yet be dripping from them and adorn their houses with the skulls and their necks with the teeth of their slaughtered victims.' He observed that these people were, however, desirous of instruction and they presented a most inviting field for missionary operations.

Having discovered the precious metals that abound in Borneo, the Chinese had been attracted in great numbers. Walter wished to visit these people and distribute his books. They were spread out through four main areas so Walter decided to first visit Mandoor, a flourishing town on a tributary of the Landak River about three days' travel from Pontianak. He organised a boat to take him and his supply of books and religious tracts there. On 3 November, he set out upriver, through thick jungle, cautiously watching out for and praying that he did not meet any headhunting Dayaks. He arrived in Mandoor on 6 November and described the sight as follows: 'Behold hills levelled, valleys filled up, rivers turned out of their course and new channels formed, yea, the very levels of earth ransacked and turned upside down.'[6]

He found the town and everything about it to be completely Chinese, as if the whole settlement had been lifted from the heart of China and set down on the coast of Borneo, populated entirely by the Chinese, under a government and laws of their own choosing. The Chinese received Walter initially with some suspicion due to the unusual appearance of a European in these parts, but as soon as he greeted them in their language, their apprehensions vanished and he was welcomed as a friend. The Chinese captain of Mandoor was most hospitable. He placed him at the head of his table, and provided guides and protection through the mining district, presenting him with a gold ring on his departure. Walter went among the miners without any impediment and they greeted him with rapture and seemed eager to obtain his books.

Walter had an interest in visiting the town of Monterado, around 40 miles to the north, but was discouraged from making the three-day trip because the Chinese there were at war with the Dutch and they would not be receptive to Europeans. Monterado was apparently more populous than Mandoor and was the first Chinese settlement on the coast. The cause of the conflict between the Dutch and the Chinese was the taxation imposed by the Dutch on supplies going to the mining centres. The Chinese had then resorted to growing rice in the lowlands by the sea but they were still required to pay taxes for clothing and other items from China. Those at Monterado were the most militant and had even resorted to attacking the Dutch fort at Mempawah. Walter concluded that this would be a difficult place for missionaries, because eventually they would have to take sides.

Walter returned to Pontianak on 11 November. After another short trip upriver to visit a Chinese settlement growing sugar cane, he departed north for Sambas, arriving on 23 November. The town of Sambas lay 15 miles on a tributary of the Sambas River around 30 miles from the ocean. The river was very wide at this point and vessels of up to 300 tons sailed up the river as safely as in the open sea. Sambas was a nest of pirates. The former sultan was a pirate by profession and frequently attacked large ships, which he captured and brought into the Sambas River. In retaliation for his capture of an English vessel of 300 tons, the Royal Navy dispatched a frigate and a brig to Sambas in June 1813, burned the town and removed any ordnance they could find. The sultan escaped into the interior, returning when all was quiet and renewing his pirate activities.

The Dutch now occupied the place and kept piracy to a minimum but all the elderly people in the settlement were formerly pirates. North of Sambas, barbarism and piracy prevailed along the coast and the interior was under the control of headhunting Dayaks. Such was the dangerous state of the north-west coast of Borneo. To the south of Pontianak, the coast was freer of piracy but the whole island of Borneo was unsafe for any vessel that was not well armed.

Walter left Sambas on 4 December and, after visiting Pamangkat at the mouth of the Sambas River, he returned to Pontianak after a stormy passage in a leaky Dutch Government proa. On 17 December, he embarked on a Malay proa for Semarang in Java and during this voyage, he wrote his report and recommendations for the directors in London.

From his observations, he did not think that Borneo would be a useful station for a Chinese missionary as the population was only around 25,000 and they were scattered over the different mining sites. Little good could be expected from Chinese schools because the Chinese seldom settled and those who did generally sent their children home to China for their education. There was, however, an opportunity for a missionary to study the Dayak language and attempt to bring Christianity to a people that he believed were ready to be reformed. Since encountering Malays and Chinese, the milder manners of these more civilised people had made the Dayaks a little ashamed of their cruel ways. They were not interested in following Islam since it restricted them from eating pork, but he had heard that some of them had embraced the Chinese system of idolatry, which showed that they were receptive to change, and so Christians should be more zealous in spreading the true faith among them.

Walter's tour and recommendations had little impact on the LMS, although its missionaries, especially in Singapore, continued to print and distribute large numbers of Malay and Chinese books and tracts via trading vessels to Borneo. The accounts of his travels influenced the American Board of Commissioners for Foreign Missions (ABCFM), which coordinated missions for several Protestant church bodies in the USA. The ABCFM periodical, the *Missionary Herald*, in September 1830, published extracts from Medhurst's journal and he was named in a lengthy article in the *Chinese Repository*, published by the ABCFM in Canton in 1836. The ABCFM ultimately set up a mission in Borneo in 1839, after which they experienced all the problems Medhurst had predicted. Walter arrived home in Batavia in January 1829, having been away for five months, to discover that his family had been suffering with severe sickness. For several months, two of his children, followed by his sister-in-law Sophia Martin, had been suffering from a violent fever and Betty had nursed them all until she too became sick. By the time Walter arrived in Batavia, the children had recuperated but Betty had broken out in an acute infection of the skin called erysipelas. Walter was immediately taken up with nursing the family, realising how indispensable his partner was to his life and family, and he prayed to God for her speedy recovery. Sophia Martin, however, was in a much poorer state of recovery and her condition completely baffled the local doctor who gave faint hope for her recovery. Walter's letter to the directors lamented the state of Miss Martin's affliction, praised her attainments in Chinese and Malay and emphasised how important she was to the success of the Chinese Female Schools. He asked them to pray for his family, but rejoiced to add that his own health was good.

It was decided that Sophia should move to Singapore for the good of her health. Batavia was known as the 'Graveyard of Europeans' because of the high mortality rates among citizens, mainly living in the walled city. The Medhursts' home at Weltevreden should have kept them safe from the worst impacts of malarial mosquitoes and polluted water supplies but their missionary work took them into the old city, especially Sophia who was working in the Chinese schools. Often a sea voyage alone would help a person recover but Sophia's case was serious. Relocation to a healthier climate was considered the only solution. Walter wrote to his friend Thomsen asking him to take care of Sophia and advised that once she recuperated, she would be a great asset to the Singapore Mission. Betty once again had to say farewell to her sister but this time she would not be as far away as India and they could assure her they would meet again soon. Happily, Sophia recovered some weeks after arriving in Singapore and became active in the mission, helping to establish and run the mission's schools. Three years later, she married Thomas Whittle, a surveyor, and in August 1833 gave birth to a daughter named Sarah Sophia Whittle.

16

BUILT TO LAST

By 1830, the old bamboo chapel was in an advanced state of decay as it was approaching nine years since Slater had arranged its construction. The visit of Tyerman and Bennet had not resulted in a very positive report on the prospects for the Batavia Mission, which meant any funding application to the directors would be a hard sell. It took up to nine months to get a response from London, and any request for funding had to be considered by a meeting of the board. It would be well over a year before a plan to rebuild the church could even be considered. Walter determined that he would have a better chance of funding the reconstruction by seeking the support of the local European population. He spoke with his friend the Dutch minister Dirk Lenting, who agreed to approach the governor general and seek the support of the government. The governor general agreed to support the subscription, which encouraged the Dutch inhabitants to follow his example, and he agreed to supply some of the building materials from the government store.

In August 1830, Walter wrote to the directors that,

Our old bamboo place of worship was found to be in such a decayed state at the commencement of this year, that I found myself under the necessity of doing something for its repair or renewal; and not expecting to be able to collect more than would be sufficient to build a thin brick wall and furnish a few wooden windows, I put round a subscription for it. The application succeeded beyond my fondest expectation, the English inhabitants subscribed willingly and the Dutch Governor General put down his name for a handsome sum and instead of a few hundred rupees, we have enabled to collect 5 or 6000...We expect that the chapel will be completed and opened for Divine worship in about two months time and then the Society may have the satisfaction of knowing that they possess a substantial and respectable place of worship on their own premises at Batavia, without any encumbrance and I hope without incurring any further expense than the small sum of 100 rupees, which I thought it right to put down in the Society's name, in order to commence the subscription.[1]

The Revd Archdeacon Scott, visiting Batavia on his way back to England from Sydney, preached the first sermon only a few weeks later, and the following month, the chapel was painted, completed and opened for regular service. Apart from extensions to the building in 1839 and 1863, the chapel that opened in 1830 still functions today as All Saints Church, Jakarta, by far the oldest English-speaking institution in Indonesia.

Shortly afterwards, the congregation agreed to a 'Constitution of a Christian Church at Parapattan, Batavia' comprising nine clauses, a copy of which was included as a handwritten document in correspondence to the LMS directors in London. It bore the strong influence of the Congregationalist tradition with which Walter was most familiar, but sought to be inclusive of the other Protestant traditions represented by the missionaries and other members of the English-speaking community.

The document stated the intention to avoid controversy over potentially divisive issues on baptism and church government, and acknowledged that a person's membership in the congregation did not break a connection with any other church or surrender the acceptance of the pastoral care of the LMS missionary. This was a pioneering document in that it was the first time in that region, and maybe anywhere in the world, that an independent church represented various Christian denominations. Since the Reformation, the Churches had fought bitterly over doctrine and practice, and this document offered a significant break from that convention. Thus the ecumenical document that Walter Medhurst wrote as the Constitution for the Church in Parapattan became the standard for the Protestant missionaries when they eventually entered China.

Walter had been busy compiling a Hokkien dictionary, which had taken up much of his time during 1830. He reported that the Chinese to English part of the work had been completed – 800 pages of closely written quarto – and that would be followed by 100 to 200 pages of preface, indexes and appendices. The East India Company had offered to take the work through to the press at no expense to Walter or the society. He was still working on revising and bringing through to the press the translation of the New Testament in Low Malay, which would be completed at the government printing office, but completion of this work was not expected until the end of 1831. A new English school had been commenced, principally for the benefit of the Medhurst children and a few neighbours, and the school had seven students. William Young taught them in the morning and Betty Medhurst in the afternoon. Afternoon teaching was interrupted on 7 January 1831 when the Medhurst family increased with the birth of daughter Martha, to join Sarah (eleven), Walter (eight) and Eliza (two).

On 20 January 1831, another new missionary came to stay with the Medhursts. The Revd David Abeel was an American from New Jersey, sponsored by the American Board of Commissioners for Foreign Missions (ABCFM) to become a missionary to China. He planned to join the Revd Gutzlaff in Siam but followed his predecessors in deciding to visit Batavia first to learn from Walter Medhurst and commence his studies in Chinese. Walter and Betty invited him to make the mission his home while he was in Batavia. Abeel spent the next four and a half months living with the Medhursts, accompanying Walter on his daily labours among the Chinese residents in the town. During this time, an extra English service was held in the chapel on Sunday evenings.

Walter was still making his regular visits to the native Christians at Depok and in his memoir David Abeel recalled joining him on one of these visits:

> We arose this morning and pursued our journey some distance by the light of the moon. The undisturbed serenity of the hour, the sombre shade of the forest and the pale beauties of the open landscape – the freshness of the dewy morning – and above all, the tranquillising influence of the moon with its thousand associations – combined to provide the most delightful effect upon the mind.[2]

He later recalled that by the time they reached their destination the heat was very oppressive and he was relieved to find that the natives were assembled for their meeting in the shade of a large tree. Living in a tropical climate close to the equator was a new experience all the missionaries had to get used to.

The climate of Batavia and the prevalence of tropical diseases for which there was little treatment or cure resulted in a very high mortality rate among the Europeans. We have seen how the Slaters both died and the Medhursts were left to care for their children until a relative could take that responsibility. The Medhursts were frequently the people that the community turned to when children were left as orphans. In 1832, it was becoming apparent that something needed to be done for the children who did not have relatives to support them and for whom adoption was increasingly difficult. The Medhursts and William Young discussed the need for an orphan asylum, which they believed could be funded by subscriptions from the European community and which would be run in combination with the Batavia Mission. They located a plot of land close to the mission in Parapattan, which the owner, Said Alowi bin Mahomed, would lease for twenty-five years with an option to purchase, and costed out a proposal to build and run an orphanage there.

On 17 October 1832, a meeting was held to raise funds for the proposed orphan asylum and a committee formed for the building, management and control of the institution under the chairmanship of Walter Medhurst. The following was agreed at that inaugural meeting:

1. That an Asylum for the benefit of Orphans and others, the descendants of Christian Parents, is highly desirable and necessary and that it be accordingly established under the name of the Parapattan Orphan Asylum.

2. That the object of the Institution be to feed, clothe and educate such Orphans and other children as may be left destitute in this part of India [as Indonesia was referred to at that time].

3. That the Institution be fixed at Parapattan and that a Building sufficient to accommodate 20 children be erected or purchased for that purpose.

4. That the management of the Institution be under the control of a Committee, which for the first year shall consist of the following gentlemen: President, Revd W.H. Medhurst; Treasurer, A.B. Young, Esq.; Secretary, W Young, Sen. Esq.; and J Davidson, C. De Haan, E. Doering, H.K. Spencer and J. Brown Esquires.

5. That Subscribers of 50 Rupees annually be considered as members and each entitled to vote in the reception of children.[3]

The response to the subscription was just as successful as the previous one to build the chapel, and in the first year they raised 7,440 rupees, with a construction cost of 5,507 rupees, leaving a balance on hand of 1,933 rupees. Judging by the speed with which the orphanage was completed, Walter must have quickly gained the support of the committee to buy the land and erect the building, and the first children were admitted to the institution on 1 February 1833. The first children to call Parapattan home were as follows:

James Cooke, aged 10; Maria Cooke, aged 8 and Sophia Cooke, aged 6; children of the late Mr James Cooke of Batavia.

Julia Todderick, aged 9, Cornelia Todderick, aged 7 and Emily Todderick, aged 4; children of the late Mr George Todderick of Batavia.

John Knoppers, aged 9 and Hendrika Knoppers aged 6, children of the late Mr Albert Knoppers of Batavia.

John MacGeorge, aged 4, son of the late Captain MacGeorge of Batavia.

During the first year, ten girls and six boys were admitted to the institution, the oldest being eleven and the youngest four. They were all orphans except for Hendrick Parapattan aged five, who was described as a foundling. The children all attended the English school run by Betty and William Young. In the first annual report of the institution, the children had made significant progress in their studies.

After the first year, the funds provided for the buildings and for maintenance of the orphans showed a respectable surplus. The rapid progress made by the children, the unanimity and cordiality of all the committee meetings, the favourable disposition of the subscribers towards continuing the charity, were all a matter of congratulation. 'It is however but a beginning,' the report went on to say.

Not only was Parapattan Orphanage extended, but it outlasted the colony itself, continuing after Indonesia became independent. Parapattan is still sheltering children as it did when it started a 183 years ago.

The success of the new English chapel at Parapattan and the Parapattan Orphan Asylum show how much Walter Medhurst had matured and improved his people skills since his days in Malacca and Penang. He might not have achieved the success he had been seeking in converting the Chinese but he had gained the support of the local Dutch and English community, built a successful missionary station and earned the respect of his fellow missionaries in building for the day when the doors to China were open. His overriding objective, however, remained focused on the vast Celestial Empire, embracing one third of the human race. It was for China that he joined the LMS and his settlements in Malacca, Penang and Batavia were intended to be merely a temporary expedient.

In August 1834 came the news that the person who had motivated Walter to choose his vocation had died. Dr Robert Morrison, the founder of the LMS Ultra Ganges Mission and the father of the Anglo-Chinese College at Malacca, had passed away in Canton and was buried alongside his first wife and child in Macao. Walter received the news of Morrison's death with a mixture of sadness and frustration. In twenty years, Dr Morrison had achieved more than any Protestant missionary but he still had not moved beyond the limits of the foreign settlement in Canton. When would missionaries get the chance to expand across the Celestial Empire? Although Dr Morrison was the early inspiration for Walter Medhurst and they had exchanged numerous letters, they were not close and they had only met once. It is strange that they laboured for so long in a cause together, both becoming giants of the missionary movement, and yet they had such little personal contact. Walter must have felt regret that he had not gone to Canton or Macao earlier to exchange ideas with Dr Morrison.

In December 1834, the Medhurst family had to say goodbye to young Walter, who at the age of twelve was being sent to school in England. His passage was booked to Rotterdam in the ship *Batavia*, from where he was to be sent to England by the directors of the Dutch Missionary Society. Walter asked the directors if they would assist in getting Walter into Mill Hill School and, if not, to suggest another equal establishment. He also suggested that his brother-in-law, Charles Baker of Cavendish Square, or his friend Horatio Hardy, the proprietor of the Jerusalem Coffee House, might be able to assist.

The other news that he passed on was that he was preparing for William Young to take over running the mission from January 1835 and that Betty and their daughter Sarah would take over running the English school. He discussed the idea of going to China during 1835 and then travelling home to England with his family in 1836.

Walter quoted from a letter he had received from Gutzlaff, who claimed it was erroneous to believe that China was inaccessible to Christian missionaries. The enterprising Gutzlaff had entered China at various times and places and intended to make a voyage up the Yangtze, through the whole of central China, up to Tibet and Bengal. Gutzlaff expressed the opinion that many fruitless efforts and expenditures may have been wasted in the Malayan Archipelago, among a few thousand emigrants, when they might have gone directly to China. However, it was not too late to retrieve what had been lost if the missionaries abroad and the Churches at home awakened to their duty. Walter was despondent about getting his opportunity to go into China and claimed that his long residence in a tropical climate may have enfeebled him. He expressed a desire to be among the first to go up and possess the land but he was not a maverick like Gutzlaff and he assured the directors that he had no desire to take such a step without first receiving the sanction of his friends and supporters at home. He asked the directors to consider this view and to let him know their views regarding their missionaries in these outstations endeavouring to get a foothold in China itself.

By the time Walter's letter arrived in London, Gutzlaff's book, *Journal of Three Voyages along the Coast of China*, had been published and the supporters of the LMS were asking when the LMS missionaries would enter China. Walter Medhurst was now the most senior of the LMS missionaries in the Ultra Ganges after the passing of Milne and Morrison, so when would he be going to China? He need not have worried, however, as the directors were thinking along parallel lines. In July 1834, the directors wrote to Walter Medhurst, requesting him to proceed to Canton, to confer with Dr Morrison, and to make, if practicable, a voyage along the coast of China to ascertain the facilities for missionary usefulness. He would have received the letter after he had written to them with the same request. By March 1835, the directors had still not received Walter's letter but they had a good measure of the man and published the following statement in the *Evangelical Magazine*:

No intelligence has yet arrived of the receipt of the above letter by Mr Medhurst, but from his own enterprise of character, the deep interest he has ever taken in the evangelisation of China and the ability of his assistant with whom he would be able to leave his station in Batavia, the Directors have every reason to believe he would, on receiving their instructions, take immediate measures for proceeding to Canton.

Walter received the letter with overwhelming happiness and would immediately have put into place plans to leave for Canton.

17

FINALLY TO CHINA

Walter arrived in Canton in the middle of June and met with Dr Morrison's son, John, recently appointed Chinese Secretary to the British Commission in China. He was only twenty but already fluent in Chinese, having spent three years at the Anglo-Chinese College in Malacca and doing much of his late father's work at the English Protestant Church in Canton. This was to be the start of Walter's long association with John Morrison. He also caught up with old friend Charles Gutzlaff, who had just returned from a trip up the Chinese coast as far as Fuzhou, and who was also employed as a translator by the British Commission. He was very pleased to see Walter Medhurst and to know that finally the LMS was sending its best missionary on an exploratory trip into China. He offered to assist in any way that he could.

Walter was accommodated at the American factory and welcomed by the American missionaries, who introduced him to D. W. C. Olyphant, Esq., an American merchant who took great interest in the propagation of the Gospel to China. The conversation turned to the propriety of a missionary taking passage in one of the opium ships, which were likely to be the only European ships going up the Chinese coast. It was forbidden by law for a European to travel in a Chinese ship. A vessel became available after around a month and the owners were willing to offer Walter a passage, but carrying opium was the major reason for the voyage, they admitted. The probability that this would be the only vessel was high and there were many books to be loaded on a ship or returned to Malacca or Singapore. There was nowhere to store them in Canton.

The objections against travelling on an opium ship were powerful, however. The connection of a missionary to the opium trade would throw disrepute on the very message that the missionary was trying to spread. The Chinese used this as their main argument against Christianity, that its proponents were vendors of an evil substance that hastened a person's ruin. An opium voyage would also restrict the efforts of a missionary: while the captain would constantly try to evade the attention of Chinese authorities, the missionary preferred to approach all Chinese openly, with nothing to hide and wanting only to communicate in friendship. Walter's strong inclination was to decline the offer.

How frustrating this must have been. Having spent eighteen years among the Chinese communities of South East Asia preparing for this moment, he now found it might be impossible to charter a suitable ship for the voyage. He was on the point of giving up when Mr Olyphant stepped in. Olyphant and Co. had chartered the American brig *Huron*, but as the cargo was not ready, Mr Olyphant was willing to make the ship available for up to three months if the missionaries could come to an agreement with the captain for his extra cost and effort for the journey. The captain, Thomas Winsor, listed the shortcomings of his vessel and crew as reasons for not being able to make the journey, and said he lacked the information needed to navigate the coastline safely. Walter listened to him carefully, and then asked if the captain would agree to the charter if Walter provided additional hands, purchased another anchor, fully provisioned the ship, and provided the requisite insurance. As to the matter of the uncharted coastline, Walter asked his friend Gutzlaff to share his experiences of previous voyages and to provide the old Dutch and French charts, notes and sketches he had available. They agreed that they could easily restrict their travels to the places visited by the East India Company Secretary, Hugh Lindsay, in the *Lord Amherst* three years previously, with Gutzlaff as his interpreter.

Thomas Winsor held out for one additional payment for the increased wear and tear on his vessel. Weighing up the extra costs, the total charge hardly exceeded the amount they originally expected to pay. With funds for the voyage supplied by the LMS, and an additional £200 promised by the Bible Society, it was considered a good offer and a deal was struck.

One of the American missionaries, Revd Edwin Stevens, agreed to accompany Walter on the voyage. A graduate of Yale Divinity College, Stevens had been in Canton for two years as the seamen's chaplain and had recently travelled with Gutzlaff up to Fuzhou. His familiarity with Chinese was not extensive but he shared Walter's zeal for seeking missionary opportunities in China. With the additional hands, the *Huron* now had eighteen passengers and crew on board, a cargo of around 20,000 volumes of books and a variety of other publications. Mr Olyphant put on board several hundred bags of rice to assist any suffering natives should there be a scarcity of provisions along the coast.

On 26 August 1835, the *Huron* set sail from the Kumsing Moon anchorage, dropping gently down the Canton River (known today as the Pearl River). For two days, they hardly made any progress but on the evening of the second day a breeze sprang up and for the next two weeks they had a succession of moderate breezes from the south and south-east and fine sunny weather. By 10 September, they were off the Shandong promontory around which they intended to commence their operations. There were various junks and other boats in sight, the crews of which were doubtless astonished to see a barbarian ship in their seas. After rounding the promontory, they headed for Weihei Bay but were kept back by offshore winds, and in the night they drifted back as far as Alceste (Haily) Island off the tip of the promontory. The next morning the breeze picked up and with the tide helping, they sailed into the harbour of Weihei and dropped anchor in the lee of Liugong Island on 11 September.

Seeing the foreign ship drop anchor in the bay, around a dozen boats set off from Liugong Island across the bay, all of them loaded with people and possessions, as if they thought the foreigners were pirates coming to raid them. To reassure the people, a boat was lowered for the missionaries and a few sailors rowed them to the beach, which caused most of the people to run back towards their village. A few brave souls stood their ground, giving Walter the opportunity to salute them in their own tongue, to which they responded cheerfully, allowing both parties to become acquainted and set aside their suspicions.

After explaining the reason for their visit, the missionaries were invited into the village where a crowd of villagers stood staring in amazement at these strange people. They were invited into a poor house built of rock walls with a thatched roof, furnished with a single platform and half filled with millet, which appeared to be their staple food source. The missionaries offered to pass out copies of their books but few, if any, could read and only one individual accepted a volume. They were, however, friendly and Walter easily conversed with them. The Chinese recalled a visit by a similar boat around twenty years before and wanted to know if they were the same people. That must have been the visit by Lord Amherst in 1816 in his unsuccessful attempt to establish a British Embassy in Peking, on which voyage Robert Morrison had sailed as Chinese secretary and interpreter. Alceste Island, which they had just passed, had been named after the ship in which he sailed. The Chinese asked about the ship and how many men they had on board. Hearing that there were only eighteen, they seemed amazed that they could raise the anchor, let alone sail the ship with such a small crew. The missionaries invited the locals aboard, and after receiving a gift of a few vegetables, they returned to the ship.

The following day, the rain and wind continued unabated and they delayed a visit to Weihei until the weather cleared. In the afternoon, however, a boat came alongside bringing a naval captain and two lieutenants, accompanied by a train of followers. Both Medhurst and Stevens recorded later that there was nothing in the appearance of these men to distinguish them from the commonest soldiers. Walter welcomed them aboard and the elderly captain asked their names, where they were from, and their destination. Walter responded, but as to where they would go from there, he answered, 'if the north wind blew, then he would go to the south and if the south wind blew he would go north', which seemed to amuse the Chinese. He explained the reason for his visit: that Europeans who wanted to share their religion with China had financed this visit in order to distribute books about Christianity. The books were produced and perused by the visitors, who raised no objection about their content. They apologised for the absence of the senior officer of Weihei who would have come to pay his respects in person but for the inclement weather. They replied that they would be pleased to meet with the senior officer on shore as soon as the storm ceased.

On the morning of 13 September, the weather cleared. A boat was lowered and at 9.00 a.m., the missionaries set off for Weihei. On their way, they passed several junks from Jiangsu riding at anchor and decided to call on them and offer them books. The captains of the junks received the books and listened to Walter with an air of politeness and respect and their crews gathered around eagerly to see and hear the foreigners. After calling on two or three vessels, they passed a hilltop fort from which a few soldiers waved a flag, trying to induce them to return. A few hundred yards from the shore a boat met them with one of the officers who had called on them, and although he greeted them politely, he tried to persuade them that they should go to another junk where the senior officer was waiting for them. Suspecting a ruse to prevent them from going ashore, Walter replied that they would see him on their return and called out to the sailors to pull hard on the oars, leaving the officer's boat in their wake. The missionaries landed among a crowd gathered on the beach where they distributed books and greeted them in their own language. The officer who followed made every attempt to stop the missionaries and even grabbed at Walter's arm to halt the activity, pleading with them to go to the junk and meet the senior officer. Walter told the officer that they should first take a walk through the town and converse with the people, and after that, there would be plenty of time to make the visit. His years of working and living with the Chinese had taught him that the people had no sympathy with authority and never assisted them, unless forced. His instincts were right and the people gave them no opposition as they walked up to a row of houses lining the beach and proceeded through one small street.

Just then, it was announced that the chief mandarin and his group had disembarked from the junk and had followed them into the town. The police runners were making way for their superiors by beating their bamboo poles on the ground and, if the people were too slow to move, they aimed them at the nearest person in the crowd. One of the officers indicated that the missionaries should return to the beach to meet the mandarins but Walter suggested that it would be better to wait where they were and let the group approach them. As the group approached, it was observed from the buttons and badges on the caps and uniforms that the first in the group was a tsan-tseang or sub-colonel, and the second was a civil mandarin, from Yantai, around 20 miles away. The civil mandarin became the chief speaker and demanded to know who they were and what they were doing there. Walter responded that he 'was an Englishman, come to do good by distributing books and medicines'.[1] The mandarin said that they could not be permitted to proceed any further since the ground on which they trod was the Celestial Empire and the emperor who commanded all under Heaven had given strict orders that no foreigners should be allowed to go a single step into the interior. Walter replied, 'Then, if it is truly the Celestial Empire, it must comprise all born beneath heaven, including ourselves of course, and therefore we shall proceed a little distance at least and then return.' The argument was ignored and they could not proceed. 'Such laws,' Walter replied, 'were evidently meant for lawless people and enemies who would injure them, but we were evidently harmless and came only to do good.' This tempered the conversation and the officers explained that they were only carrying out their orders in enforcing the law. 'At least,' said Walter, 'this is no place, among a crowd, for gentlemen to converse about so important affairs; you cannot do less than invite us into some house and give us a cup of tea, when we can arrange matters.' 'Well then,' said the colonel, who up until now had been silent, 'we may go to the temple over this way.' 'No, no, no,' said the mandarin but he spoke too late, for Walter cried out, 'Yes. To the temple, to the temple,' and the crowd echoed the expression, made way for them to pass, some even showing them the way.

The temple was on a hillside a little above the village and they proceeded quickly towards it, leaving some of the mandarins behind. Ignoring the cries of the people behind, they walked onwards and upwards rapidly until they left the mandarins, police and most of the crowd behind. Before they reached the summit, which afforded an extensive view of the country and of Weihei Bay, one of the police runners came huffing and puffing and sat down with them, complaining of their fast pace, and slowly a group of their colleagues joined them. They chatted very pleasantly, asking them if the land they came from looked any different to this. They pointed out the real position of the town of Weihei, which it seemed they had missed by landing at a small village further up the bay.

After resting, they walked to the summit and saw the sea in the distance on the south side of the promontory and the location of the different villages and towns through which they might travel. They descended and at the foot of the hill, encountered the junior officer who had first met them at the beach and proceeded with him to the temple, to be ushered into one of the adjoining buildings where the mandarins were awaiting them.

Walter knew that being particular in matters of etiquette in dealing with the Chinese was necessary for undertakings to be successful. He understood that Chinese authorities generally treated strangers with contempt in order to degrade them in the eyes of their own people, and this prejudiced the business of the foreigner. They had resolved, therefore, that if they found the mandarins seated, and no accommodation had been provided for the missionaries, they would decline the conference rather than submit to the indignity of standing while the rest were seated. To their surprise, however, they found the mandarins standing to receive them and Walter was invited to take the chief seat on the left, which with the Chinese, is a post of honour. Tea was brought in and Walter began by stating their objective in coming to Shandong, giving him the opportunity to go over the principal doctrine of the Gospel and point the way to salvation. The Chinese replied that they were well assured of the friendly intentions of the missionaries but indicated that their orders left them no discretion to permit open intercourse with the people. They had read some of the missionaries' books and found that although they differed in some respects from their own classics, they contained many good things and saw no objection to their distribution. If they wanted any water or supplies, the Chinese would supply them gratis.

Walter responded that he understood that foreigners were not allowed to visit other ports than Canton for trade, but trade was not what they came for, so they did not see how they could be breaking any law. If the law forbade all intercourse, the true intention of such a law must be to keep off spies, robbers and enemies, none of which they were, and as such those laws would surely not apply to them. After some complimentary expressions in response, the conference broke up.

Arriving at the beach, they were anxious to distribute a few more tracts before departure but the officer in attendance said that as the mandarins had a supply of books it was not necessary to spread them among the people. Medhurst and Stevens were of a different opinion and told a sailor to bring a basket full of books from the boat. As soon as Walter opened it, the crowd could no longer be restrained and rushed forward and seized the books. The rush was so sudden and unexpected that it was impossible to avoid or withstand it and, in a few minutes, every leaf disappeared.

After returning to the vessel and obtaining refreshments, they loaded the boat with more books, set off once more for Liugong Island, visited two villages, and distributed books without hindrance. The locals exclaimed in amazement, 'These strangers speak Chinese! Where have they learned it?' They could not believe that Walter was a foreigner, staring at his face and checking the back of his neck to see if he plaited his hair in a queue. They were interested in the apparel of the missionaries, more interested in their waistcoats, shirts and cravats than in the religious message they brought. Later that afternoon they crossed to another part of the mainland where they entered a village pleasantly situated among the trees, going house to house, distributing their publications and conversing as freely as they might have done back in Batavia. The women, who appeared very shy, retreated to their houses.

They came across a woman driving an ass round a mill to grind millet. The ground millet appeared very fine and clean. Observing their approach, the woman left the mill and walked quickly into the house, while the blindfolded ass kept on his accustomed round as though his mistress was still there behind him.

Through this village ran a beautiful stream and they passed over a small bridge to the other side of the village and gave books and pamphlets to all those who could read or were inclined to accept them. They met two schoolmasters, both of whom accepted the books gladly, and one of the inhabitants presented them with a bunch of grapes in a display of gratitude. Outside the village, they observed a white tombstone that reminded them of Western tombstones. It was found to be a memorial of the virtue of a departed wife. Such tombstones were subsequently observed quite often in Shandong, leading Stevens to comment, 'Which makes it probable either that the wives of Shandong are more faithful, or the husbands more grateful, than in the southern provinces of the empire.'

Encouraged by the disposition of the people they had recently met, the next morning they went ashore on the east side of the bay and proceeded from village to village towards the western side. With one sailor to help carry the books, they left the boat to follow them around the bay. At a public threshing floor by the entrance of the village, a few people met them and in a few minutes, a large group assembled with the local schoolmaster as their spokesperson. The missionaries announced their mission and gladly gave books and pamphlets to those who accepted them. The Chinese had nothing to give in return but a pipe of tobacco and could not understand why the missionaries did not wish to receive it, but the sailor gladly accepted on their behalf. After completing their message and giving out some books, they moved a mile or two to the next village. In all of Shandong, they never saw a house standing alone, but everywhere the people lived in clusters of twenty-five to five hundred houses.

After taking refreshment at the boat and obtaining another supply of books, the missionaries set off across the fields towards a distant cluster of trees through which they saw whitewashed houses. Their arrival to the village was blocked by a small stream and they waded through it and called the people to them in the shade of two large trees in front of a temple. The crowd was large and they rushed forward to help themselves to a book. They placed the basket on the ground and Walter addressed the crowd, saying that they would not give out a single book until the crowd behaved in an orderly manner. The missionaries then took out half a dozen books and passed these out, then another six books and passed these out until the crowd appeared satisfied. As proof that the people understood the books, several of them who had received the first or second volume of the Harmony of the Gospels came to request the corresponding volume, delighted that they could make up a complete set.

The missionaries did not take the eagerness of the people as a sign that they had any relish for the subject, as was evident from the preference expressed by some for a book with a red cover or one with a brown cover. They understood that this was driven by an eager curiosity to obtain something that came from abroad and especially something for nothing. The hope was that the book would be read or passed on to someone who would read, resulting in a curiosity to learn more about the subject. Once the books were distributed in each village, Walter would stand and address them on the doctrines of the Gospel and the life, death and resurrection of our blessed Saviour, to which one man exclaimed, 'Oh! You are come to propagate religion!' 'Just so,' Walter replied, 'and happy you will be if you receive it!'

At the end of the day, they reached the boat tired out, having visited eight or nine villages, thankful for the successful work completed. They discovered that the mandarins had paid a visit in two junks with about a hundred men. Using a card written by Walter, the sailors had communicated that the missionaries and some of the crew had gone ashore. They appeared so friendly that the captain allowed them on board to look over the ship. They had asked the crew for some books and about fifty volumes were given out. After waiting for some hours they departed, highly pleased with what they had seen.

During their first two days in China, Walter and Stevens had distributed a thousand volumes, each containing a hundred pages, in a place where they had expected an unwelcome reception. That augured well for the future and especially for the way the people would receive them when free of the influence of the officers of government.

The building known as John Kyrle's House, formerly The Kings Arms, Ross-on-Wye, Herefordshire.

'The Post Office, St. Paul's Cathedral, and Bull and Mouth Inn, London.' A coloured engraving by G. J. Emblem, from a picture by T. Allom, about 1830. © Museum of London.

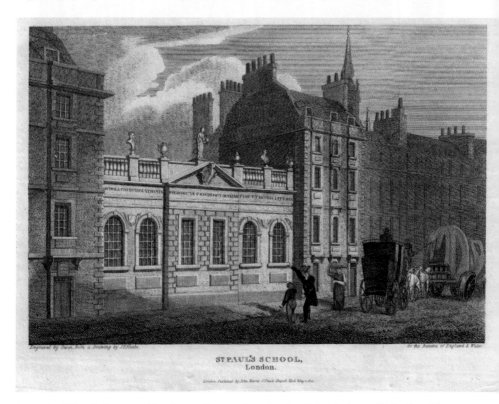

St Paul's School. Engraved by Owen from a drawing by J. P. Neale, published in *The Beauties of England and Wales*, 1814.

Portrait of Walter Medhurst before he left London in 1816 by W. T. Strutt. Collection of the SOAS Archives.

British officer
of the Madras
Native Infantry.
From the
*Historical
Records of the
XIII Madras
Infantry*, 1898.

O.Baxter Sculp.

Dr & Mrs
Milne, from
*The Life and
Opinions of Rev
William Milne*,
London, John
Snow, 1840.

Robert Morrison DD by John Robert Wildman, engraved 1824. © National Portrait Gallery.

Left: View overlooking Georgetown, by James Wathen. Collection of the Penang State Museum.

Below: Map of Batavia in 1846. Created by Eduard Selberg.

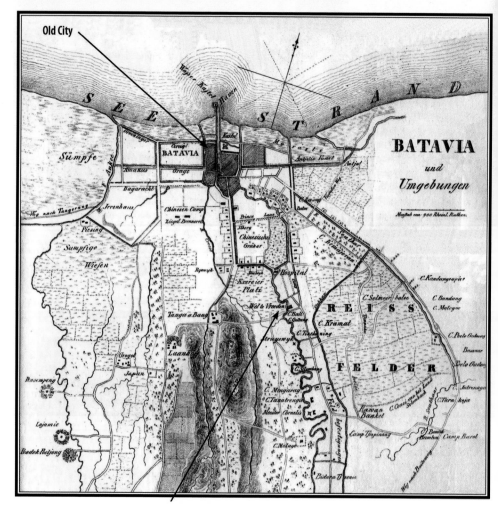

View of Engelsche Kerk Weg (English Church Road). Photographer: Woodbury &
Page, mid-1860s. Collection of Scott Merrillees.

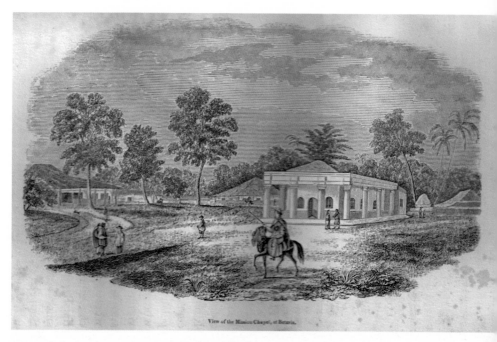

View of the Mission Chapel at Batavia. Drawn and engraved by G. Baxter. From *China: Its State and Prospects*, by W. H. Medhurst, London, John Snow 1838.

The Batavia Mission Chapel, now All Saints Jakarta. Photographer: Woodbury & Page, mid-1860s. Collection of Scott Merrillees.

Above: Landing at Woosung, 1835. From the *Evangelical Magazine and Missionary Chronicle.*

Right: Preaching in the Chinese temple. From *Missionary Magazine & Chronicle* 1852.

THE IDOL ÆSCULAPIUS.—SCENE IN A CHINESE TEMPLE.

Medhurst in conversation with Choo-Tih-Lang attended by a Malay boy. From *China: Its State and Prospects*, by W. H. Medhurst, London, John Snow 1838.

Medhurst in England, 1838. Collection of the SOAS Archives.

Hackney in 1840, by Caleb Turner. © Victoria & Albert Museum.

Torquay in 1842.

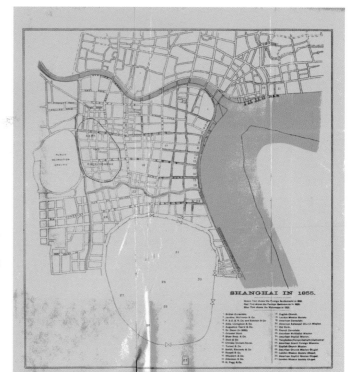

Map of Shanghai
in the 1850s.
Note the Mission
Centre at 18
and the chapels
at 28 and 31 in
the walled city.
Author H. Pott,
*A History of
Shanghai*, Kelly
& Walsh 1928.

PRINTING THE CHINESE SCRIPTURES.

The printing press at the Shanghai Mission. From *So Great Love: Sketches of
missionary life and labour*, by Cecilia Lucy Brightwell, London, John Snow 1874.

Dr Medhurst in the 1850s, from *Sunday at Home Magazine*, 1857.

William Lockhart, FRCS. Engraved by J. Cochran from a photo by Maull &
Polyblack. US National Library of Medicine.

Betty Medhurst in the 1870s.
From a locket owned by the
author's mother.

The grave of Dr Walter Henry
Medhurst at Abney Park
Cemetery, London.

On 15 September the *Huron* weighed anchor and set out to sea but spent most of the day becalmed. That night a breeze sprang up, allowing the ship to proceed slowly along the coast to the west, arriving at a harbour at Keshan.

When they arrived during the evening, the sails were taken in but the ship was still moving forward when the mate observed some birds ahead standing on a sandbank not a ship's length away. He called for the immediate hoisting of the foretopsail in an attempt to bring the ship's bow around so that they would miss the sandbank. The crew jumped into action and the ship turned less than half the ship's length from the bank, with only six inches of water to spare. Had the mate not seen the birds, the ship would have gone straight into the sandbank causing serious damage, if not a total shipwreck.

The next morning the weather was fine and the extensive bay seemed dotted with little groves indicating numerous villages, while the town of Keshan, adorned with a white tower, was visible around the edge of a hill. They immediately landed to commence their operations among the villages before venturing towards the larger town. The first place they came to did not present the same welcoming appearance as in the previous days and the people they met strongly opposed their entry to the village. Before long, a very officious man joined them and resisted their attempts to move any further. They told him that their objective was only to do good and ask for nothing in return, but he said that it was forbidden for foreigners to enter their country and consequently they should go. Not wanting to anger the other people, the missionaries turned back to the beach and walked along to another village. On the way, they met several friendly and civil people who gladly accepted books. At the next village, they were met by several people, including one old man who thought they had come to take his country. He wanted to know how many ships they had and when told only one, he asked how many men they had on board. When told there were only eighteen, he exclaimed, 'A very likely story indeed! You come all this way with only eighteen people, merely to distribute books? You expect us to believe that?'

Having been rebuffed at two villages, they determined to go directly to Keshan and face any officers who might be there. On the beach was a makeshift customs house attended by a few policemen, behind that a market and a temple, and a little beyond were the houses where the people lived. With no landing place in front of the town and the muddy beach, they stood off to some rocks on the eastern side of the bay. This enabled the people of the town to get a good sight of the foreigners as they landed and induced many to come down to meet them. Stepping ashore, they began giving away books and no sooner had they been taken than others began calling for more. The sailor accompanying them opened the basket when the whole crowd rushed forward, tumbling the sailor and the books over into the sand. In no time at all the books from that basket were gone.

They moved forward surrounded by a dense crowd, while the sailor went back for more books. Walter climbed up onto a junk that was hauled up on the beach and addressed the crowd, trying to calm them down and assure them that there would be books for all. Without much success in controlling the crowd, they suspended the work of distribution and proceeded to the customs house, where they met the officer in charge, who was displeased at the disturbance they had caused. Seeing that the police had seized a man from the crowd for having taken part in the scramble, Walter approached the officer and asked him, in a friendly manner, to let the poor culprit go as he had not been noisier than the rest and it was quite excusable to be a little excited on such an extraordinary occasion. The officer suggested that Walter should mind his own business. 'Sir,' said Walter very properly, 'it is my business to interfere, because I am the occasion of his offending. If he suffers for this affair I shall consider it an intended insult to me.' When the officer replied that he would be released after they left, Walter assumed a bolder tone and said that he would not move until he saw the culprit released. This firmer approach had the desired effect and the officer immediately released the man and became civil with the visitors.

When Walter expressed interest in buying fresh provisions, the officer replied that it was past noon and the market people had most probably gone home. Walter said they would go to the market to ascertain for themselves but as they entered the market, they could hear the police running on ahead ordering the people not to sell to the foreigners. The missionaries returned to the officer at the customs house, who initially denied having given any such order, but Walter asked the crowd gathered around and they agreed, forcing the officer to back down. The order was rescinded and when they returned to the market, every stall was open and all the market people wanted to sell to them. Now, another problem arose. Spanish dollars were not accepted there. Fortunately, a solution presented itself when the captain of a junk from Fujian agreed to buy the provisions for them and accept their silver coins in payment.

The next day they landed on the western side of the bay and passed through all the villages on that side, and again, they were treated with a level of suspicion, but not entirely without friendliness. At one village, two elders approached them. One said, 'Will I obtain forgiveness of sins by reading this book?' 'You will,' replied Walter, 'if you follow the book and trust in Jesus the only Saviour.' 'What will this Saviour bestow upon those that believe?' 'He will take them to heaven.' 'Have you believed?' 'I hope I have.' 'Has he taken you to heaven?' 'I trust he will when I die.' 'Die! Oh! You have to wait till death for all this. Give me present enjoyment; who cares what happens after death?' Before they left the village, however, the old Confucian disciples received the books.

In one of the villages they passed through, they saw in a shop some of their own books, together with native works, being offered for sale. Being ever positive, the missionaries concluded from this that the Chinese set a value on the publications and instead of bemoaning the fact that they were being disposed of, they rejoiced that the books would be further distributed as a result. From this village they visited the fort on the hill, which they found to be small and ill equipped for any form of battle. The whole garrison, it seemed, amounted to only five men who, as far as they could see, were unarmed.

Back at the vessel, they learned that several mandarins had again been on board wishing to see them. The mate had fired two six pounders to alert them of the visit but the missionaries had heard nothing. At the end of their visit, the mandarins left the following notice in writing: 'The civil and military mandarins of the Celestial Empire have come to pay their respects and to say that the general of the district waits at Kensho where he requests the strangers to go on shore and arrange matters.'

The next day, 21 September, they moved the brig nearer to the town and prepared to comply with the invitation from the general. Meanwhile, they were visited again by a boatload of officers, including an army captain and the commander of one of the war junks. These were very hearty and cheerful men and the chief speaker's name was Tae-lou-yay. He asked their names, country and profession together with the reason for visiting this place. This gave Walter the opportunity to explain the doctrines of Christianity and to make them acquainted with the contents of the books they had brought for distribution. Tae-lou-yay asked about the voyage and wondered how they could come so far without seeing land or stopping for fresh supplies. Walter explained the system of navigation and showed him how, by means of a sextant and a chronometer, they managed to ascertain the exact latitude and longitude of any place they happened to be. He also explained that since they carried so few men, the provisions they required occupied very little space. Tae-lou-yay then requested the visitors to furnish him with a list of supplies, which the Chinese promised to provide, and invited them to meet again on shore.

Immediately after their departure, the missionaries got into their boat and arrived at the shore well before the mandarins. A large crowd had gathered on the shore and a junior and flustered officer requested them to stay in the boat until the senior mandarins arrived. Walter objected that they could not wait in the boat in the rain and urged the young officer to offer them a place to shelter. They easily gave in and the party moved back to the customs house accompanied by a dense crowd. Unlike their previous visit to the customs house, chairs of state had been placed for the missionaries while they awaited the return of the mandarins from the brig. The crowd grew and pressed more heavily around the visitors while the police brandished their bamboo sticks over their heads and shoulders. Observing that the police never attempted to strike the Fujian sailors from the junks, Walter took up conversation with them in their own dialect, which pleased them but seemed to antagonise the police, to whom it was quite unintelligible.

The mandarins returned in due course but as the wait for the general stretched out to several hours, Walter informed Tae-lou-yay that unless they were introduced to him soon, they must return on board before dark. He replied that the general was about to be introduced but first they had to discuss what ceremonies might be observed on their meeting such a great officer. Their custom was to kneel down and touch the head on the ground when coming into his presence and asked if the missionaries would do the same. Walter told him that they were not in the habit of prostrating themselves before fellow mortals but were willing to pay the same deference to Chinese mandarins of high rank as they did to their own superior officers. 'Well,' he said, 'I will speak to the general and try to arrange that matter for you.' 'But further,' Walter said, 'when the introductions are over, we expect to be allowed to sit down in the presence of the General, otherwise we beg leave to decline the conference.' 'That also,' he said, 'shall be arranged to your satisfaction.'

With these procedural matters taken care of, the missionaries were led out towards the temple where two officers, who allowed only Walter and Stevens to pass, guarded the outer gate. The pavement from the gate to the temple was lined with twenty-five unarmed soldiers, whom Stevens described as the finest he had ever seen in China, of a size fit for grenadiers. Inside the temple, sitting rigidly before the gods, sat two officers. Walter and Stevens came to the threshold before them, removed their hats and gave a respectful bow. The Chinese responded by slowly raising their hands and slightly inclining their heads. One of the attendants motioned the missionaries to take seats arranged on the lower left-hand side. The Chinese officers comprised a civilian officer, who did most of the talking, and a military general named Chow. The civil mandarin started by asking them their names, where they were from, when they had left Canton, where they had called on the way, and what their business was in coming here. Walter took every opportunity to explain the doctrine of Christianity and impress on the Chinese that the only reason they were there was to do good. Here, the general interposed and asked gruffly how they could think of coming to China to exhort people to be good; did they suppose that there were no good people in China before? Walter assured them that they had no doubt that the people of China were good, but they were far from perfect and knew nothing of the way to salvation, which was their business to inform the people. The civil mandarin replied that the Chinese had Confucius and his doctrines which had sufficed the people for ages so what need did they have of another sage? Walter observed that Confucius guided the people in their duties of social relations but Christianity gave information about divine and eternal things. One was a teacher and the other a Saviour and it was by no means superfluous to follow both.

The conversation then switched to questions about their ship. Did they own it and if so, where did they get the money to buy it? The missionaries explained the concept of the society, which had raised the funds to send them here to spread the message of Jesus Christ to all parts of the world. They also asked how the missionaries managed to become fluent in Chinese, and they replied they had had relations with Chinese emigrants in other countries within the region over many years.

They asked about Edwin Stevens and discovered that he was from New England. Was there a New England and an old England, the mandarins wanted to know. Walter explained. The mandarins were incredulous to hear that the new country was governed by two great assemblies elected by the people, and how the president was elected for a four-year term. What happened to the old president, they wondered; how could they stop him from inciting rebellion to retain the power he once had? To the Chinese mind, once a person had held supreme authority, they were never willing to be deprived of the reins of power. They also asked how an old Englander could so easily agree with a new Englander. Walter responded that as Christians they were both tied by their religion and that both countries were influenced by liberal views. The civil mandarin referred to Lord Amherst's visit some twenty years previously when he tried to establish a British embassy and how the emperor returned the ambassador's gifts, showing how indifferent they were to dealing with foreigners. He also referred to the visit of Lindsay and Gutzlaff three years previously, showing the visitors how well acquainted they were with previous attempts at negotiation with the Chinese.

By this time, it was getting dark and the conference ended. The missionaries made the same salutation on leaving as on their entrance and they departed on friendly, if not cordial terms. This was much as Walter expected. Accustomed to receiving nothing but servile obedience from the people around them, the Chinese mandarins could not be expected to respond in any different manner. Expressions of curiosity, surprise, fear, or joy would be unworthy of such exalted beings and terror, awe and respect were the only feelings they wished to engender in others. They had seen the old general examining with curiosity their dress, which showed that he was probably bursting to know more. The civil mandarin sent for Mr Stevens' pencil to examine it, and seeing how pleased he was with it, Stevens was about to ask him to accept it, but before he could the sly fox pocketed it. This kind of trick was typical of the Chinese mandarins they met, leaving the opinion that the highest officers of government achieved their positions by chicanery and deceit.

They returned to the boat, accompanied by military and naval captains and by Tae-lou-yay, who advised them to accept the gifts of provisions, or the general would be very displeased. A little while afterwards, instead of a few provisions from their list, there arrived a shipment including ten pigs, ten sheep, bags of flour, peas and millet, and several ducks and chickens. The pigs and sheep had been thrown together with their legs tied so that when they arrived alongside, seven sheep and three pigs were dead and had to be returned. In return for the gifts, the missionaries insisted on sending back twelve bags of rice. The police officers initially objected but then returned these to shore. The next morning the boat returned with the rice and a message that on no account could the rice be received. The messenger said that he had orders to return the rice and if it was not accepted then it should be thrown into the sea and if he returned with it, he would be beaten. Assuring him that the great officers of his imperial majesty could hardly be so unreasonable as to beat a man for what he did not do, the poor man was sent back to the shore. About two hours later, they observed the same boat returning with a mandarin on board, bringing the rice; but before he could get alongside, the brig was under way and in a short time in full sail, bidding adieu to Keshan and to the mandarins.

On the 23rd, they set out for a small walled town, which from an old Jesuit map they took to be Tsinghaewei. The town had originally been surrounded by a mud brick wall but was now dilapidated, with many houses in ruin. The town had sadly deteriorated since the Jesuits had made their map. The town was built, they were told, in the Ming dynasty as a defence against the Japanese, but like other military preparations of the peaceful Chinese, the battlements had since fallen into decay for want of use. Stevens made the same observation of the whole of Shandong, writing that 'everywhere there are towers on the hills, fallen to ruins, forts dismantled or nearly so and the miserable remnants of a fortress, where perhaps the enemies of their country were once withstood'.

They returned to the vessel in the evening to find that a mandarin had been to the brig, remained for two hours and been impressed with all he saw. Four or five boatloads of people had also visited and most had left with books. The next day they tried to get under way but the wind and tide worked against them and they made very little progress, anchoring that night in almost the same place they had left. The next day the wind continued blowing fresh ahead and the seas were rough so they remained at their moorings all day. On the third day, they did get under way but only managed to make it across to the western side of the bay where the ship came to anchor over a gravel bottom, with many rocks on each side of them. When they reached the shore, Walter landed alone with a basket of books and arranged to meet Edwin Stevens at a distant village further along the shore. The going was difficult due to the deep gullies that he had to cross. He was about to descend into one of these when a group of Chinese called out to warn him and show him a safer way to cross. Several people he passed received books but on approaching the first village, the inhabitants were frightened, ordering him to leave as quickly as possible. As he turned to go, a respectable man came forward and said he had heard of the books and would like to see them. This encouraged others to come forward, and soon, the entire village was receiving Walter and the books with great friendship.

Having a long journey to complete before sunset, he pressed on to the next village, wading through a wide stream and avoiding treacherous quicksands. On the opposite side, most of the villagers fled at his approach and he left a few books with those who remained before moving on to the next village. Had there been time to remain among them, he would have removed their fears through friendly conversation but the rendezvous place was a long way off and Walter had to move fast if he was to get there before dark. The plain was highly cultivated and as far as the eye could see, thickly studded with villages, but Walter had left insufficient time to approach any more and was compelled to make for the shore. He spotted Stevens in the distance and together they made it back to the boat before darkness, arriving at the vessel tired and frustrated by the lack of success. Arriving on board in the evening, they decided to proceed to a more favourable region.

After leaving Shandong, they concluded that nowhere had they been treated roughly or placed under any threat, the people had mostly been harmless and peaceful, they had seldom seen weapons, and the few soldiers manning the forts and guardhouses were without arms. Although the people were inoffensive, they had seldom offered help and with the exception of drinking water, had offered little else. As to the effectiveness of their message, they had hardly scratched the surface. They had found that the people all spoke Mandarin, which meant they could easily communicate with them, but their time with each person was so short, the messengers so unusual, and the subject so strange that they could hardly expect to have made any lasting influence. They had distributed three thousand books on the north shore and another six hundred on the south side of the promontory, leading them to believe that a seed had been planted which might one day support others in the spread of the Gospel.

In his book, Walter summarised his observations of the people of Shandong:

The men, were for the most part, robust and well fed, hearty and hard working; while no want, so far we could perceive, prevailed....

The women were...pale faced and sickly in general and seldom exhibited the ruddy complexion observable in the other sex.

It is well known that the Chinese have a method of binding up the feet of their female offspring, from their earliest infancy. For this purpose they use ligatures, wound very tight round the foot and instep, with the toes bent inwards, until they grow into the sole of the foot. Thus diminished and compressed, the foot is reduced to three or four inches in length and as many in circumference, tapering towards a point at the end. Of course, the anklebones become proportionally large, while the club feet produced are but ill adapted for walking. Indeed, some of them are scarcely able to walk at all and are obliged to use sticks to support them or to lean on a servant, in order to move along the streets.[2]

On 1 October, they set sail for the south, heading for the province of Jiangsu and the city of Shanghai, one of the greatest emporiums of commerce on the east coast of China.

After visiting Shanghai, the missionaries distributed a load of books to the native junks lying off the town of Wusong. They soon observed a boat from the customs house giving orders against communicating with the foreigners. With this impediment to their work, they moved towards the town and landed along a creek that ran into the main river. The shore was lined with hundreds of people who eagerly accepted their books, even as the mandarins came among them. With books nearly depleted, the missionaries walked up through the streets followed by the mandarins and a large crowd of people. The town of four or five hundred houses was much larger than at first imagined. The people were unwilling to sell anything, but with a bit of persuasion, they were allowed to purchase a few provisions. The people seemed well fed and the women were better looking than those they had seen in Shandong. They observed many teashops where people met for entertainment. They also saw liquor shops and in one place a distilling apparatus.

In one street, they came across a notice from the chief magistrate stating that anyone who traded or bartered with the barbarians would be severely punished. On reading this, Walter turned round to one of the officers following them and said, 'We are not barbarians, but a civilised people and we do not need these insults applied to us.' The officer replied that he had nothing to do with the notice and could not answer for it. On the shore, they observed a line of military drawn up on the embankment discharging a round of musketry, while a salute was fired from each fort. Out on the river, the general's barge was passing by, his flag flying from the masthead. The troops kneeled as he went by and rose again after he had passed. About twenty-five war junks followed, which all fired blank cartridges as they came abreast of the brig, no doubt to infuse terror into the minds of the crafty barbarians. When the war junks had all anchored, instead of showing fear in the face of this show of force, the missionaries walked up to the soldiers to inspect their military presence. The troops consisted of about a hundred men in single file and at the head of the formation stood two officers. The missionaries passed along the front of the line, examining their arms and noting their slovenly appearance. Their matchlocks were longer and thinner than common muskets and many of them were noticeably rusty, to the point of having holes in them. The only reason these weapons did not burst when fired was probably due to the weak powder used in them. They discussed with the officers at the head of the line the poor quality of the military equipment and were told that the emperor did not provide the troops with any better dress or weapons. It appeared odd that this demonstration of military power was intended to raise fear in the minds of the foreigners and yet they made no attempt to stop the missionaries from wandering among the soldiers.

In the afternoon, after returning to the boat to replenish their supply of books, they went to one of the forts from which the guns had been fired on their first arrival in the Huangpu River. Half of the fort was already in ruins and the other half was in such a precarious state that it was not safe to walk around the ramparts. On the embankment adjoining the fort were four long eighteen-pounders placed on partly rotting wooden frames, one of which had already collapsed. They went into the adjoining barracks and were soon surrounded by a group of officers and other people who willingly accepted copies of the books. One old man remembered the visit of Mr Lindsay, who had fired off his fowling piece to amuse him. With the rain pouring down, they ceased operations and returned to the boat.

The next morning they received a visit from an officer who said that he had come on behalf of the general to pay his respects, but of course, this was just a polite way of asking them to go. Because he spoke in such a friendly manner they invited him on board and gave him tea and entered into conversation about the reasons for their visit. His curiosity was taken by the red curtains pulled across their beds and he wanted to know if that was the altar for their gods. This gave Walter the opportunity to explain the basis of Christianity and the existence of only one God, but the mandarin had no interest and turned the conversation to something else. He was particularly anxious to know when they would be leaving. He said they had received an overland dispatch from Shandong about their visit up there, stating that they had fifty men on board. They assured him that it was indeed this boat but that they only had eighteen passengers and crew.

On the morning of the 12th, they decided to cross the Yangtze River to an island inhabited by about a million people. As the weather was unsettled and the estuary was wide and rough, they took the long boat. Although she was a poor sailor, she would better handle a rough sea than the small boat. They set off at four in the morning to take advantage of the tide, and almost as soon as they got under way, they found that they could not make the planned course to the north and were heading more to the north-east, which would see them end up on the southern shoal. The best course of action would be to return to the vessel but when morning dawned, they found they were two or three miles to the lee of the brig with the tide taking them out to sea. Sailing or rowing the boat back to the brig was impossible so the only thing to do was to find a creek or cove on the island where they could shelter. This they did but found that with the tide ebbing, the boat would soon be left high and dry until the tide turned. Deciding to turn a problem to an advantage, they went ashore to visit villages and distribute books.

One of the mandarins in Wusong had told them that the people on the other side were likely to beat them but the missionaries did not believe him, so they took a basket of books and set off through the villages. The fields were producing rice, cotton and vegetables. The people were dirty but friendly and when word got around that free books were being given out, the people came running from their houses and over the fields to receive them. Several times, they sent a sailor back to the boat for replenishments. They observed every now and then coffins above the ground that were made fast with stakes to stop them being washed away. Passing on they saw large jars, which, on inspection, proved to be full of human bones. From this, they inferred that dead bodies were not interred due to the frequent flooding of the ground, but left to decay and then the bones collected for preservation.

Back at the boat, they were anxious to get it afloat as soon as possible to take advantage of the turning tide and return to the vessel. Being unable to move it themselves, they asked the natives to help them, offering to pay them in coin. This they declined but said they would do it for more books. Then they got to work, some of them up to their waists in mud. They started demanding their books as soon as the boat was afloat. Walter refused to pay them until the boat was safely across the bar, which they did and the books were passed over, but not before one of the rogues stole a pair of shoes. Now a party of soldiers was approaching them and they were called on to help tow them along the beach for which they would be paid. Payment was arranged up front and then they waited while the soldiers tried to commandeer others to pull the boat. Eventually the boat was pulled about a mile along the beach and a decision was made to cast off and row the boat with the tide, towards the brig. In a few minutes, the brig was spotted under way, intending to meet them near the island. The crew in the boat rowed all the harder to be able to meet the brig, but she passed within gunshot without seeing them. Eventually the people on board caught sight of the boat but the vessel was so far away by then, and without sail on the boat, it was not possible to reach her. They rowed over to a nearby junk where they could get some stability to hoist the mast and put on sail. They now found the wind so strong that several times the boat nearly capsized and she went over so far that the gunwale was lapping the water. They shortened sail and after much soaking, fatigue and danger, they arrived back at the boat at 2 o'clock, thankful to their Divine deliverer.

They learned from the captain that as soon as they were about to weigh anchor in the morning, the war junks came down and anchored alongside the brig, each one again firing blank cartridges as they came. After that, a boatload of mandarins came on board, completely filling the quarterdeck. When they learned that the missionaries were not aboard, they were furious, since they had been keeping the brig under surveillance, but because the long boat had left in the dark, they had been duped. The poor subalterns on guard duty would be severely punished for allowing this to happen.

Now the brig was out in the estuary and out of sight of the mandarins, several trading vessels approached them, calling to see whether they wished to trade. It was further evidence that the Chinese people wished for an open relationship with the foreigners, free from the regulations of the government.

On 13 October, they left the mouth of the Yangtze, passed what they knew as Gutzlaff's Island and out into the East China Sea, heading for what they thought was Jintang Island. After anchoring for the night, they discovered that the charts and notes they were using were incorrect at this position. They were in fact out in the Zhoushan group of barren islands, at least thirty miles east of where they thought they were. So it was the evening of the 15th before they found themselves anchored between Jintang Island and Ningbo. On the morning of the 16th, six war junks came alongside, the commanders of which were very civil. They supplied the crews with books and conversed with the officers for about an hour when suddenly another war junk hove into view, having on board the commander of the squadron. This resulted in the Chinese returning to their boats and, having anchored under the stern of the brig, they commenced to fire blank cartridges, whether to salute their commander or to warn the barbarians, nobody was sure.

The missionaries decided to go ashore on Jintang Island and none of the Chinese from the war junks followed so they were left to carry on their operations unmolested. They landed at the head of the bay and entered a town where they found people to be uncommonly friendly and where their books were taken up quickly and with thanks. The women also came forward to solicit books here, showing no fear or shyness. At the edge of the town, they saw a poor boy lying down in the last stage of dropsy and evidently dying. The missionaries had no medicine with them but they also saw that his state was so advanced that it would have been impossible to save him anyway. He was lying on the cold ground, exposed to the elements, which would have been enough to bring anyone to a speedy end. The poor boy had probably been turned out to die in the streets, a practice very common in China, to prevent a person dying in the house and thereby bringing bad luck. Outside the town, they climbed the hills covered with firs, planted to serve as fuel for the inhabitants as it was the only thing growing on the hillside. In contrast, the plains were filled with waving grain, which obviously yielded a good produce.

On 19 October, they weighed anchor and set sail for Putuo Mountain, on the other side of Zhoushan island. The whole island of Putuo Mountain was covered in temples and grottos, where six thousand priests spent their days reciting prayers to Buddha. Walter had heard of this island many times and in his mind, this was where the ideas that he must compete with had come from. The missionaries ignored the Chinese fleet of war junks that had followed them. They loaded the boat with tracts and books and headed for the shore. As soon as they landed, they found a broad and well-beaten pathway leading to the top of one of the hills, at every crag and turn of which they espied a temple or a grotto with a garden tastefully laid out with walks lined with aromatic shrubs, spreading a pleasant fragrance through the air. The view from the top was magnificent, with numerous islands far and near, a mountain monastery on a nearby peak and in a distant valley a great temple with a golden tiled roof. The scene was absolutely lovely and enchanting, but to the two evangelical Christians, it represented a picture of moral and spiritual death. Nevertheless, they spent the whole day visiting the temples, caverns and monasteries trying to understand what motivated and sustained these beliefs so that they would be better equipped to argue against them in the future. They found a school taught by a disciple of Confucius, but the scholars were all young shaven-headed boys destined for the Buddhist priesthood. When asked whether the priests taught the boys under their care, they were told that the sole employment of the holy men was to recite prayers to and employ themselves in contemplations upon Buddha.

Over the whole island, their books were readily accepted and some that had been left by Gutzlaff on a previous visit were also found. Walter wrote that he was gratified to see that the temples were in a state of decay, earnestly hoping that this was a sign of a declining philosophy as a competitor to the one true religion. Priests were eager to see them, thinking that they were visiting to worship at the different shrines, but Walter was quick to tell them that his adorations were paid only to the living God, the maker of heaven and earth, to whom alone they were due.

At the brig, they found the commodore of the Chinese fleet and one of his naval captains had come to pay their respects. The former was Te Laou-yay with the rank of lieutenant colonel and the latter was Sung Laou-yay. The colonel said very little but the captain was very friendly and talkative. Walter asked the Chinese why they were honoured with the escort of their vessels from place to place and they replied that they merely came to show them the way and to ensure that they did not fall foul of rocks and shoals. Walter observed that if their object was to prevent them trading, they could be spared the trouble since they were not traders, but merely wanted to distribute books and ideas. The captain agreed that they perceived their object to be a benevolent one but there had been many vessels in their area before, vessels engaged in the opium trade, which was illegal and immoral, and they were there to prevent it. As for regular intercourse, they confessed that it would be better for both countries if it was allowed and they complained that the laws of China were too severe in prohibiting all commerce with foreigners, except at Canton. They spoke highly of Mr Lindsay and had felt for him when he had to leave Ningbo without being able to effect his purpose. When dinner for the missionaries was ready, finding the officers to be so candid and open, they invited them to share a meal together. The group spent a pleasant afternoon and parted as good friends.

On the 21st, they left Putuo and headed south for the province of Fujian. After two days' sail, they came to an unknown and uncharted part of the coast and as the weather was deteriorating, they endeavoured to move into a bay. They came to anchor in the lee of a few islands. They had scarcely dined, before they saw, by the falling tide, an extensive reef of rocks within a few hundred yards of them, with breakers crashing over them as high as the masthead. Had they continued on course before anchoring, they would have been dashed to pieces.

For the next three days, the storm continued and they were confined to the vessel without any hope of going ashore. Finally, on the 27th they set off in the jolly boat and when they arrived safely on the beach, the people came in droves and readily accepted books. The missionaries then moved through the villages, distributing as they went, greeting the people in their own dialect. The women, who were particularly anxious to accept the volumes, exhibited more taste and skill in their appearance and make-up here than their sisters further north. Their hair was tastefully arranged, sometimes with artificial flowers, and they wore dangling earrings. Their feet were the smallest they had seen and when they measured the impression of one they found it to be four inches long. The soil seemed exceedingly poor, producing only sweet potatoes and groundnuts, while the people mainly subsisted by fishing. Their houses were built of stone and were generally thatched but some were covered in tiles. On the roofs were many stones, placed there to prevent the tiles being blown away by the strong winds that blew along that coast. The insides of their dwellings were filthy and the stench about them very offensive to the visitors, although the locals seemed little bothered by it.

Having returned to the vessel at about 2 o'clock, they were able to get under way that same afternoon and headed south, sailing down the coast of Fujian until on the morning of 29 October they came on the fine harbour of Dongshan. Having anchored at some distance from the town of Dongshan, the boat was not seen until they were close and they landed before the people had time to gather on the beach. It only needed five minutes, however, before hundreds of smiling faces were rushing towards them. The missionaries were getting low on books and, thinking they had given out enough in this part of the town, they took the boat across the bay to reach the other end of the town, where they landed in the midst of a huge crowd. The second mate, a powerful man, stepped forward with another sailor to help the missionaries and took the bag of books to distribute them. When he climbed up on a wall with a second bag, someone jumped forward, grabbed the bag and ran off triumphantly into the crowd. The second mate was having none of that, however, and sprang forward, grabbed the bag back from the thief and did not let go until he had slowly and carefully distributed all the books one at a time. Just as he was distributing the last of the books, they heard a clattering of bamboo poles on the ground and the crowd started to scatter. The noise came from two petty officers who beat the ground but also took swings at the heads of some among the crowd, at one time almost hitting Walter Medhurst. As all the books had been distributed, the missionaries were not concerned about the people being dispersed but they commented to the officers that it was unnecessary to strike the people for their enthusiasm. Edwin Stevens burst out in English, demanding to know how they could think of striking his friend. A discussion ensued and the officers mellowed in their attitude, leading to an invitation to accompany them to the castle and partake of a cup of tea.

The officers led the way to the upper room, which to Walter looked only just strong enough to bear the weight of the group. One of the officers appeared very upset and turned quite pale as he enquired with quivering lips about the outburst from Stevens. The officer could not understand what was said, but guessed it was not good from the black look that Stevens had given him. To calm the officer down and to prevent a real misunderstanding, Walter explained that it was the American's humour and merely a joke. This seemed to settle the man down and after conversing for a short time the group broke up and the missionaries proceeded to the market to purchase a few provisions, to which the officers had no objection.

The streets were narrow and it was difficult to make any progress due to the size of the crowd, almost all of whom were there to see the strangers. Whenever they stopped to purchase anything, the crowd halted and people climbed up on walls and houses to get a good look. The market was well stocked and surrounded by shops selling a large choice of wares. The people were astonished at the fluency with which Walter spoke not just the Fujian dialect, but more specifically his accent, which was identical to that in the district where Dongshan was situated. Walter had employed a man in Batavia who came from this region, from whom he had picked up the accent. It left the people totally puzzled though. They felt sure that his parents must have been from the region but they could not account for his light hair and round eyes. The people said that they had seen foreign ships pass by the coast before but this was the first time that one had stopped and the first time they had ever seen a foreigner.

The next day, the anchor was raised for the last time and they sailed out through the western entrance to the harbour, keeping Nan'ao on their starboard side and heading back to Macao. They arrived at Lintin Island in the Canton River on 31 October 1835, having been away for two months and five days. They had given away about eighteen thousand volumes among cheerful and willing people without meeting the least aggression or injury. They thanked God for their safe return and prayed that the seed sown would one day bring forth an abundant harvest.

18

HOME AND HOME AGAIN

The *Huron* arrived at Lintin Island before the end of the Canton trading season, which ran from September through to December, and there must have been a hundred sailing ships in the harbour, with hundreds more barges and lighters servicing Canton and Macao. It was a sea of activity and industry compared to the places that the *Huron* had been to. In another two months, with the arrival of the north-east monsoon winds, the harbour would be almost empty with most of the ships halfway to India and Europe.

As soon as he arrived, Walter sent a message to Charles Gutzlaff and John Morrison in Canton to meet him in Macao. With the trading season in full swing, there would be no room to stay in Canton. The Chinese were also getting very restrictive about missionary activities in Canton and the authorities had recently shut down the printing operation, from which Keuh-a-gang, one of the mission's local converts, narrowly escaped apprehension to the safety of a ship at Lintin. His son was arrested and might not be seen again.

On 10 November, an edict from the Imperial Court at Peking charged the men with distributing books designed to seduce the people with lies. The edict instructed the governor to explain immediately the order to the foreigners as follows:

> … they must not abruptly enter every province, disorderly scheming to obtain extraordinary gain. If they again indulge their thoughts and act so irregularly, instantly drive them forth out of the port and do not permit them to trade: let them not involve themselves in subsequent repentance. Respect this.[1]

After arriving in Macao, one of Walter's great pleasures was to receive correspondence from Betty, his family and friends in England and the directors in London. This last information included a request for Walter to return to Batavia long enough to secure a passage to England, along with his family, for discussions with the society about extending the mission into China. He resumed his work, as is shown in a letter to his old friend from Gloucester, John Tucker:

> Macao, China, Nov 15, 1835
> My dear friend,
> It did my heart good to read your well known signature and to peruse your friendly and welcome epistle. I have just time to return you a hasty reply, more with the view of convincing you of my continued friendship and regard, than of communicating much information to you. Do you still remember the time when you and I used to compare notes together as good Mr Bishop called it in the vestry and when we joined together the Church of Christ at the Southgate Meeting. How is it, my Brother, have we kept our vows? Full well I know, not one good thing hath failed of all that the Lord hath promised, but alas! … I am now indefatigably

busy with the devoted Gutzlaff in remodelling the translation of the Chinese Scriptures and from all you have heard of his ardour and zeal, you must indeed think that diligence and effort are necessary to keep pace with one who soars on such eagle's wings, who runs without weariness and walks without finishing. Though he has been engaged half the time I have in the study of Chinese, he has already attained a more extensive acquaintance with the character than I can aspire to, though as might have been expected his style and idiom are still a little deficient. Drs Morrison and Milne, being called to their rest and the call for a revision of the Chinese translation being loud and urgent, that labour has devolved upon us, in conjunction with Dr Morrison's son, a pious and talented youth. When we are through the New Testament, which I hope will be in a little more than a month, I expect to leave China and proceed to Batavia; from which place I hope (God willing) to sail with my family to England, the Directors of the Missionary Society being desirous to confer with me on the best means of prosecuting the Mission in China and I myself, standing in need of some change of climate after more than 19 years absence from my native land.

It will afford me unspeakable pleasure, should I be spared to accomplish the intended voyage to meet you and the other dear friends whom I once knew and still love. But when I come, I mean to beat up for recruits for the Chinese Mission and therefore I would have you look out for talented and zealous young men to come forth...Make enquiry and have all things in readiness when I come.

Remember me to your wife and accept of the best wishes yourself, from

Your affectionate friend, W.H. Medhurst[2]

Walter Medhurst, Charles Gutzlaff and John Morrison were now fully engaged in revising the translations of the New Testament by Morrison and Milne and it would be another month before Walter could free himself and return to his family in Batavia. He wanted to take the finished job with him so that he could start printing the new translation of the New Testament before leaving for England. He also committed to discuss a completely new translation of the Bible with the society's directors, for they had identified the need for a thorough revision of the work done by Morrison and Milne.

A few weeks before the *Huron* arrived back at Lintin Island, two missionaries from the American Episcopal Church arrived in Canton, the Revd Henry Lockwood and the Revd Francis Hanson, both desiring to learn Chinese and join the work of the other Protestant missionaries in the region. With the growing restrictions on missionary activities in Canton and Macao, Lockwood and Hanson were forced to reconsider where to locate in order to commence their studies in the language. They had been considering Singapore as a possible location, when along came Walter Medhurst, fresh from his expeditionary tour of China, and invited them to Batavia, where they could learn the language and assist the mission during his absence in England. The opportunity seemed ideal and the two Americans departed for Singapore and Batavia, where they arrived on 22 December with the news for Mrs Medhurst that her husband was safe and well and would be home within a few weeks.

The revised translation was completed in mid-December, and Walter arrived home in Batavia in early January. Betty and the children were all well. William Young had again managed the affairs of the mission well during his absence. It was a hive of activity and the two Americans had blended well into its operations. The print shop under the direction of Benjamin Keasberry was working long hours to produce Chinese, Malay and Javanese literature and by

1835, this operation had printed almost two hundred thousand copies of publications varying in size from five to two hundred and eight pages. The largest of these publications was a Catechism in Malay, written by Betty, of which a thousand copies were produced. The Chinese, Malay and English schools were full, with daughter Sarah running the English school. Sundays were devoted to ministering to the English and Malay congregations as well as teaching Sunday school, which had become Betty's favourite task. The Parapattan Orphanage continued to grow, housing twelve girls and thirteen boys. Two of the older boys worked part time at the printing works, while many of the children were being trained in needlework, some even making clothing for themselves. Finally yet importantly were the activities to assist the constant stream of European and American missionary recruits coming through Batavia to receive basic orientation before leaving for other parts of South East Asia.

With all the family, friends, employees, and visiting missionaries at the mission centre, Walter's welcome home left little opportunity to share close moments with Betty, until eventually, people drifted away and the children went to bed. Now they could relax and catch up on their six months of being apart. Both of them were hard-working individuals who had come to share the same vision of building the evangelical team for China and they supported each other in their chosen roles. Betty had to discuss a pending family problem. Their eldest daughter Sarah had fallen in love with the visiting American, Henry Lockwood, and she was distraught at the idea of leaving Batavia for England and being parted from her beloved Henry. Sarah was only sixteen years old, although she was mature beyond her years and had shown herself to be as driven and hard working as her parents. Both Betty and Walter liked Henry Lockwood and believed him to be a good man, but at twenty-nine, was he too old for their daughter, or was it just that she was too young? They believed it too harsh to insist that she accompany them to England but then again, they could not leave her alone for up to two years without a suitable chaperone. The only alternative seemed to be marriage, but first Walter would have to discuss the situation with Henry Lockwood to find out his intentions.

The next day, Walter caught up with Henry Lockwood and Henry made the discussion easier by coming right to the point, declaring his undying love for Sarah and requesting her hand in marriage. If Sarah had been just a few years older, Walter and Betty would have been doing their best to arrange a union such as this and, apart from her youth, Sarah and Henry Lockwood appeared to make the perfect couple. It seemed churlish to insist on making them part for as much as two years and so he consented to Henry's request and declared that a marriage must be arranged before the Medhursts departed for England.

The wedding was set for 17 February, only eight weeks after Sarah and Henry first met. The service was conducted by the Revd Francis Hanson, with Walter giving his daughter away. The mission chapel was packed with friends and well-wishers and the happy couple moved into the family home, preparing to take over some of the duties of running the mission while the Medhursts were away.

Now the family had to prepare to leave Batavia for England, expecting to be away for about eighteen months. Before he left, Walter wanted to get the printing of the newly revised translation of the New Testament started and he called on the assistance of his friend, the local Confucian scholar Choo Ti Lang, to help ensure that the final drafts were correct. He reported to London that there would be a run of two thousand copies, which would take about eight months at a cost of one rupee per copy. Choo Ti Lang came from Guangdong province in China and had assisted Walter several times in the translation of the Scriptures. He was a master calligraphist and had presented Henry and Sarah with a beautiful picture of an ancient Chinese proverb as a wedding gift. With a long sea voyage ahead of him and much work yet to do in further translations of the Scriptures, Walter asked Choo Ti Lang to go with him to London.

On 6 April 1836, Walter and Betty said farewell to Sarah and her husband and together with daughters Eliza and Martha, son Ebenezer and Choo Ti Lang, they set sail from Batavia to Rotterdam and then on to London. It had been almost twenty years since Walter had left England, during which time he had always lived and worked in a tropical climate and had survived cholera and at least one bout of malaria, so he was relieved to be going to a cooler climate. For Betty, this would be her first visit to England, the land of her father and many of her friends, a place that she had dreamed about all her life. Having always lived in the tropics, she did not know whether to look forward to the cooler weather or not. For the children, it was the beginning of a new adventure and for Choo Ti Lang, a journey into the unknown.

The journey home took them about four months. Walter continued to work on his writing and translations, with Choo Ti Lang's assistance, while Betty kept the children occupied with their school lessons. For most of the voyage, they enjoyed smooth sailing and cool sea breezes although they encountered occasional storms and the other extreme of the doldrums in the tropics. Finally, at the end of July, they came tantalisingly close to England when they sailed past the white cliffs of Dover, but then they sailed on across the North Sea to Rotterdam. The twenty-first-century-traveller complains if there is more than an hour's delay waiting for a travel connection, but for the Medhursts it would be another week before they finally arrived in London.

19

ENGLAND

The final leg of their journey took them across the North Sea and up the River Thames to London. After an overnight anchorage in the Margate Roads, a flood tide made for an early morning start and favourable winds meant they would reach London that day. After four months confined within four wooden walls, the prospect of being able to wander freely wherever they chose was a dream come true. Walter was returning to London after twenty years in the Far East, with the intention of winning support from the society for the next stage of his life's dream. Betty was coming for the first time to her father's home and for a reunion with her sons, George Braune and Walter junior. The ship finally came to an anchorage at the Isle of Dogs and the passengers were ferried to shore.

The Medhursts arrived in London on 5 August to be welcomed by the Revd Henry Burder, the minister of the St Thomas Square Congregational Chapel in Hackney. The society provided the family and Choo Ti Lang with a house close to St Thomas's Square, just round the corner from the Hackney Theological Seminary on Well Street, which Walter attended back in 1816. The society made it clear to Walter that he had earned a rest from his almost twenty years out in the field and he should spend some time showing his family around London and reuniting with his family. Difficult as this would be for Walter, he had many family members and friends to become reacquainted with, or in many cases for Betty to meet for the first time.

High on the list was Walter Henry junior, who was now thirteen. It being school holidays, young Walter had been staying with his Uncle Charles and Aunt Mary, waiting anxiously for his parents' ship to arrive. Both of Walter senior's sisters were living in London, Clara with her second husband Stephen Clinton and Mary with her husband Charles Baker. News arrived that George Braune, after graduating with a BA from Cambridge, had followed his stepfather's footsteps and been ordained in the Church of England. In October 1834, he had married Emma Halsted, the daughter of Admiral Sir Lawrence Halsted, and he was now the Curate at St John the Baptist in Frome, Somerset, just eight miles from where his grandfather George Martin came from. Not only that but they had a daughter named Emma, so Betty had become a grandmother.

If the society thought that Walter Medhurst would take time off and relax with his family, they were greatly mistaken. Within a month, he had organised to tour the country, preaching and lecturing about his experiences, calling for support for the LMS, and urging recruits to join the cause. An invitation to speak at the anniversary of the Bristol Auxiliary Missionary Society was the trigger for a tour of the West Country. Betty would join him, starting with a visit to their son George in Frome and his family. It had been seventeen years since George had been shipped off to England to school and apart from the twice-yearly exchange of letters, they had been isolated from one another.

Knowing the Medhursts had an interest in visiting Frome raised the attention of the newly appointed Foreign Secretary of the society, the Revd Arthur Tidman, who for ten years had been the pastor of the Zion Congregational Chapel in Frome.

Arthur Tidman was very pleased to arrange for Walter to speak at his former town, providing another reason for the Medhursts to visit the area. Even so, they only had a few days there and they made sure that every day counted. Since they were staying over a Sunday, Walter preached in his stepson's church and at the same time imparted his message about China. George had kept in touch with some of Betty's cousins from her father's side, whom she now met for the first time. For both Walter and Betty this was a wonderful reunion but it reinforced the fact that a missionary and his family must pay a high price to reach the aspirations of their vocation.

Another of Betty's relatives lived not far away in the town of Warminster, her stepbrother Francis Martin, who was born in Bellary, India, shortly before their father had died. Betty had only met him once when her stepmother lived for a short time in Madras and Betty was living at the Blacktown Mission. Betty's son George had become friends with Francis and a visit to Warminster was arranged, where the Martins lived at Eastleigh Lodge. Francis Martin had recently graduated from Wadham College at Oxford University and on 30 June, had married Julia Augusta Collier, the eldest daughter of Rear Admiral Sir Francis Collier, who served on Horatio Nelson's flagship at the Battle of the Nile. It appeared that for a young lad left as an orphan in India, Francis Martin had done well for himself. His success continued when he became sheriff and deputy lieutenant of the County of Dorset.

From Frome, the couple travelled to Trowbridge where Betty's father had come from, then through Bath to Bristol, where the twenty-fourth anniversary of the Bristol Auxiliary Missionary Society would be held all week from 17 October. The Bridge Street Chapel was where Walter had attended a meeting some twenty years earlier, inspiring him to become a missionary. Now he would preach at various chapels around Bristol, as well as speak at a public meeting at the Castle Green Chapel, which was filled to overflowing, even though it was the largest venue available. The public meeting was chaired by the Mayor of Bath and there were four missionaries making presentations, the Revd Dr Philip from South Africa, Revd Lord speaking about Upper Canada, Revd Williams from the South Seas, and Revd Medhurst speaking on China. Dr Philip spoke of the great success that the LMS was having in Southern Africa.

Walter observed that the population could not be less than three hundred million and it concerned him greatly to know that ten million people annually were passing into another world without knowing the truth about the one God. He noted that they had already heard of the glorious effects resulting from missionary labours in South Africa, but they would hear far different statements from him. 'The isolated condition of China was considered an insuperable bar to missionary efforts.'[1] He described how the Chinese regarded their country as situated at the centre of the earth, beyond which were barbarians, and that there was nothing that could be learned from those outside the empire. Their superiority, however, was not real. It was necessary to teach them about secular matters including science, medicine, political, and social affairs, as well as the message of the Gospel.

The anniversary celebrations were a success. Three of the chapel meetings and the public meeting were full, with standing room taken and latecomers turned away. The funds raised during the week amounted to £11,019, which was considerable for 1836, proving that the activities and adventures of missionaries were matters of great public interest in those days and the Evangelical movement transcended all denominations and barriers of social class.

After Bristol, it was time to head back to Gloucester for Walter to catch up with John Tucker and his other old friends and acquaintances and to introduce Betty to the people and places of his upbringing. He would also visit the grave of his brother William.

The independent chapel on Southgate was going stronger than ever, although the Revd William Bishop had passed away three years before. Walter's old friend John Tucker introduced him to the current minister, who had arranged for a special public meeting at which Walter would speak about the Ultra Ganges Mission and promote his call for recruits. Again, the public meeting was filled to overflowing and record funds were raised for the society.

Walter's presentation again referred to the desirability of including secular as well as religious matters in communicating with the Chinese, applying this tactic to all his audiences in England, incorporating general information about China that had little to do with missionary activities, thereby increasing the interest of his listeners and raising his image as an expert on China.

Before returning to London, Walter took Betty up to Ross-on-Wye to show her what he considered one of the most beautiful English towns and the place of his earliest memories. They visited St Mary's church and met with the Revd Thomas Underwood, who remembered the Medhurst family well, having been the rector since 1801. He had followed Walter's career as a missionary and he was so pleased to see them that he insisted they stay with him at the rectory and meet some of the town's dignitaries. A meeting was hurriedly organised for the next day so that Walter could make his presentation to whoever could attend the meeting and a message was sent by the morning stagecoach to London informing them of their delayed return. Walter and Betty took the opportunity to relax and enjoy a walk out on the Prospect to gaze on the views across the River Wye towards Bridstow and as far as the Welsh mountains. It was early November and a cool breeze was blowing down from the hills, giving Betty an indication of what winter might mean. They wandered through the churchyard, paused for a while at his sister Martha's grave and then visited the memorial to John Kyrle, the Man of Ross. It was a time of peaceful renewal after the hectic week in Bristol and Gloucester.

After spending two days in Ross, Walter and Betty boarded the London stagecoach, this time taking inside seats, to make the twenty-four-hour journey back to London. This mode of travel would soon disappear from England as railway lines were under construction throughout the nation and, within five years, the journey would be possible by steam train.

In London, it was time for Walter to brief his colleagues at the LMS on the situation in China and the satellite Chinese communities in the region. The society wanted to extend missionary activities into China at the earliest opportunity, but Walter's experience showed that it was not yet possible for a missionary to take up residence anywhere in China proper. In the meantime, Walter's heart was set on a project for a complete revision of the Chinese translation of the Scriptures. To his utter dismay, the directors did not approve this project and he would have to return to Batavia without achieving one of his major goals for the trip. His suggestion was premature, but at least he had planted the seed and the project would later be approved and come to fruition, resulting in what became known as 'The Delegates Version' of the Bible. The directors encouraged Walter to continue his travels around England, speaking at chapels and meeting rooms about the need to support the society's efforts in China, and suggested he write a book about the Ultra Ganges Mission so that a record of his experiences might be left after his return to Batavia. This was just the thing to help him rise above the disappointment of having his translation project refused and he quickly switched his exuberance to writing and publishing a book about China.

Walter met up with the Revd Richard Knill at the society's headquarters. They had previously met in Madras when they had shared an attraction for the young widow Eliza Braune. After Madras, Richard had been sent to St Petersburg where he served for thirteen years before returning to England in 1833. He had obviously overcome his disappointment of losing out to Walter for Eliza's hand, as he had married Sarah Notman, a native of St Petersburg, with whom he had five children.

In early December, the Medhursts received the very sad news that their eldest daughter Sarah Sophia, whom they had left in Batavia in a picture of happiness, having just married Henry Lockwood, had passed away. After five months of a new life as a married woman, she had come down with a fever from which she did not recover. This was heartbreaking for Walter and Betty and they once more leaned on their faith, understanding that this was God's will, confident they would meet again in heaven. By the time they returned to Batavia, a marble memorial had been placed on the church wall, which remains today.

Sacred to the memory of Sarah Sophia Lockwood. Born November 16, 1819. Died August 9, 1836. A young wife and a young Christian, but beginning early and labouring hard, she did much in little time; benefited her generation during her short pilgrimage and speedily ripened for glory, leaving her husband and parents to lament her loss.

Christmas 1836 was a new experience for the Medhursts. During Walter's absence from England, Christmas had become a much more popular religious festival as the country moved away from its Puritan heritage. Christmas trees were appearing, gifts were exchanged and carol singing became a popular pastime, introducing illiterate people to the message of Christmas. The most popular new book of 1836 was *The Posthumous Papers of the Pickwick Club*, by Charles Dickens, where Mr Pickwick advocates Christmas as the season of hospitality, merriment and open-heartedness. Since Betty and the children had never experienced an English Christmas, let alone seen any snow, they looked forward to 25 December with some excitement after the dreadful loss of Sarah. As if on cue and especially for their benefit,

England was hit by a north-east gale and a record-breaking snowstorm on 25 and 26 December, dumping three feet of snow and making roads impassable for several days.² The coal fires would have been stoked up in Hackney that Christmas. March, April and May of 1837 were recorded as the coldest on record, with snow showers recorded in London as late as 22 May.

The severe weather restricted Walter's movements and his speaking tour was held up until May, leaving him lots of time to dedicate to writing, one result of which was published in the February issue of the *Missionary Magazine*, where he made an appeal on behalf of the Ultra Ganges missions. In a four-page article, dated 8 January 1837, he provided an overview of the activities and achievements of Morrison, Milne and the other missionaries who had laboured in the East for almost thirty years.

The directors of the LMS had passed a resolution to send six additional agents to the Ultra Ganges, with a view to China, as soon as they could be found. Walter expressed his fervent wish and confident anticipation that not only would these men be found, but double the number would offer to join him when he returned to his station. He reassured potential applicants that the difficulties they would face were not insurmountable.

He compared the climate of China to England's, and he asserted regarding learning Chinese, that a missionary would be able to converse fluently within two years. The written language constituted a difficulty, but not such a mighty one. It was a question of becoming familiar with the basic two hundred and fourteen characters.

Walter wrote another article for the May issue of the *Missionary Magazine*. He appealed to medical and surgical practitioners to volunteer as missionaries. He wrote from his own experience about opening dispensaries for the relief of various common ailments, which had been well accepted by the people and received financial support from the East India Company. He

gave examples of the achievements made by individuals over
the years, starting with Dr A. Pearson who, in 1805, introduced
vaccinations into China. These were readily accepted and over
twelve months, several thousand people were vaccinated. It was
evident that the Chinese would place themselves willingly under
European treatment and the skill of English physicians had been
firmly established. Much of the prejudice against foreigners had
been overcome by the efforts of pious surgeons and in time, the
contributions of medical missionaries would help to eliminate that
prejudice. It was likely that the Chinese authorities would tolerate
the residence of medical practitioners in China sooner than that
of merchants or missionaries. Let those who have acquired the
necessary qualifications and whose souls burn with desire to
accomplish lasting good, come forward and join this great and
glorious purpose, Walter exhorted. He announced the support of
the directors of the LMS and promised his personal attention to
anyone who applied, hoping that on his return to China one or
more such devoted and qualified men might accompany him. His
wishes were to be fulfilled and his rationale for including medical
practitioners among future missions was justified, as would be seen
when he established the Shanghai Mission.

20

TOURS OF BRITAIN

The English winter of 1837 finally ended and the opportunity for comfortable travel with a reliable timetable became a reality. Before he left London, however, Walter attended the Annual Public Meeting of the LMS held on 11 May in the main auditorium of Exeter Hall in The Strand. This held over four thousand people and was used by religious and philanthropic groups so often that its name became synonymous with the Anti-Slavery Society. The LMS took over both auditoriums, the attendance surpassing all previous years.

The state of the society's operations was reported. The society now had four hundred and twenty-eight stations staffed by one hundred and fourteen missionaries and four hundred and eighty-two assistants who supervised eighty-four churches and operated schools with thirty-four thousand two hundred and twenty-two scholars. Receipts for the year, including legacies, amounted to £64,372 16s 5d and the expenditures totalled £63,160 9s 0d.

Among the speakers were Captain Fitzroy, Commander of Charles Darwin's ship, HMS *Beagle*; Charles Lushington Esq., MP for Ashburton; a Caffre chief from South Africa; Richard Knill for the society; missionaries from America, Africa, India; and, of course, Walter Medhurst speaking on China. Walter said:

I stand alone, single handed to plead the cause of nearly half the world; three hundred and sixty millions of people. I could shrink into my own insignificance and sit down in silence, did I not feel that if I held my peace, the very stones would cry out. When I consider that so great a population has been held together in one empire, under one form of despotic government, led astray by one false philosopher and are bowing down to one absurd superstition: and when I consider that this system has been going on for ages... and when I consider that the Christian Church is almost asleep with regard to that object, which should constitute the great design of every Missionary Society, I seem almost overwhelmed by the idea.[1]

The audience hung on his every word and for most, it was the first time they had heard from someone who had visited China. Walter spoke of the success of Morrison and Milne, as well as his own efforts, right up to his recent visit along the coast of China. He described how his feet had trodden on forbidden ground and how the celestial mandarins had confronted him, but said the people themselves were pleased to receive him and appeared friendly and favourable to the cause. Walter said that when he returned to China, he hoped to embark in a vessel funded by an association in New York, together with a noble band of physicians who would commit themselves to this worthy cause.

He asked not just for their monetary contributions, but also for zealous and devoted men to join him on his return. 'My soul is with the Chinese,' he said. 'Where they are, I will be; where they dwell, I will dwell. When I return I shall be accompanied by brethren in the ministry, but also by several devoted physicians, who will attend to the healing of bodies, as well as improving the minds of the inhabitants of China.'

On 25 May, with other foreign missionaries, Walter set off for Lancashire where their first meetings were held in support of the

Mid Lancashire Auxiliary Missionary Association, covering the towns of Preston, Blackburn and Burnley. His visits followed similar formats, speaking with groups of people at independent chapels in each town and preaching at Sunday services. Northern England was a very prosperous part of the country in those days, mostly arising from the growth of manufacturing and the development of new railways. Walter's visit was almost always carried out by stagecoach but everywhere he went the construction of cuttings, embankments, viaducts, and bridges displayed evidence of the upcoming railway age.

On Saturday 17 June, the group moved to Manchester to support the East Lancashire Auxiliary. Meetings had been arranged from Sunday through to Wednesday 21st. There was to be another family reunion for Walter in Manchester.

Over the years, Walter had supported his mother. Part of the reason was because of his parents' break-up shortly after he left England in 1819. His mother moved to London and his father to Manchester with another woman. Very little contact was maintained between Walter and his father but his sisters had kept him informed. William Medhurst had followed his son's career and was justifiably proud of his achievements. It was unthinkable that they should not meet while he was visiting Manchester. Walter not only met his father, but also his father's new wife Susannah and their sixteen-year-old son, Walter's stepbrother, William.

To conclude the missionary activities in Manchester, a public breakfast was held in the Rusholme schoolroom, where the organisers announced that their concerns about the society's ability to raise sufficient funds that year were unfounded and that a record collection had been raised. Following the breakfast meeting, as the delegation was about to depart for London, news came through that King William IV had died from a heart attack at Windsor Castle on the 20th. Since none of his ten children was legitimate, the throne would pass to his eighteen-year-old niece,

Princess Victoria of Kent, who became Queen Victoria. England passed into the Victorian age.

Walter returned to Hackney for most of July, writing his book, speaking at meetings in the London area and preaching at the Chapel in St Thomas's Square on Sundays. Towards the end of the month, he was on the road again to revisit his old colleagues in Gloucester and Bristol, seeking recruits to his cause. On 2 August, he spoke at a public meeting at the Eign Brook Chapel in Hereford. There, he received a message to return home to London as soon as possible, where his son Ebenezer had fallen ill with scarlet fever. The next day he took the early morning coach from Hereford and twenty-four hours later arrived in London only to find that his young son had passed away, just short of his fourth birthday. Having now lost five of her nine children, this was a particularly hard loss for Betty. She had assumed that in England her children might be safe from the dreadful diseases that she had become accustomed to in India and in the East Indies, but here she was again lamenting the loss of another infant. The little boy was laid to rest in St Thomas's Square cemetery and once more, the family fell back on their faith to help them through the tragedy.

Taking into consideration Betty's distress, Walter decided that it would be beneficial if the whole family spent some time away from London. Betty's son George had left an open invitation to join him at his wife Emma's family home in Devon and this seemed like the perfect opportunity to revive Betty's spirits and see some more of England. True to his nature, Walter arranged to combine business with pleasure and looked for a way to tour that part of the country, advocating his missionary ideals. Another deputation with the Revd M. Hodge, recently returned from the West Indies, was shortly to leave for Devon and Cornwall, which Walter arranged to join. A planned return to Yorkshire was cancelled, the newspaper reporting that Mr Medhurst was prevented from attending by a 'severe domestic affliction'[2].

Torquay had become a fashionable seaside resort in recent years and the Medhursts found a hotel on the seafront facing the harbour, a short walk from where the girls, now aged nine and six, could enjoy playing on the beach. After a few days of rest and relaxation with his family, Walter joined the Revd Hodge and set off on a tour of the meeting halls and chapels around Devon and Cornwall, starting at the New Independent Chapel in Falmouth.[3] Two weeks later, he returned to spend another week with Betty and the children before they took the stagecoach back to London, revived and refreshed.

During November, Walter attended several meetings with members of the Anti-Slavery Society, lending his support to the cause and sharing his experiences from the Far East, especially those involving John Slater. Although the Slavery Abolition Act was passed in 1833, it only covered the British Empire and even then, with some onerous conditions unacceptable to abolitionists. The founding members of the Anti-Slavery Society were William Wilberforce, who had passed away in 1833, and Thomas Clarkson, a former student of St Paul's whom Walter had heard speak many years before.

One of the conditions of the ban on slavery in the British Empire was a transitionary apprenticeship system to be used in the West Indies. Under this system, workers would have to work forty hours per week without pay before they would qualify for paid work. Although intended as a transitionary program that would slowly be phased out, the abolitionists wanted it to end immediately. A public meeting of the opponents to the apprenticeship system was held at Exeter Hall on 23 November. The hall, seating over four thousand people, was full. Twenty-three members of parliament and twenty ministers of religion, including the Revd Medhurst, were seated on the platform. Speaker after speaker addressed the meeting, outlining the horrors of slavery, and proposing actions to end it. The report in the next day's *Morning Post* showed how passionate both the speakers and the audience were.[4]

The Medhursts experienced another cold winter in 1837/38, with the lowest temperature for the nineteenth century recorded at Greenwich. By the end of January, the Thames was frozen over. They must have been pleased that this was the last cold winter they would experience before returning to Batavia. Walter was now working full time on his book, which he was determined to have printed and on sale before he returned to the East. It was a challenging and time-consuming task. Apart from writing the six-hundred-page book, it was to contain illustrations. George Baxter, the illustrator and engraver, assisted him. Many of his illustrations were completed from Walter's own drawings, because Baxter would not have seen any of the images depicted. Walter must have been quite an accomplished artist himself. The book, *China: Its State and Prospects, with special reference to The Spread of the Gospel,* was finally published in May 1838 and generated sufficient demand to be reprinted several times.

There was one more thing that Walter wanted to do before he returned to Batavia: visit Paris to evaluate a new composite Chinese type font designed and manufactured by M. Marcellin Legrand, an expert type founder in France. In June, he set off across the English Channel and was away for two weeks. Legrand had developed a new system of Chinese matrices, which could be combined to produce over twenty thousand characters. Sets of his new matrices had been ordered by the king's printing office in Paris and by the Presbyterian Missionary Society in America. Walter was very impressed by what he saw at M. Legrand's office, claiming it was as beautiful a display of the typographic art as he had ever witnessed. Walter and M. Legrand discussed the only shortcoming there seemed to be, which sometimes threw the characters slightly out of proportion, and together they worked out a solution. The copper matrices would be used to cast type fonts of the characters required and these matrices were fashioned from steel punches, which Legrand had made. His customers had the option of purchasing just the matrices or the punches and the matrices.

Walter recommended that the directors proceed with the types. Since the Presbyterians would be in possession of the matrices, perhaps they could ask the Americans to cast the types for them, replacing the current type cast by Samuel Dyer in Malacca. If the Americans would not supply, or if the price was too high, then the society could purchase their own set of matrices, leaving Dyer to produce a type of a smaller size to the Parisian fonts, the result giving them the ability to print a range of books in different font sizes. From Walter's report, it can be seen that he was very keen for the society to make the change to these type fonts but he was diplomatic in not wanting to get Samuel Dyer offside. This visit would go on to be a very important contribution to the future success of the mission presses in Hong Kong and Shanghai.

The coronation of Queen Victoria took place on 28 June 1838, an event that very few Londoners would want to miss, especially Betty, Eliza and Martha. Queen Victoria was the first monarch to live at Buckingham Palace and her coronation procession started at Hyde Park Corner and proceeded along Piccadilly, Pall Mall, Charing Cross and Whitehall to Westminster Abbey. The crowds would have been huge by the standards of the day but there were plenty of vantage points from which to view the procession. Choo Ti Lang went along with them so that he could give his countrymen from the Celestial Empire an eye-witness account.

Choo Ti Lang had so far not become involved in the meetings and activities of Walter, the reason for him being in London having been revoked by the directors. However, he had made himself busy at St Thomas's Chapel, learning English and conducting some Chinese lessons. Some of the ladies at the church had taken a particular interest in him, helping him with his English and explaining the sacred Scriptures. As he became acquainted with the language, he also developed an interest in Christianity, to the extent that he decided to ask Dr Burder if he would baptise him. His reasons were set out in a letter to Dr Burder who decided that the baptism should occur before he returned to Batavia with the Medhursts.[5]

In the meantime, Walter attended meetings as far north as Lincolnshire and decided to ask Choo Ti Lang to accompany him, which added another interesting perspective to his presentations. Choo Ti Lang would address the meeting in Chinese and Walter would translate for the listeners, but afterwards the public found that Choo's English was sufficiently fluent for a full and interesting conversation.

One of the last meetings that Walter was asked to attend was the AGM of the Coggeshall branch of the LMS in Essex in July 1838.[6] This was held close to the school at Chipping Ongar where the LMS trained its new missionaries. The students that year would undoubtedly have attended Walter's address. David Livingstone, a young Scottish medical student, was motivated by Walter's experiences and he volunteered to join the LMS with the objective of going to China. His plans were disrupted by the outbreak of the First Opium War and he was redirected to Africa, where his experiences were to make him one of the most famous missionaries of the nineteenth century.

21

RETURN TO BATAVIA

On Tuesday morning 31 July 1838, the Medhurst family sailed from Gravesend in the *George IV* under Captain Drayner, heading for Batavia and China. As well as their daughters, Eliza and Martha, they were taking with them their son Walter, now fifteen years old. It was Walter's intention that his son should learn Chinese during the three-month voyage. Also travelling with the Medhursts were Dr William Lockhart, who had been assigned as the first medical missionary that the LMS would send to China, Choo Ti Lang, who would be returning to his family in Canton, and Thomas and Elizabeth Fursey, who were going out as superintendents of the Parapattan Orphanage. The Furseys' first-born, George, was born on board. Two other passengers on the *George IV*, orphans Catherine and Isabella Parkes, aged fifteen and thirteen, were going out to join their cousin Mary, who was married to Charles Gutzlaff. Catherine helped to pass the long days teaching Eliza and Martha music and singing. Walter wrote that the family circle at their domestic altar was large and asked the directors to pray that they would be preserved from dangers, spiritual and temporal, and brought in safety to their haven.

The voyage started very slowly due to unfavourable winds and they did not lose sight of England until 12 August, but then the winds picked up and blew strong and steady so that in eighty-one days they came in sight of Java. The winds were not so heavy as to interfere with Walter's writing, for during the voyage he composed an English-to-Chinese dictionary of fifteen thousand words. His only regret was that the voyage was not long enough for him to complete the task before they arrived in Batavia. Writing the dictionary was additional to his other duties of preaching to the passengers and crew on Sunday, supervising the teaching of Chinese to Lockhart, and teaching Chinese and natural sciences to young Walter. He would have been a hard taskmaster but from his report back to the directors, he was very pleased with their efforts.

They arrived back in Batavia on 5 November to find that William Young was so sick that Walter sent him on the *George IV* to China, where the coming winter season might help to revive him. William Young's assistant, Lucas Monton, had also been sick, but he briefed Walter on the situation in Batavia. Their son-in-law, Henry Lockwood, had left Batavia the previous May to escape the oppressive heat and he was to return the next day on a ship from Singapore. It was a sad reunion with Henry and an opportunity to share the memories of their lamented daughter Sarah.

Walter Medhurst junior would be going on to China with William Lockhart, who was assigned to assist in the hospital in Canton, and both would concentrate on their language studies. The events in China, however, were about to take a dramatic turn, one that would lead to the expulsion of the English from Canton and Macao. This forced Lockhart to return to Batavia and Walter junior to take a position in government service.

In the absence of William Young, the Batavia Mission imposed a heavy workload on Walter and he was again prompted to write to the directors asking them to send additional support. He was fortunate that many other missionary organisations had followed his example and used Batavia as an entry point for future missionary activities to China. Although Lockwood's colleague

Hansen had returned to the United States, another American, William Boone, had settled in Batavia while the Medhursts were in England, and Mr Boone had been assisting with the English services in the chapel. Henry Lockwood's health was deteriorating and he finally left Batavia for America in April 1839.

The Chinese day schools had fallen into neglect during Walter's absence, when key staff members had drifted away. He decided to close the day schools and established in their place a Chinese boarding school with funds solicited from friends in England. Within eight months of his return to Batavia, he wrote that the school had twenty-three pupils who could already read and spell in English and were translating passages from the New Testament from Chinese into Malay. The cost of maintaining each pupil was only £4 per year. Furthermore, Mrs Medhurst had a school for twelve Chinese girls, which she taught herself, giving lessons in Chinese and Malay and in the art of embroidery.

One of the reasons Walter Medhurst ran such a successful mission station was because he drew assistance from a range of sources. He received support from local European residents and colonial governments by calling for subscriptions to build his chapel and the orphanage. During his visit to England, he recruited the assistance of numerous friends and acquaintances to donate to his cause. In addition, he took advantage of the many Evangelical organisations operating in England and in America and he was constantly writing letters requesting support in one way or another. The Religious Tract Society, the British and Foreign Bible Society and the Prayer Book and Homily Society were but three of the organisations that made grants of cash and kind to the Batavia Mission. Other organisations sent their own missionaries, with whom Walter worked closely, as he did with Lockwood, Hansen and Boone of the American Episcopal Missions. By the time the Medhursts had returned to Batavia, an English group, the Eastern Female Education Society, had set up two girls' schools staffed by three single ladies with whom the Medhursts built a close working relationship.

The mission chapel was enlarged during 1839 and opened on 21 September in the presence of clergymen from the Dutch Established Church. The press was printing in Chinese, Malay, Japanese, Javanese, and English and during 1839 produced over twenty-six thousand books and various tracts. The Parapattan Orphan Asylum was now looking after fifty-two children under the care of Mr and Mrs Fursey, supported by funds raised from the congregation of the mission chapel.

Betty Medhurst gave birth to her tenth child on 1 August 1840, a daughter who was named Augusta Liberta. Eliza at twelve and Martha aged nine were excited to welcome their new sister and were willing assistants in caring for the new baby.

22

THE FIRST OPIUM WAR

The First Opium War was a watershed event that marked a new stage in China's relations with the West and would lead to the opportunity for foreigners to expand their activities beyond the limitations of their allocated warehouse space in Canton. Under the Qing Dynasty's regulations, Western traders were restricted to conducting trade only in Canton and only through the guild of Chinese merchants, the Cohong. Traders were only allowed access for a few months of the year and were not allowed to bring their families with them. Missionaries were forced to make arrangements with the traders in order to gain a foothold. The British Government was less open to such arrangements than were the Americans. Dr Morrison had set a precedent by acting as a translator initially for the East India Company and subsequently for the British Government. Charles Gutzlaff and other missionaries followed that lead and became a resource for the traders and the government, a situation complicated by the absence of diplomatic channels between the British Government and the Qing court.

During the 1830s the opium trade more than doubled, the major source being British opium grown in Bengal and shipped in East India Company ships. In 1839, this amounted to about two thousand five hundred tons. The opium trade was so large and profitable that both Chinese and foreigners wanted to participate in it. The Qing Dynasty regarded opium as an illegal commodity that brought no customs revenue, but local officials demanded bribes to allow the trade to continue. In the 1830s, it was estimated that around 30 per cent of government officials regularly consumed opium, and even the Daoguang emperor himself was an addict. The Qing court debated whether it should be legalised and thereby taxed and controlled, or the prohibition enforced and the major source of supply through Canton destroyed. The British side was similarly plagued by the dichotomy between their dependence on the trade and the evils that resulted from it. Even the Chief Superintendent of British Trade, Charles Elliott, was against the trade and in 1839, he wrote to Lord Palmerston, the Foreign Secretary, that the opium trade was a disgrace and a sin. Missionaries like Charles Gutzlaff opposed the trade but allied themselves with the opium traders for transportation and communication.

Ultimately, the Daoguang emperor decided to support the hardliners who called for complete prohibition, and sent the influential official Lin Zexu to Canton as the Imperial Commissioner to clamp down on the trade by whatever means possible. He arrived in Canton in March 1839, shortly after Walter Medhurst junior and William Lockhart arrived there from Batavia. Walter had been given an introduction to Dr Morrison's son John Morrison and was given a job as a clerk in Charles Elliott's office, from where he continued his studies in Chinese. William Lockhart did not stay long in Canton as he was appointed to the Medical Missionary Society to take charge of their hospital in Macao, leaving Dr Parker to run the medical practice in Canton.

In Canton, Commissioner Lin ordered the merchants to hand over all stocks of opium and demanded that the traders sign an agreement not to import opium, a breach of which would be punishable by death. He closed the channel leading into Canton, effectively holding the merchants and the government officials hostage. Charles Elliott got the merchants to hand over the opium with the promise of eventual compensation from the British Government. The promise was never kept, however, because of the political backlash it would have caused in Britain. The subsequent British offensive was in part due to having to do something to substitute this broken promise. Over twenty thousand chests, about half a year's supply of opium, were handed over and destroyed in June 1839. Commissioner Lin wrote to Queen Victoria in an attempt to stop the trade, describing the harm it caused to the Chinese population. Whether free trade advocates intercepted the letter or whether it just got lost is not known but the letter never reached Queen Victoria. It was published, however, in the *Chinese Repository*, the Protestant periodical published by the American missionary Elijah Bridgman.[1]

Not all merchants supported the opium trade and the next event leading up to the war happened when Captain Warner of a British ship, the *Thomas Coutts*, decided that he would continue to sail up to Canton and unload his cargo. The Quakers, who were opposed to the opium trade, owned this ship and Warner was prepared to sign the agreement offered by the Chinese. To prevent other ships from following Warner's example, Charles Elliott ordered a blockade of the Pearl River. When a second ship, the *Royal Saxon*, attempted to sail to Canton, the Royal Navy frigates HMS *Volage* and HMS *Hyacinth* fired warning shots across the bow. The Chinese force of sixteen war junks and thirteen 'fire-boats' answered by firing on the RN ships and the battle was on. Several of the junks were sunk or severely damaged and on the British side, one sailor was wounded. Commissioner Lin reported to the Qing court that a great victory had been won but the reality was that the genie was now out of the bottle. Charles Elliott requested reinforcements from the British authorities in India, and a British fleet of forty-eight ships and four thousand fighting men was assembled for despatch to China. It was not until 31 January 1840 that the British India authorities would issue a formal declaration of war against China, and June 1840 before the fleet would arrive.

After this initial altercation, Commissioner Lin ordered the removal of all British citizens from Chinese territory, including those living in Portuguese-administered Macao. The Macao authorities complied with the request and the British departed, many of them leaving on ships that remained in Hong Kong anchorages. Others departed for Manila and Singapore, while William Lockhart and William Young returned to Batavia in September 1839. This presented the opportunity for the missionaries to discuss what outcome the war might bring and whether this could ultimately mean the opening up of China. The directors had become tired of Walter's repeated message of 'send more missionaries for China' and for now, Lockhart had taken up the call and it was his letters that were printed in the *Missionary Magazine*. By the middle of 1840, it appeared safe for Lockhart to return to Macao, and he reopened the hospital in August. Among others who decided to return to Batavia were two new missionaries sent out by the LMS, the Revd W. C. Milne, son of the late Dr Milne, whom Walter and Betty had cared for as a young child, and a medical missionary by the name of Hobson.

Meanwhile, young Walter's position as a clerk in the British trade office had him front and centre in all the preparations for war. After the fleet's arrival under the command of Admiral Sir George Elliott (Charles Elliott's cousin), the British issued a demand including compensation for the seized opium, abolition of the restrictive Canton trade system and the right to occupy one or more islands up the coast. Rather than attack Canton, where Commissioner Lin had assembled his forces, the British imposed a blockade of the Pearl River and decided to move north, in an attempted diplomatic approach by Charles Elliott. The hope was that they could meet with more open-minded Chinese officials who might be persuaded to take their ultimatums to the emperor in Peking. As the fleet prepared to move, additional warships joined them, including the first steam- and sail-powered iron warship, the *Nemesis*, on which Walter Medhurst junior would sail. Later reinforcements brought additional iron steamers and increased the number of forces to around twelve thousand.

By the beginning of July 1840, the British had arrived off the coast of Chusan (Zhoushan) and the admiral, with Charles Gutzlaff as interpreter, held discussions on his flagship, HMS *Wellesley*, with local Chinese officials, trying to persuade them to surrender peacefully. He was unsuccessful and the following day the British bombarded and then occupied the city. An occupying force was left in Chusan and the fleet moved on to blockade Ningpo (Ningbo) and moved north to Tientsin (Tianjin) and the strategic waterway leading to Peking. The two Elliotts, with interpreter Charles Gutzlaff, meanwhile succeeded in meeting with officials in Tientsin and in conveying the British demands to the emperor. Back in southern China, the British had moved to destroy the Chinese military force that threatened Macao and thereby secured access to Macao and the island of Hong Kong.

The emperor responded by stripping Commissioner Lin of his powers and replacing him with a mandarin by the name of Qishan. Qishan persuaded the British to return to Canton where they could engage in negotiations when talks started in December. The British Government had refined its instructions to Charles Elliott and would now demand the opening of the five ports of Canton, Amoy, Foochow (Fuzhou), Ningbo, and Shanghai and the surrender of an island such as Hong Kong, as well as compensation for the surrendered opium and the costs of the war. By January, the British became aware that Qishan was not prepared to make any substantial concessions and the negotiations were called off.

On 7 January, the British attacked the two forts guarding the Bocca Tigris strait, which led to Canton, in a battle that lasted an hour and resulted in an estimated five hundred Chinese killed and British wounded of thirty-eight. The *Nemesis* featured in this battle, the first time it saw action. Being flat bottomed with a shallow draft, it proved to have a real advantage in the shallow waters of the Pearl River. It was an ill-matched battle, with the *Nemesis* and its sister ships easily destroying the Chinese junks.[2]

On 20 January, Qishan acknowledged the threat of such a superior force and indicated that he would cede Hong Kong, pay an indemnity of six million dollars, enter into official diplomatic relations, and re-open Canton to trade. This so-called Convention of Chuanbi was submitted to the emperor for his approval. The emperor flew into a rage, imprisoning Qishan and sentencing him to death. As it happened, Charles Elliott was also castigated by the British Government for settling for the lowest possible terms and removed from his appointment. Given the slowness of communications, Elliott was not to find out about this until late July with the arrival of his replacement, Sir Henry Pottinger.

Before news of his dismissal arrived, Elliott had assumed that the emperor would not accept the terms and initiated a series of attacks further up the river, allowing British warships to move close enough to besiege Canton itself. The Chinese losses again were heavy, including an admiral, whom one of the British warships honoured with a cannon salute when his family took his body away. The result was that by the beginning of May, the British were able to bring up a large enough force to take the forts guarding the city and begin bombarding Canton. Local officials and the merchants of the Cohong responded quickly by offering Elliott a 'ransom' of six million dollars to desist and a truce was agreed to on 27 May.

Under the truce, the British and Chinese troops started to pull back from the front lines, but a local militia, furious at the destruction caused by the foreigners, gathered to continue the fight. On 30 May, they encountered a detachment of Indian sepoys, led by English officers, caught in a torrential downpour near the village of Sanyuanli. The sepoys were mired in the mud and the rain caused their flintlocks to misfire, which resulted in a minor defeat for the British troops. To Elliott and the British officers on the scene, the encounter at Sanyuanli was insignificant, but the Chinese rumours soon reported the British dead at about ninety, with many others wounded. In present-day China, Sanyuanli stands out as the major victory of the war and the first spontaneous struggle by the Chinese people against the foreign aggression.[3]

Pottinger replaced Elliott in August 1841 and his orders were to withdraw from the siege of Canton and take the war further north, towards the Qing court itself. In late August, fourteen warships, including four steamers, successfully took Amoy (Xiamen), Chusan and Ningbo. Amoy was taken without much opposition but the battles at Chusan and Ningbo were particularly gruesome for the Chinese, with several mandarins choosing to commit suicide rather than face the humiliation of defeat and the wrath of the emperor. In some cases, the battle turned into a massacre when British officers were unable to stop the butchery by their own troops. At the completion of the battles, the British fleet wintered over at Chusan, where Walter Medhurst junior was left as the official interpreter, which showed that he must have inherited his father's linguistic skills given he was only eighteen.

The war continued in March when the Chinese unsuccessfully attempted to retake Ningbo, before the British moved up to the Yangtze River and attacked Wusong and Shanghai on 16 June. As usual, plunder and pillage followed in their wake, firstly by the foreign troops and then by mobs of Chinese looters taking advantage of the breakdown in law and order. These events sowed the seeds of civil disorder that would rock China for decades to come. After Shanghai, the British turned their attention to Nanking (Nanjing), the former Ming Dynasty capital. The gateway to Nanjing was the walled city of Chinkiang (Zhenjiang), which the British attacked on 21 July in what turned out to be the last major battle of the war, during which most of the city was destroyed and left to the mobs to plunder. This battle left Nanjing open for similar treatment and the Qing court finally realised that the foreigners were in a position to take the whole country unless they agreed to a treaty.

Under the Treaty of Nanking, signed on 29 August 1842, China agreed to open the five ports requested (Canton, Amoy, Foochow, Ningbo, and Shanghai), pay an indemnity of twenty million silver dollars, abolish the Cohong monopoly that hitherto had controlled trade in and through Canton, and adhere to a fixed schedule of customs duties. Additionally, the British were granted the right to occupy Hong Kong in perpetuity; this was their sole outright territorial acquisition.

Walter Medhurst junior had served as a clerk in the Chinese secretary's office throughout the war and had been awarded a campaign medal for his services as an interpreter. After the signing of the Treaty of Nanking, he was appointed to the staff of Captain George Balfour, the British Consul at Shanghai, to act as his interpreter.

23

LEAVING BATAVIA

Back in Batavia, Walter and Betty followed the progress of the war in China as closely as possible. Ships called into Batavia every few days and brought news of what was happening, sometimes bearing letters from young Walter, Lockhart, Gutzlaff, and others, and copies of articles from the *Chinese Repository*, the newspaper published in Canton. After returning to Macao, William Lockhart had moved north with the campaign and opened a hospital for the benefit of the natives in Tinghae, the capital of Chusan, but by the end of 1841 he had returned to Macao. The Medhursts received news that he had married Catherine Parkes, one of the young ladies who accompanied them all from England on the *George IV*.

All this time, Walter planned his next move once the war was over, as it seemed certain that China would be opening up to foreigners. Following the predictable pattern of his relationship with the directors, he lobbied them for support to move his mission operations into China, waiting for a commitment that at most would provide an indefinite guide and often would arrive too late to be of great assistance. It was a time of great frustration, as he knew he was missing opportunities that others were taking. He knew that the greatest single goal of nineteenth-century Christian missions was about to unfold, that of taking the Gospel to the largest population in the world, and he wanted to ensure he did not miss that moment.

Walter decided that he should take steps to close down the Batavia Mission and move his family first to Hong Kong and then to one of the five ports listed in the Treaty of Nanking. Arrangements were made to sell the land, the buildings and the chapel to an entity set up by a group of local Batavian businessmen, the British Protestant Community of Batavia (BPC). The BPC elected a committee of five trustees, borrowed the equivalent of £600 sterling from the Dutch Trading Company, and took on the responsibility of recruiting a chaplain. The Parapattan Orphanage was already structured independently from the Batavia Mission, so that could be left to continue as it was. Both of these organisations could now be left to continue under the guidance of others, and continue they did. In 2015, over a hundred and seventy years later, both are thriving institutions.

By early 1843, the Medhurst family was ready to leave Batavia. As had happened with many of Walter's previous decisions, his move to China seemed to end up in accordance with the views of the directors in London. The directors called on all the missionaries in the Ultra Ganges missions to meet in Hong Kong in August to discuss and formulate the society's plans for China, the conference to be chaired by Samuel Dyer. Samuel Dyer had recently returned from London where he had discussed with the directors the manufacture of a smaller version of the Chinese type as proposed by Walter after visiting M. Legrand in Paris. The intention of the directors was to relocate the type foundry and the Anglo-Chinese School to Hong Kong.

In June 1843, the Medhursts left Batavia for the last time, stopping en route at Singapore where Betty could visit her sister Sophia and the Medhurst daughters could meet their aunt. William Young travelled as far as Singapore, where he was to join the mission there. It had been twenty-one years of hard work in Batavia and they were leaving behind a lot of friends and happy memories, but they were probably not sorry to be heading for a cooler climate. What Walter Medhurst had actually achieved during his time in Batavia was debatable. Based on making converts to Christianity, the mission was a total failure, but its achievements in other areas were considerable. The mission press had produced almost two hundred and fifty thousand copies of various publications in multiple languages, many of which were written by Medhurst himself. They trained many of the missionaries who went on to achieve success in other places. They provided a basic education to thousands of children, and they helped to prepare the society for its original goal of taking the mission to China. The legacy of the mission can still be seen today in All Saints church in Jakarta and the Parapattan Orphanage.

Although the future was dependent on various factors, including the outcome of the forthcoming conference, the Medhursts were already considering Shanghai as their next home. Their son Walter was established there as a key member of the consular staff, it was a place Walter had already visited, and it was a city he considered most likely to benefit from the new trade regime.

From Singapore, the Medhursts travelled to Hong Kong with Samuel Dyer and the brothers John and Alexander Stronach, who were gathering in Hong Kong for the conference of the LMS. They would join William Milne, son of the builder of the Anglo-Chinese College, John Morrison, son of the founder, and James Legge, the most recent manager of the college. The society had closed down the missions in Penang and Malacca and were most concerned that the Anglo-Chinese College should be relocated to Hong Kong with the hope that the new government there would grant them land for a new college building. To this request, the Governor, Sir Henry Pottinger, responded that land had already been granted the previous year to the Morrison Education Society, with the understanding that this society was to supersede the Anglo-Chinese

College. The governor also remarked that his invitation during the recent war with China to applicants from Penang, Malacca and Singapore for the posts of Chinese interpreter had evoked not a single response. So much, the governor concluded, for the results of subsidising the education of overseas Chinese in those centres.

So, the gulf that existed between Morrison and the society back in 1818 – about the purpose and direction of the Anglo-Chinese College – still seemed to exist, and the legacy of the founder continued through his son and the Morrison Education Society. The missionaries of 1843 were content to see the college become little more than a training school for Gospel preachers, just as the missionaries in Malacca had in 1818. A year later, the directors of the LMS reported that in accordance with the recommendations of the Hong Kong conference in August 1843, they had resolved to convert the Anglo-Chinese College into a theological seminary. This was contrary to what Morrison and Milne wanted but the LMS always got what it wanted in the end. Of more interest to Walter Medhurst were the discussions regarding a new translation for the Bible. It was decided that the work of translation would be shared, with committees formed at five stations to manage the work. Each committee would assign a person to join a central committee of delegates to determine the final version of the work. This translation became known as 'The Delegates Version'. Samuel Dyer, the chairman of that first meeting, would not see the progress of his efforts. After leaving Hong Kong, he came down with a fever and was forced to stay in Macao, where he died two months later.

Before the conference even began, Walter had spoken with his colleagues about his intention to proceed to Shanghai at his earliest convenience and take William Lockhart with him. Knowing how independently minded and determined a man Walter Medhurst could be, none of his colleagues challenged him for the position, accepting his obvious knowledge and familiarity with the place and his contacts via his son with the British Consul. With that, the conference broke up with everyone agreeing that Walter Medhurst would head the Shanghai Mission.

Accommodation was scarce in Hong Kong at that time, with insufficient housing available for the influx of Europeans from Macao. The Medhursts were staying with an American, the Revd Samuel Brown, and his wife. Brown was the headmaster of the Morrison Education Society's school, which had recently moved from Macao. Walter had intended to move up to Shanghai as soon as possible but unfortunately his daughters Eliza and Martha fell ill so he delayed his departure and then accepted the Browns' invitation for the family to stay so that he could go on ahead.

Walter set off in the *Argent* on 4 October with William Milne, who was heading back to Ningbo, but after four days at sea, they were hit by a north-east gale, which the following day developed into a full typhoon. At the height of the storm, the captain was accidentally knocked overboard and drowned. Soon after, and perhaps from carrying too much sail, the foretopmast and main topgallants came crashing down, leaving only one rag of a sail. With this being supported by the main rigging, they were able to keep the vessel close to the wind and avoid broaching, allowing the sea to make a clean break over the ship. The sea was mountainous, the wind sounding like a continuous scream, and everyone on board thought that the ship was lost. The storm lasted thirty-six hours, during which the vessel leaked so much that it had two feet of water in the hold.[1] Forced by the storm in a southerly direction, the vessel eventually limped into Manila on 20 October, some three hundred miles south-east of Hong Kong.

A local merchant, Mr Diggles, kindly offered Medhurst and Milne his hospitality while they planned their next move. The *Argent* would not be ready to sail for several weeks. They decided to return to Macao and there take a steamship north, no longer trusting to sail. By chance, a Dutch man-of-war was leaving Manila on 28 October and Walter persuaded the captain to give him passage as far as Macao. There was only room for one passenger, however, so William Milne had to wait for another opportunity to get home. No sooner had the Dutch ship left the bay than they encountered another typhoon. This time the stronger and better-manned ship was able to cope and despite rough seas, they reached Macao after nine days and thence Walter made his way back to Hong Kong.

What a surprise it was for Betty and the family when Walter walked in through the door, and hearing of his ordeal, they were so relieved to have him safely home. Walter was also pleased to see that his wife and daughters were now in full health and happiness. 'But I have a surprise for you,' said Betty, waving a newspaper in her hand. 'Two days ago, our host, the Revd Brown, gave me this copy of the *New York Daily Tribune* dated July 1, 1843[2] and I quote from the front page. *At the Commencement of the University of the City of New York[3], held on Thursday June 29th, 1843, the degree of D.D. was conferred on Revd William H. Medhurst of Batavia, East Indies.* Welcome home Doctor Medhurst! The reporter seems to have written your name down wrong but hopefully when your citation arrives, it will be recorded as Dr Walter.' This was recognition for the huge body of work Walter had written and translated over the years, which had achieved wide circulation particularly via the American missionaries, and it placed Walter in the rank of his mentors Dr Morrison and Dr Milne.

Meanwhile, Walter Medhurst junior sailed as interpreter to the new British Consul to Shanghai, Captain, later General, Sir George Balfour, arriving in Shanghai on 8 November 1843. The first point of business was to find a residence for the consul and after some difficulty in finding a suitable house, a large dwelling of fifty-two rooms was secured in the walled city for $400 per annum. All other foreigners would be restricted to the area agreed on for the foreign settlement and the British Consulate would move there when a suitable building could be constructed. The settlement area was bounded by the river road (known today as the Bund), the Wusong River (foreigners knew this as Soo-Chow Creek), the Yangjingpang Creek (approximately where Yanan Road is today) and stretching back almost to where the Shanghai People's Square stands today. George Balfour took a large parcel of land at the confluence of the Wusong and Huangpu rivers, where the British Consulate would later relocate (now known as 33 Waitanyuan). Within the settlement, the Chinese were obliged to move out and foreigners would buy their land under an arrangement considered a perpetual rental from the emperor. Along the riverfront, the land was divided up and sold to the foreign merchants, including some of the trading companies that had been previously established in Canton and Hong Kong. Shanghai was officially declared open for trade on 14 November 1843.

The streets of Shanghai were narrow and winding, often along the banks of canals that may originally have followed a natural watercourse. Narrow as the streets were, they served for wayfaring, the conducting of retail business, drainage, sewerage, and as receptacles for rubbish. Most Chinese lived in houses that Europeans would consider hovels. They were low, dark and damp, so constricted as to be very hot and unhealthy in summer, yet without heat and comfort in winter. They had unglazed windows, no ceilings and often mud floors, so any Europeans coming to live in the city would have to build their own houses. Their senses, too, would be bombarded by the stench of sour rice, rotting vegetables and excrement, not to mention the sounds of dogs howling, children crying and the clashing of cymbals to drive off evil spirits. It was going to be quite a challenge for Walter Medhurst to establish the LMS here in Shanghai.

In November 1843, Walter set off from Hong Kong again and reached Chusan, where William Lockhart had set up a mission with William Milne and was living with Charles Gutzlaff, who had been appointed as a magistrate. Lockhart had decided he would be better employed on the mainland and agreed to accompany Walter to Shanghai. At Chusan, Walter was given the news that his library, having been shipped separately from Batavia, was wrecked. A severe flood had destroyed the building that the books were stored in and most of them were ruined. What remained of the library, along with the medical instruments and supplies of Dr Lockhart, were loaded aboard a small steamer and they set off on a grey, overcast morning for Shanghai. They crossed Hangzhou Bay and entered the Yangtze River, heading up towards Wusong, the Huang-pu River and Shanghai. Eight years had passed since Walter had last made this journey and this time he was coming back to stay.

They landed on 20 December 1843, very close to the Tianhou temple, where Walter had landed in 1835, but this time, a familiar face was waiting on the dockside to greet him. His son Walter was waiting with a carriage and servants to help unload the missionaries' possessions and take them to the consulate, where they could stay until they found a house to rent. This was the first time Walter had seen his son in five years, during which time young Walter had seen action in Amoy (Xiamen) and Chusan. He had been attached to the Chusan garrison as interpreter for fifteen months, for which he had been decorated with the Opium War medal. Now, as the consular interpreter for Shanghai, he was in a good position to assist his father and Dr Lockhart in setting up the Shanghai Mission.

Within a few days, they had bargained for a house to accommodate two families at a modest rent. Walter was surprised that the Chinese authorities seemed to take no notice of them and no objection was raised to their living just outside the walled city. Although this was not his first visit to Shanghai, he looked at the city in a different way. Everything was new and strange but he observed that they would have no difficulty living here. For the first time he realised that there were thousands of Catholics in the city who were free to worship. He also noted many Fukien people, which meant that he would be able to converse with them in their own language. He had only been in Shanghai for a few days but he had already warmed to the prospect before him. This would be his greatest challenge and one that he could undertake with confidence.

Always looking over his shoulder at what the society might decide elsewhere, he recorded an official minute for the directors:

At a meeting of the local Committee of the Chinese Mission for Shanghai, Ningbo and Chusan, held at Shanghai on the 26th of December 1843, present W.H. Medhurst and W. Lockhart, it was resolved:

1. That having inspected all the stations included in the northern section of the Chinese Missions, we fix ourselves at Shanghai, as most eligible in respect to overflowing population of the city, as well as for the numerous Fukien strangers resident here.
2. That Mr Lockhart return immediately to Chusan to bring up his family and that Mr Medhurst remain at Shanghai during the winter, and then make arrangements for bringing up his family also.
3. That a house fit for the accommodation of 2 families be rented on behalf of the Society.[4]

Possession is said to be nine-tenths of the law and on that basis, Walter had taken possession of Shanghai, making it very difficult to remove him from his new mission centre.

24

SHANGHAI

The new home of the Shanghai Mission was located outside the walled city, in what today is the business centre of Shanghai. The main portions of the land were raised and under cultivation; other portions were lower and marshy. There were numerous creeks, ditches and ponds, and the lower grounds in summer were covered with reeds. Innumerable grave mounds dotted the land and the purchasers were obliged to agree that the former owners could visit them at stated periods and perform the customary religious rites. The Bund was a towing path with a wide foreshore, covered or uncovered according to the tide.

For a considerable period, the foreign residents had to be content to live in native houses outside the city walls and the conditions of life were not pleasant. One of the first neighbours of the missionaries was a Robert Fortune, on commission from the Royal Horticultural Society to find new plant species, who recalls what it was like. 'Rain and snow would blow in through the windows of our fireless lodging and we would often wake to find ourselves drenched. Whenever we left the house, hundreds of people crowded the streets and followed in our wake. People gazed as if we had been inhabitants of the moon.'

Robert Fortune held similar ideas to Walter about building the relationship between the British and the Chinese, and he believed that they should earn respect from the Chinese not by force, but from the civilisation and achievements of the British. 'Nothing, I believe, can give the Chinese a higher idea of our civilisation and attainments,' he wrote, 'than our love for flowers.'[1] Perhaps more in Walter's mind regarding civilisation and attainments were the numbers of patients presenting themselves to the Chinese Hospital, the horse-drawn carriages, the regular monthly steamer service from Hong Kong, and the development of roads and buildings taking place in the settlement. Either way, they both agreed on the evils of the opium trade and regretted the tragedy of the Opium War.

For the first month Walter was on his own, William Lockhart having returned to Chusan to close his operation there and return with his wife and sister-in-law. This was a busy time for Walter. He needed to have his printing presses and what was left of his library unloaded and moved into the house, and to make the house more habitable for the Lockharts and his own family. Having the consul's staff available to assist in finding tradesmen and suppliers of furniture was helpful but they had only been in Shanghai for six weeks ahead of him, so it was very much a case of using his own initiative, which he was good at. He was not the only foreigner in town, the first trading ships having arrived within two days of the port being declared open. Chinese entrepreneurs saw this as a great opportunity for them too. There would be no shortage of offers of help at a price.

At the end of January, William Lockhart returned to Shanghai with his wife Catherine (Kate) and her sister Isabella. They would have been among the very first foreign families to arrive in Shanghai, presenting another spectacle for the locals. Medhurst and Lockhart would now build a formidable team for the next twelve years, founded on shared enthusiasm, as expressed in Lockhart's words: 'A wide field is now open before us in China, the door hath burst asunder that formerly obstructed us.'[2]

The division of labour between the two missionaries was straightforward, with William Lockhart establishing the hospital and Walter running the mission and the printing works, initially operating out of the house they shared. Very soon, the hospital was attracting more patients than William Lockhart could cope with and there was a need also to accommodate in-patients, with patients coming from as far away as Nanjing. At the end of May, the Lockharts moved out to another house that included several outbuildings that could be used as a hospital for in-patients.

In June 1844, Betty arrived from Hong Kong with Eliza, Martha and Augusta and the Shanghai Mission started to feel a lot more like home. Eliza was in a sullen mood, having left her new love in Hong Kong. She had met and fallen in love with Charles Hillier, the assistant magistrate in Hong Kong, and although Betty had married at the age of fourteen, she had decided that her daughter should wait until she was at least sixteen before getting married. Eliza accepted her mother's decision but made it clear that there was no one else for her but Charles. The Medhursts and the Lockharts formed a close friendship and were frequently at each other's houses and Walter junior visited whenever he could get time off from the consulate. Walter junior was taking quite an interest in Isabella and in August 1844, the young couple declared their engagement. William Lockhart was not convinced, however, and persuaded them to wait until the following spring. Eventually the engagement was broken off and within two years, Isabella married another missionary.

By the end of 1844, William Lockhart was treating up to three hundred patients a day with every imaginable complaint. As was the case in the American hospital in Canton, they found that conditions of the eye were very common, with William frequently operating for cataracts. Chinese medical knowledge and skills were extremely primitive so it was hardly surprising that people flocked to the hospital. Once or twice a week Walter held services at the hospital for around a hundred and fifty people, handing out books and tracts. On Sundays, there was a service for the foreign community and Walter held daily services for his servants and friends. He was encouraged by the Chinese in Shanghai taking to his services with far more enthusiasm than had been shown by the Chinese in Batavia. Most weeks, Walter and William would spend a day touring the country around Shanghai, preaching in the villages and handing out literature. Most of the travel was on foot but sometimes by boat along the many canals that crisscrossed the land. Wherever they went, people would stop and stare because this was the first time in their lives that they had seen anyone who was not Chinese.

The Shanghai Mission Press also made rapid progress during 1844 and the Chinese Repository reported that it had produced a nearly three-hundred-page book of *Chinese Dialogues, Questions and Familiar Sentences*, written by Dr Medhurst with a view to promote commercial intercourse and to assist beginners in the language. This would be a popular little book with all the new residents and visitors moving into Shanghai.

On 31 March 1845, Walter wrote to London campaigning for better living accommodation and for the funds to build a new chapel and printing office. He stated that their dwellings were far from convenient for their operations, neither were they conducive to their health and comfort. In pressing his point, he reminded the directors that the board had resolved that the proceeds of the sale of the Batavia Mission were to have gone towards the proposed theological seminary in Hong Kong, which had not happened.

In his forthright manner, he informed the directors that the Shanghai missionaries had heard of the ordination of Mr Fairbrother and of the board's intention that he join the Chinese mission, and while they greatly rejoiced in this decision, they wanted to ensure that he was destined for the Shanghai Mission. To add to his argument, he suggested that the society restrict their operations to three stations including Hong Kong, Amoy and Shanghai. The Baptists and the Presbyterians from America had already occupied Ningbo, while Shanghai would for many years have sufficient scope for the energies of all the missionaries that the board could send out.

In his letter, Walter also recounted the visit of a native from the interior, Wang Sho Yeh, who had been a regular attendant at the chapel and who had shown a great interest in the Scriptures. He belonged to a group of religious reformers and spoke with great admiration of his master, who he said was too old and frail to make the journey to Shanghai, yet he would welcome a visit by one of the missionaries. This triggered a plan in Walter's mind to embark on an expedition to the interior of China with Wang Sho Yeh as his guide. He explained to the directors that should this journey be accomplished, he must undertake it in the garb of a Chinese and should he be successful, communications with the Chinese in the interior would be established and the way paved for future operations.

He went no further in this correspondence, but his preparations for the trip must have been very advanced, for three days later, William Lockhart completed the letter to the directors, stating that Dr Medhurst had already set out on his journey into the interior.

25

TRAVELS WITHIN CHINA

Walter Medhurst was fascinated by China and his enquiring mind longed to know what was over the next hill, or round the next bend of the river, and what lay beyond the distance they were allowed to travel under the treaty. He would engage travellers from the interior in conversation, probing them for information about where they were from. Being a foreigner, however, meant that he was restricted to the places he could travel to and from in one day. If he were to go to the interior, he would have to go as a Chinese man, taking on the appearance of a Chinese, eating food in the Chinese way and conducting himself in every manner that would convince all who met him that he was one of them. Both Morrison and Gutzlaff had successfully passed themselves off as Chinese and Walter's communications skills were every bit as good as theirs, giving him confidence that he could travel the interior of the country without his origins being discovered. He decided therefore that he would take two months and travel through the silk and green tea countries of the interior, through the provinces of Zhejiang, Jiangxi, Anhui, and Jiangsu.

Walter was a very complex person and his missionary calling was only one part of what motivated him in life. Travelling clandestinely in the guise of a Chinese man meant that he could not even hint at the subject of Christianity, let alone come anywhere near attempting to preach and make converts. He would need to forget that he was a missionary for two months and spend his whole time learning about China and the Chinese. In this, he was very successful, as evidenced by the book he wrote on his return, titled *A Glance at the Interior of China, obtained during a Journey through the Silk and Green Tea Countries.*[1]

The first half of his book described his preparation for the trip and since it was written with nineteenth-century British readers in mind, he described the daily practices of the Chinese as they went about their lives. He explained how Chinese men dressed, the food they ate and how they ate with chopsticks, the eating-houses and teashops he encountered along the way, and the various modes of travel including Chinese boats and Chinese roads. All of these differed from their British counterparts, especially when it came to road travel, where wheeled carriages were rare and roads were designed for foot passengers or the occasional wheelbarrow, donkey or sedan chair.

In order to achieve a suitable complexion matching a Chinese, he achieved this in the same way that the Chinese complexions were tinged; by never using soap for washing. The Chinese washed their hands and face several times a day, but without soap.

The trip was undertaken with serious concerns for the safety of the guide, Wang Sho Yeh. Had the poor fellow been discovered leading a foreigner into the country, the repercussions on him and his family could have been horrendous. He seemed fully alive to the danger but willing to accept it. Walter admired his manner, his solidity, earnestness and apparent sincerity, and a friendship soon sprang up between them.

The evening before they departed, Walter travelled down to Wusong and summoned a barber from the town to meet with him on board one of the ships in the harbour. The barber seemed not at all surprised at the request to shave the hair from the front of his head in the Chinese style and to have an artificial queue (plait) attached to his remaining hair. (The braided queue was considered a sign of subjugation by the Chinese to their Manchu rulers.) With his queue covered under a cap and still wearing European clothes, Walter boarded a passing ship heading for Shanghai and proceeded below to one of the cabins, where he changed into the Chinese clothes he had brought along with him. When he re-appeared on board, he astonished the ship's company because they had not seen this individual come aboard.

The captain kindly offered to take him ashore in his own boat, but just as they manoeuvred to find a landing in the dark, a thunderstorm came on and the heavens opened. The captain was a stranger to Shanghai and did not know where to put ashore. At length, they saw a light on shore and guided the bewildered traveller over some sticks of timber and on to firm ground. Gaining a foothold and looking around, Walter soon discovered that he had landed at the native customs house, whose officers he was well acquainted with. Those on duty, however, appeared too lazy or too frightened by the storm to look out the door, and he was very pleased to escape their observation. It soon became dark and he risked falling into one of the pits he knew to be in that area. He stopped to ask at a blacksmith's shop for a candle. The blacksmith asked him where he came from and where he was going and after much hesitation and suspicion, he gave him a small length of candle. With this, he proceeded a little further but the wind soon blew the candle out. By degrees, he adjusted his eyesight to the darkness and being well acquainted with the streets, he managed to reach the neighbourhood where he had agreed his guide would meet him. Here, he spied a glimmer of light and approaching it, found his faithful friend, Wang Sho Yeh, true to his promise, standing at the rendezvous, dripping wet from the rain. They proceeded to the riverside, to the boat they had arranged, along with Wang's friend who would be travelling with them. They embarked and crept into the hole that was allocated as their cabin, changed out of wet clothes, crawled under the bedclothes, and went to sleep.

The next morning the boat was already under way, although not for long. After fifteen minutes of rowing, they reached an entry point to the canal they wanted to travel through but were held up waiting for the tide, which would not be high enough until the afternoon. Since they were surrounded by other boats and close to one of the English merchant houses, Walter felt it too risky to test his disguise in an area where there were so many foreigners, most of whom would probably recognise him. Soon after midday, however, the tide had risen sufficiently for the boat to enter the canal and after the crew rowed the boat a short distance upstream, Walter was able to appear on deck. To his relief, the boatmen gave no sign that they had noticed anything unusual about this new passenger.

This was his home for the next six days as the boat made its way to the city of Huzhou, which was then the principal seat of silk cultivation in China. Along the way they visited several walled cities, some of them dating back to the Ming Dynasty, which Walter described in detail in his book, complete with sketches of views and plans of street layouts within detailed pictures of city walls. He described the changing topography as the boat passed hillocks topped with pagodas, gradually transforming to a region of hills and lakes, about which he wrote, 'Soon to be surrounded by lofty mountains which did delight and bewilder us by their beauty and magnificence.' They passed numerous other boats and rafts along the canals, some of them carrying timber and bamboo building materials, bound for the cities of Hangzhou and Suzhou. Two of the boats each carried about twenty fishing cormorants that the fishermen had under their control. At a given signal, they were made to dive into the water after fish, which the fisherman retrieved from the bird's gullet, the birds having a ring around their necks that stopped them from swallowing the fish. The birds returned again and again, retrieving fish until the fishermen were satisfied, and when the cormorant's ring was taken off they were allowed to fish for themselves. They frequently observed people working in the rice fields, while others were employed in getting mud from the bottom of the lakes and canals for enriching the rice fields. In more elevated areas, mulberry trees were cultivated for the production of silkworms.

One evening along the way, they anchored at the boatman's cottage and his children came running down to greet him and see who was travelling on their father's boat. 'The appearance of the children indicated the health and happiness of the family,' he wrote. 'Their little chubby faces were so begrimed with dirt, that it was difficult to tell what colour they originally were.' This could be a test of Walter's disguise as many family members and friends milled around scrutinising the travellers. To his surprise, however, they scarcely gave him a second glance, which was even more surprising since for more than a year he had been stared at and followed by the Chinese wherever he went. Now, dressed as another Chinese, the people did not appear to notice anything unusual about him.

As they approached Huzhou, they passed many grain junks receiving on board the emperor's tribute to be carried to the capital. They watched the process by which rice was loaded from smaller boats alongside by means of a rope strung over a pulley attached to the top of the mast. Walter wrote, 'A dozen men were attached to the rope, in order to raise one bag of rice, which could not be done, even with all that manpower, without much singing and noise.' The junks were larger and newer than anything he had seen in Shanghai, often gaily painted, and the sailors were particular about keeping them clean. Since the sailors could each take aboard anything that could be sold for profit in Peking, the decks were covered with birds, dogs and various other animals. At least five hundred grain junks were moored along the canal in a line that extended for more than a mile. Arriving in Huzhou in the evening, they passed through a water gate in the city wall with an arch at least twenty feet high. As they passed through the gate, an old man demanded payment for entry, the amount of which seemed to be negotiable, and they entered the city. The canal was wider here than on the outside, with many vessels coming and going, while the banks were lined with stores and warehouses, giving the appearance of a populous and commercial city. In the middle of the city, they came to a large bridge of three arches, each about fifty feet wide. The name of the bridge was 'hold your tongue bridge' and every Chinese passing under it held their tongues more out of superstition than obedience to any public order. There were many temples and pagodas around them but since it was late, they thrust their boat among others and after the din of voices around them subsided, they fell asleep.

Silk was one of the products from China in high demand in Europe during the nineteenth century. Silkworms had originally been domesticated in China five thousand years before and although the Chinese had long since lost their monopoly over silk production, the processes for cultivating silkworms and producing silk in China were still little known in the West. For this reason, it is not surprising that Walter Medhurst took up almost twenty per cent of his book to describe the growing of mulberry trees, the cultivating of silkworms and the winding of the silk. He also included illustrations of the various tools and implements used in the silk trade. The surprising thing is that he provided so much detail after only a brief stop in Huzhou. He must have gleaned a lot of this information from other stops in the area, probably picking up material that he could study during the many hours travelling the canals.

After Huzhou, the travellers headed west towards the town of Sianzhen where they would leave the boat and continue their journey by road. That night they stayed at a tavern where the host received them very politely and invited his honoured guests to take tea. 'Of the accommodations however, I cannot speak flatteringly,' Walter wrote.

After the meal, several rough-looking coolies came to check the baggage, to ascertain its weight and determine how much they would charge to transport it. The next part of the journey would take fourteen days of walking about thirteen miles per day, over hill and dale, in all kinds of weather. Each coolie would carry about a hundred and fifty pounds (68kg) and any variance to what they had to carry during the trip would require a renegotiation of the agreed payment. After much haggling, a bargain was struck and the coolies agreed to return in the morning to start the trip. The baggage was piled up in one corner of the room, benches and boards were brought out and sleeping places were constructed on the floor surrounding the baggage so that nothing would be stolen during the night.

After an early breakfast, the coolies arrived and loaded up and the party moved off along the road. The narrow pathway was sometimes crowded with other travellers bearing burdens or wheeling barrows going in both directions. It was striking how some of the travellers made little attempt to allow room to pass, noticeable to Walter who was accustomed to seeing the Chinese avoid Europeans. He felt pleased that he had succeeded so well as to be treated like one of them. His friend commented that it was the custom for empty-handed people to give way to those carrying burdens, for coolies to give way to chair bearers and for chair bearers, in their turn, to give way to those on horseback. The only reaction he generated from passers-by was in reference to his dark-coloured spectacles, which were unusual in this part of the country, and as a result, his guides advised him to change his glasses.

On this first day of travel, the land looked barren, with the occasional fertile patch laid out in wheat or mustard plant, the seeds of which were used in the manufacture of oil. On the parts where nothing grew, whole tracts of land had been converted into one broad and uneven road where wheelers of barrows had perpetually chosen out new tracts of land for their vehicles.

In places, the lines converged for travellers to cross a bridge over a stream. After about twelve miles, they came to a more level and fertile region where the road narrowed to pass between fields of wheat and rice. Then it led over a wooden bridge spanning a stream flowing to the north-west and into the suburbs of a larger city, which was to be their stopping point for the night. The lodging house was no better than the previous night and Walter stated that he was almost afraid to enter the room allotted to them. There was no window and the only light came through the door that opened into another room, but as they had no choice, they could only take their seats and wait for their evening meal. Added to this, Walter was feeling unwell through exposure to the sun and sleeping in a draft of cold air on the previous night.

The following morning, heavy rain was falling and they decided to delay their departure until the weather cleared, which it did by 10 a.m., but by then the coolies had already seated themselves at a table to play cards. Not even a command from the emperor would have persuaded the men to leave their game and attend to the needs of their employer. There seemed nothing could be done about it so Walter and his companions settled down to spend the day in this village.

They started early the following day, wearing the spiked leather shoes they had brought with them especially for travelling over muddy and slippery roadways. After about half an hour, they reached the city gates and at the guide's suggestion, walked on top of the wall, thereby avoiding closer observation from the crowds at street level. Walter was pleased to agree to this suggestion since it gave him the opportunity to view the city from a higher vantage point. As with most of the places they were passing through, Wang Sho Yeh was well informed about the history of the city and provided details of the military force stationed there, the population and the area of arable land in the region.

On this occasion and many others during his travels through the interior, Walter waxed poetically, drawing from his classical education and perhaps even the writings of Robert Bloomfield (from *The Banks of Wye*) to describe what he saw.

> We entered a most romantic valley, on each side of which the hills were covered with the blue bell and convolvulus, while the crystal stream murmured through the dell and the feathered songsters warbled in the grove, altogether contributing to cheer the heart and lighten the fatigue of the way.

They came to a Buddhist temple where three priests were busy boiling rice and preparing tea for the travellers who passed by. The temple was in good repair and tastefully adorned and the accommodations appeared clean and decent. Walter observed that this might be a good place for a Western botanist or naturalist to spend a few days, searching out specimens in the mountains. He described some of the unusual flowers and blossoming trees that he saw there for the first time. Rumour had it that frequent robberies took place in this valley and that the perpetrators were sheltered by the priests, but the guide was quick to point out that the priests had since been changed and all was now safe.

That evening, their accommodations resembled those of the previous night except that this time they had a boarded floor. The room was just as dark, however, and the space so small that the three bed spaces and luggage completely covered the floor and their hands could touch the ceiling above their heads. In the shop they discovered a notice which asked people to bury their dead speedily and not to listen to the stories of the Feng Shui teachers who pretended to find lucky sites and by this means kept the dead out of graves for months or years. That evening the coolies took up their gambling game again, where they thumped the table and rattled the cash for more than half the night, keeping the other guests awake.

Over the next few days, they travelled through small hills and narrow valleys, with a small strip of cultivation on each side of the road occupied by wheat and mustard. The streams were mostly flowing northward towards the Yangtze River, and all this land formed part of its basin. They came across a bridge three hundred feet long and twenty feet wide, consisting of eight arches and crowded with travellers. While crossing the bridge, Walter was noticed by several people, perhaps on account of the long strides he took in his attempt to measure the bridge, or by the fact he held an umbrella low down to conceal his face. Some curious individuals looked under the umbrella and inspected the hair at the back of his head. The guides became nervous about Walter's identity being discovered, compounded by comments they overheard in the street. They decided that the two guides had better split up, one to continue with Walter travelling by sedan chair, and the other to follow with the luggage. The guides were anxious to put the plan into action but there were no sedan chairs available from the current location and they would have to wait until next day. That night, one of the guides became very agitated at the thought of their secret being discovered. He claimed to have overheard people talking about the devil's son, with reference to a supposed foreigner, and to top it all, Walter was heard speaking in the Malayan language in his sleep.

They were glad to be away in the morning but they were no less concerned when at the next village they saw three mandarins making offerings at the temple, raising the concern that their attendants might consider something unusual about their little company. Still no sedan chair bearers were available but they were assured that they could hire some at the next village, where they would spend the night. The next morning, sedan chair bearers were found and an agreement was reached for the hire of the chairs at a fixed amount and the supply of food and wine for the bearers. This proved to be costly since the bearers were determined to eat three hearty meals a day, amounting to half the cost of the hire charge.

However, the chair bearers moved much faster than the coolies and in the first day they had covered more than twenty miles. The journey was much easier on Walter and his companion, although they had to get out and walk whenever there was a hill to climb.

The plan to travel separately by chairs was successful, for neither the bearers nor the many people they passed paid any attention to the travellers. In one town, the bearers insisted that the travellers alight from the chairs and walk through the town, and they insisted in taking a rest by the city gate, where hundreds of people were coming and going and Walter had to sit exposed for about an hour. Outside this gate, they passed several memorial arches commemorating various females who had served the local community. Again, Walter indicated admiration for the local culture by observing the value that the inhabitants placed on female worth.

By the middle of April, they had reached the prefectural city of Huizhou, where he saw more commemorative arches dedicated to various virtuous females. 'These arches are in such numbers and so lavishly adorned,' he wrote, 'as to lead a stranger to imagine that all the feminine virtue in the empire has been congregated in Huizhou.' The next day they took a southerly course to the town of Tunxi, one of the largest places of commerce in the green tea district. The population there was about a hundred thousand inhabitants. It was the base for the leading tea dealers, who purchased the teas grown in the surrounding country and after preparing and sorting them, despatched them by canal to Shanghai or over a range of hills to the west and then south to Canton. Walter's travelling companion was well acquainted with the manager of one of the tea establishments and they stayed at his house for the night. Here they received a very hospitable welcome and during the evening, they were treated to a feast in the dining hall. The only problem was that the light was very dim and Walter's dark glasses made it very difficult for him to see what he was eating. Added to this, his poor skills with chopsticks resulted in a trail of fallen food between the bowls and his plate. The host took pity and picked up the fallen pieces and placed them on Walter's plate. With the other guests appearing to suspect something unusual about the strange man in dark glasses, Walter was relieved when the meal ended and they moved to another even gloomier part of the room. Here the host posed questions about the status of business in Shanghai, to which Walter was able to respond with some confidence, and when it became apparent that Walter was familiar with the Fukien dialect, the conversation turned to the customs of the Fukien people.

They set out early the next morning and for the next two days travelled through tea country over a dividing range, from which all the rivers they had passed previously flowed back towards Hangzhou Bay, whereas the rivers on the other side flowed south and west to Poyang Lake. The second night, the chair bearers stayed up all night drinking, gambling and arguing with other lodgers at the inn, the result being that they did not want to work the following day. An argument ensued, whereupon the bearers shouldered their chairs and left, leaving Walter and his companion to continue their journey on foot. Wang found places on a boat travelling down river, but as they were all seated close together, face to face, any foreigner would surely be discovered by such scrutiny. The passengers seemed more interested in passing around a smoking pipe than in observing their fellow travellers, so once again, Walter passed as just another Chinaman. The river was fast flowing and the boat crossed at least ten rapids, where the skills of those on board were indispensable to their safe arrival at their destination.

The boat took them to the home of Wang Sho Yeh, near the town of Wuyuan, where they stayed for the next four days until their fellow traveller, with whom they had split up earlier, arrived with the coolies bringing the baggage. It was interesting for Walter to observe the reception Wang received from his family after being away for two years. Both his mother and sister appeared to be only interested in the things he had brought them and his brother merely gave him a nod and continued with his work. Walter was surprised by the casual manner and lack of emotion in the meeting, but he later surmised that this lack of displayed emotion was normal when a stranger was present.

The house was small. The front and central room where family meals were eaten was a sort of shed, open in front and surrounded on the other three sides by the remaining rooms of the dwelling, one being a pigsty and the other Walter's sleeping quarters. The floor was bare earth and very uneven, for every foot that entered in wet weather brought an additional quantity of earth with it. Walter's description continues: 'As to the maintenance of cleanliness, such a floor offered peculiar advantages; all liquids soaking at once into the earth and smaller particles being easily trodden into it; while the bones, which fell occasionally from the table, were gladly carried away by the half famished dogs. The stench arising from such a floor however, combined with the pig's sty on one side and an uncleaned drain in front, was rather disagreeable to those unaccustomed to it.'

However poor the dwellings of these people, the provisions of their table were by no means deficient. The hostess was proud to bring forward something new and different at every meal. Although forbidden by Chinese etiquette to sit down at the same table with a stranger, she would stand on one side and frequently insist on him eating more. Her daughter of about eighteen frequently went in and out of the front room and was always well dressed and had remarkably small feet, the shoes of which would not have been more than four inches long. Her principal employment seemed to be to feed the pigs, which she did about every half an hour. Thus she was seen, all day long, hobbling through the front room with her slush bucket, going to feed her pets, which later would become their food. In one of the outbuildings was equipment used for heating and drying the tea ready for market, which occupied the attention of every household in the district at certain times of the year. The tea trees were growing at every spot of ground that could be spared from rice cultivation, not in plantations but along pathways, between buildings and anywhere land could be made available.

During Walter's stay in the house, the death occurred next door of a young man who was intended to be married to a cousin of the family. Since the grief seemed to be so severe, Walter enquired as to the relationship of this person. He had been taken into the family as an infant, with the intention that he should be raised to marry a daughter at some future time when the family could afford the expense of the wedding ceremonies. There had been an exchange of infants in this case; one family having two daughters and the other family having two sons, with a daughter being exchanged for a son. It was common in China for arranged marriages. Furthermore, they were kept single until the parents could afford the funds to celebrate the wedding appropriately. In this case, the intended bridegroom had died, leaving his fiancée to wait until someone else asked her to marry him.

After the second guide arrived, they set out for Fuliang, where the religious reformers resided. This was a two-day walk through hilly but scenic country, where they once more had to contend with extremely basic accommodation. That night, after a tiresome journey, they arrived wet and tired at a poor inn where the host had to be roused from his sleep to attend to his guests, which seemed to annoy him profusely. The tea that the wife supplied was inexcusably bad, considering that they were in the land of tea. It was boiled in the pot previously used for rice and vegetables and even the Chinese could scarcely bear it. Other guests soon filled the little room they occupied. First a dealer in chickens, with his stock in trade, followed by a couple of travelling tinkers, with their stock of pots, pans and tools, all requiring space in the crowded room. Finally, a couple of vagrant-looking, soaking wet travellers, looking as if to see what they could pick up to their advantage. The dinner was shared by everyone and consisted of rice, putrid mustard vegetable and soup to wash it down. It was a relief to find their room, six feet square, in which the three of them would sleep. At least it had a door and after closing it and spreading their mats on the floor, they lay down thinking they would be alone until the morning. Far from it. As soon as they had put out the light, they were attacked by untold millions, which bit them on every part of their bodies and ensured that sleep was impossible.

The next day, the fresh air and beauty of the scenery soon erased the inconvenience and lack of comfort of the previous night. That afternoon they climbed the last of a range of hills to look out across the Fuliang district's rice fields and tea plantations stretching as far as the eye could see. The descent was pleasant and easy but distances were deceiving, as the onward journey was still over six miles and it was getting dark. They arrived late at night at the residence of Wang's friend, and Walter, overcome with fatigue, was much relieved at the opportunity to rest and relax in a hospitable environment. The atmosphere was warm and welcoming and the cordiality of these friends meeting after a long separation was a striking contrast to the cold indifference displayed by the family reunion. Walter determined that the family was reluctant to display their affections, whereas groups of friends were fully expected to display their feelings.

The next six days were spent in the house of Wang's friend. Walter could relax and let down his guard a little since the host had been informed that he was a foreigner. Once the surprise was over, the host appeared rather pleased to have a foreigner in his house and he was full of questions about where he was from, how far it was from China, and the population, culture, manners, customs, and religion of all the other places he had visited. Walter held frequent discussions with him and the rest of the school of religious reformers on religious subjects, including the nature and being of the Deity, the creation of the world and an agreement and declaration on peace and happiness for those who embraced these truths. Their desire seemed to be to follow the system of Confucius and to cultivate the virtues of benevolence and righteousness as laid down by him. Walter wrote, 'Some of their observations and sentiments regarding self-examination, victory over evil desires, searching after their own errors and confession of them when ascertained, were tolerably good and would not have disgraced a Christian moralist.' In spite of these positive statements about the group and his support of what he saw as open-mindedness, Walter was unable to convince them to take the step towards becoming Christians. In addition, the aged leader of the group who had been unable to visit Shanghai excused himself from paying Walter a visit here, again on the grounds of poor health. With time on his hands, Walter took the opportunity to write a brief summary of the Christian religion to be passed on to the aged leader.

While living at this house an incident occurred that highlighted the danger Walter and his guides had exposed themselves to by undertaking this trip. After retiring to his room one night, Wang rushed after Walter with something in his hand, exclaiming they had just escaped a fearful danger. Walter's queue had fallen off. If this had happened anywhere but their friend's house, Wang would have been exposed and possibly imprisoned and ruined. To prevent this from happening again, Wang tied the queue back on so tightly that it pulled at Walter's hair. Better safe than sorry, suggested Wang, and Walter accepted this.

Having finished their business in Fuliang, it was time to return to Shanghai. The route via Hangzhou might be the most direct but the Hangzhou customs house had a reputation as the strictest as far as examining a traveller's baggage and therefore it would be good to avoid them. The other course was to proceed northward to the

Yangtze River and then via Nanjing and Suzhou to Shanghai. They decided on this route.

Having thanked their host for his hospitality, they stayed the first night with a brother of one of the guides, who ran a mixed business shop. The shop did not appear to be doing very well and the chief customers appeared to be rats, which visited the shop by night, keeping Walter awake as he lay on one of the counters. The owner of the shop later visited Shanghai and swore that he had never met Walter before, much to the amusement of bystanders who knew the full story. The following day they once again engaged sedan chairs and chair bearers to take the journey north towards the Yangtze. Three days later, they reached a tributary to the Yangtze, where they booked a passage on a boat heading to Tungliu where they would join the main river. They were on the Yangtze at a point where the majestic river was almost a mile wide and the waves rocked their vessel as if on a small sea. After anchoring overnight at Anqing, they continued their journey down the mighty river in a moderate breeze, which by late afternoon had increased to a strong gale. This forced them to take shelter in a small creek, intending to anchor overnight, but the storm continued throughout the next day, forcing them to wait until the gale had passed.

After four days, they reached the city of Wuhu, where they encountered their first customs house. Wang was very anxious about the customs officers becoming suspicious of them and he asked Walter about the notebook he had been writing in. It turned out to contain a description of the whole journey from the time they left Shanghai, and Wang considered this exactly the kind of thing that could be their undoing. He insisted that the book be destroyed. Walter expressed a feigned objection to the destruction of his notebook, knowing that he had taken the precaution to transcribe a copy during the several days' stay at one of the houses. On arrival in Wuhu, the concerns of Wang proved unfounded since the customs officer was only interested in finding out if they had any goods for sale.

At Wuhu, they left the Yangtze and entered a smaller river, which took them as far as Gucheng Lake, where an isthmus divides the eastern and western rivers. This was the main point of transfer to the canal systems, which feed off the Grand Canal and flow to Suzhou and Shanghai. It was serviced by many coolies, transporting goods from the rivers to the canals. Accommodation was found for the night and passage arranged to depart on a boat for Shanghai the following morning.

Wang Sho Yeh travelled with Walter as far as the last customs house in Suzhou and there they parted company, leaving Walter to continue to Shanghai. Just seven weeks after leaving home, travelling over seven hundred miles through four Chinese provinces, Walter arrived back home, along with two boatmen to assist with his baggage. He closed the story by writing, 'I discharged them and quietly walked in; those who had accompanied me not knowing who I was and those at home not dreaming of the direction in which I had travelled, or the way in which I reached home, except in so far as I chose to inform them.'

26

GROWTH OF THE SHANGHAI MISSION

The years 1845 to 1847 were a time of growth and consolidation for the Shanghai Mission. After returning from his trip to the interior of China, Walter's first task was to locate a suitable block of land for the site of the new chapel and hospital. He acted on the assumption that the directors would approve of the expansion he had proposed in his letter of March, but at the same time, both he and Dr Lockhart solicited support from other sources. By the end of 1845, they had acquired a couple of acres of land along what would become known as Shantung Road and had arranged for the erection of a mission house and a chapel. Dr Lockhart had raised funds through a subscription for building his residence, and through friends for the building of a hospital.

The move to Shanghai appeared to mark the end of Betty's work in translation and teaching. Her translation of the catechism into the Malayan language was one of the largest works of the Batavia Press, but in Shanghai, there was no call for that language skill. It was a difficult time for her to adapt once more to the new culture, further from her Indian roots, but one she no doubt had become accustomed to as the wife of an ambitious and relentlessly driven man.

In July 1845, they welcomed the arrival of a new missionary and his wife, Mr and Mrs Fairbrother, who were relieved to have survived a calamitous journey from England. Travelling via Calcutta and Singapore, their ship caught fire at sea and had to be abandoned, leaving them adrift at sea for some time, after which they were rescued by another British ship, which took them to Hong Kong. On the last leg of their journey, they sailed into a typhoon, which dismasted the ship, leaving them dangerously close to a rocky shore, before the storm finally abated and a jury-rigged sail got them to safety. Their troubles were not yet over. Two weeks after their arrival, Mrs Fairbrother experienced an attack of diarrhoea, which brought on premature confinement, and she sank and died on 18 September. After her death, Mr Fairbrother also became very sick and Dr Lockhart wrote that he deemed it necessary for him to return to England as the only means not only of restoring his health, but also of saving his life. Thus, another opportunity to add a worker to the missionary team was denied them.

In November of that year, however, the mission team was increased with the arrival of William Milne and his wife Frances, who moved into the house with Walter and Betty. It was like having family come to stay. William had been one of the four-year-old twins whom Betty had taken care of in Malacca when his mother Rachel Milne had died. Walter was particularly pleased to welcome William to the mission because he already had four years' experience working in Canton, Hong Kong and Chusan and, like Walter, he had made a journey through the interior of China. They had seen each other last in Manila after nearly being shipwrecked together.

Family milestones were prominent in 1846, the first being the news received from England early that year that Walter's father, William Medhurst, had died in London on 27 October 1845[1] and was buried where he started life, in Shoreham, Kent, along with his parents and Uncle George. Walter had not had a lot of contact with his father over the years, but William's death was newsworthy throughout England because he was the father of the Revd Dr Medhurst, missionary to China.

The other family milestone that year was a happier event, the marriage of daughter Eliza to Charles Hillier, now the Acting Chief Magistrate in Hong Kong. At the insistence of her parents, Eliza had waited two years following their departure from Hong Kong and since the couple still declared their love for each other, it was agreed that they should marry at the Colonial Chapel in Hong Kong on 28 May. The unfortunate part of the arrangement, however, was that Charles could not get leave to come to Shanghai and the cost of taking the whole family to Hong Kong was beyond that which a missionary could afford. This would be a huge disappointment to the Medhurst ladies, expressed openly by Martha and Augusta, but accepted quietly but reluctantly by their mother. It was decided that Walter should travel down to Hong Kong to give his daughter's hand in marriage and to arrange meetings with his fellow missionaries, which meant that the travel was at the cost of the society. Similarly, Walter junior was able to travel with them, having government business to attend to in Hong Kong. The ladies had the small consolation of being able to attend another wedding in Shanghai at about the same time, that of Isabella Parkes, Dr Lockhart's sister-in-law and for a short time the fiancé of Walter junior. She was to marry the Revd Thomas McClatchie of the Church of England on 29 May.

One final happy task for Walter to perform before leaving Shanghai was the baptism of his guide to the interior of China, Wang Sho Yeh. Baptisms of Chinese had been very rare during Walter's long career as a missionary, so this was an important milestone that he hoped augured well for the future.

Two days after Eliza became Mrs Charles Hillier, Walter was in Canton preparing to take part in the first ordination of a Protestant minister in China. James Granger Bridgman, a member of the American Board of Foreign Missions, was ordained at the home of his cousin, Dr Elijah Bridgman, on 31 May by an ecclesiastical council consisting of Dr Medhurst, Dr Bridgman and the Revd Liang Fa, assisted by the Revd Peter Parker and the Revd Pohlman of Amoy. Liang Fa had been an assistant of the late Dr Milne and he returned to Malacca with Milne after Walter was first left in charge of the Malacca Mission. Dr Morrison had ordained Liang Fa in Macao in 1821 and he became the first Chinese Protestant minister and evangelist. Much to Walter's fascination, Liang Fa had travelled widely in China, to the extent that the Imperial Chinese Government became incensed by his activities and he was forced to return to Malacca, where he had recently worked with the late Samuel Dyer. Walter was intrigued to know what success he had achieved in converting some of his countrymen during his travels. In fact, Liang Fa had been responsible for the conversion of Hong Xiuquan, which would have a profound effect on the future of China, but at the time, the impact of that conversion was unknown.

While in Hong Kong, Walter's intention was to meet fellow delegates and other missionary colleagues to discuss the progress of the translation of the Scriptures and to set a date for the first meeting of the delegates. The five delegates in 1846 were Dr Medhurst of the LMS, Dr Bridgman of the ABCFM in Canton, Bishop Boone of the ABCFM in Shanghai, John Stronach of the LMS in Amoy, and the Revd Walter Lowrie of the American Presbyterian Board in Ningbo. Walter met with all the delegates except John Stronach and the Revd Lowrie. John Stronach's brother Alexander was visiting Hong Kong at the time, where he was setting up the Chinese type foundry created by the late Samuel Dyer in Malacca. He was planning shortly to leave for Amoy, which meant that Alexander could brief his brother about the proposed meeting set for the summer of the following year in Shanghai.

One aspect of the translation prompted major discussions among the delegates and filled the columns of Christian publications around the world: determining the correct Chinese word for 'God'. Walter published a hundred-and-seventy-page book on the subject, *An Inquiry into the proper mode of rendering the word God in translating the Sacred Scriptures in to the Chinese Language.* The discussion of this almost derailed the whole translation project and led to a major dispute between the LMS delegates and those of the ABCFM. In some ways, this was understandable since before a word could be translated, agreement had to be reached on the meaning of that word in English. To achieve agreement today on a single English definition for the word 'God' would be difficult, especially if it had to encompass the way the word was used in the Old and New Testaments and take account of the modern usage of the word. Furthermore, the way this word was translated into Chinese would have enormous influence on the acceptance of Christianity for a very long time. This was an extremely important matter and they had to get it right.

The delegates' meeting commenced at the Medhurst home in Shanghai on 1 July 1847. The Revd Elijah Bridgman and the Revd John Stronach took up residence in Shanghai, almost for the duration of the translation project, which continued for several years. Bishop Boone attended the meetings for four days, but then objected, with Bridgman, to the term being used for the Chinese name for 'God'. Unable to reach unanimous agreement about the term, Bishop Boone left the meeting and never returned. After that, he claimed that ill health prevented him from attending any other meetings until the conclusion of the work in 1850. The argument on the proper Chinese word for 'God' then moved into the public arena, with Bishop Boone writing essays for the January and February issues of *The Chinese Repository*. Walter Medhurst hit back with articles supporting his side of the dispute, which were published in all the issues from March to December. Readers must have been tiring of the discussion by the end of 1848. Walter's daughters followed the controversy and Eliza's opinion was revealed in her letter to Martha where she wrote, 'Poor Papa has got into hot water again with those dreadful Americans about some new term they have hit upon for the translation.'[2]

The Revd Walter Lowrie was the delegate responsible for the translation work of the Ningbo committee and he participated at this first meeting before leaving to return to Ningbo on 16 August. On a ferry halfway across Hangzhou Bay, the passengers observed a pirate craft bearing down on them, manned by about twenty men armed with matchlocks, spears and swords. Not able to outrun the pirates, the boatmen submitted to the pillaging of the boat, the theft of all the boatmen's possessions and clothing and the destruction of the rigging and the rudder. When the pirates had stripped the boat of valuables, they turned their attention to Mr Lowrie. Would he report them to the authorities? Should they kill him or just throw him in the sea and leave him to drown? Three men took hold of Mr Lowrie, who to this point had been reading his Bible, and threw him overboard. His last act was to turn around and throw his Bible down on the deck and kick off his shoes to be able to swim. He swam for some time but eventually tired and sank out of sight. With Mr Lowrie gone and the boat disabled, the pirates left and the survivors managed to reach the shore, where the alarm was raised and a reward offered for the capture of the perpetrators.[3]

The information reached Shanghai on 29 August and although the authorities in both Ningbo and Shanghai took up the matter, it seemed unlikely that the pirates would be apprehended. Chinese pirates were becoming an increasing problem in the islands of the Zhoushan archipelago, reported by the *China Mail* as being several thousand strong and organised under the direction of a youth of about twenty. They posed a continuing threat to native shipping and the Chinese authorities, and were a constant reminder that outside the European governed treaty ports, China was often a wild and ungoverned country. Back in Shanghai, where the delegates were now another member short, Walter's response was to appoint William Milne to the role. Perhaps this placed the balance of the delegates a little more towards the London Missionary Society. It would certainly not help the dispute with Boone and Bridgman over the Chinese word for 'God'.

On 26 August 1847, three more assistants arrived to join the Shanghai Mission: the Revd Benjamin and Mrs Southwell, the Revd William Muirhead, and Alexander Wylie as superintendent of the Shanghai Mission Press. The missionaries had a relatively smooth passage from England. They arrived in Shanghai the same day that two small French boats rowed up the Huangpu. The reason for their appearance demonstrated the huge risks of sea travel on that coast. Two French ships of war, *La Gloire* and *Victorieuse*, had been wrecked on 10 August on a shoal off the Korea coast, largely due to the lack of good charts of the coastal waterways. There had been no loss of life but over five hundred men were stranded on an island while twenty-four men took sixteen days in their two open boats to reach Shanghai to raise the alarm. By this time, the French Government had signed a treaty with China and had established a consulate in Shanghai, so the rescue of the five hundred-odd French sailors would be a job for the French Consul. Fortunately, the British fleet was in the area and three Royal Naval frigates were able to pick up the marooned sailors on 12 September.

Alexander Wylie was a young cabinetmaker who was self-taught in Chinese. He was sent on a short period of training in printing before sailing to China with a brand-new cylinder press capable of producing three times the output of their existing press, made possible by a grant of £1,000 from the Bible Society. The only problem was that this press was designed to be powered by a steam engine, which the Shanghai Mission did not have and had no funds for. As a unique merging of centuries-old technology with the new, the cylinder press was installed so that it was driven not by steam but by bullocks in the adjoining wheel works.

In October 1846, Walter Medhurst junior was sent back to England, leaving his sisters to care for his dog Henry. He wrote back to Martha from Hong Kong, asking her to let Henry smell the letter as he would be sure to recognise his scent and be comforted by it. Being an ambitious young man, Walter took the opportunity while in England to further his education and build his relationships with those who could help his career in the diplomatic service. He was evidently successful in attending the correct social events as it was noted in the *Court Reporter* that he attended the Queen's Levee at St James' Palace in February 1847.[4] He also changed his domestic situation, and on 20 October 1847 married Ellen Gilbert Cooper at St John's church, Notting Hill, in a double ceremony with Ellen's sister Harriet.[5] Interestingly, Harriet's bridegroom was Charles Baker, the son of Mary Baker, *née* Medhurst. So Walter had gone a'courting with his cousin and together they had married sisters.

Walter junior and his new bride returned to Shanghai in 1848 before Walter was sent to Amoy (Xiamen) as Acting Vice Consul and Ellen was able to meet his parents. By the time they arrived in Shanghai, however, Ellen was in an advanced state of pregnancy and it was decided that she had better stay with her in-laws for the birth of the baby while his father went on to Amoy. Walter Henry Balfour Medhurst was born on 16 December but the mother was in labour for two days and the delivery was complicated, so much so that Ellen did not survive the delivery. Once more, Betty was called on to take care of a motherless baby in the face of another family tragedy.

Tragedy was again followed by a happy occasion, the marriage of Martha, who was engaged to a Shanghai businessman, Robert Saul, known by his second name of Powell. They were married in the mission chapel on 28 February 1849, and this time Betty and Augusta could participate in the wedding.

Powell and Martha moved into their own house very close to the Shanghai Mission and by the summer of that year, announced that Martha was expecting their first child. A little girl was born on 27 April 1850 and named Eliza Margaret. This time, both mother and child were healthy and well.

27

THE GRAIN JUNK MEN
AFFAIR

In addition to all their activities in Shanghai at the hospital, the chapel, the mission press, and the schools, Walter Medhurst and William Lockhart still made regular visits to the villages and towns around the city. Under the agreements between the Chinese and the British Government, they were free to visit anywhere that could be travelled within a day. On 8 March 1848, Walter, Lockhart and Muirhead travelled about thirty miles west of Shanghai to the town of Qingpu where they distributed tracts from door to door to anyone who appeared able to read. Unfortunately for the missionaries, on this day, Qingpu had been visited by a group of grain junk men.

The grain junk men, who normally navigated the canal junks, had been thrown out of work because of the emperor's grain being shipped that year by sea-going junks. Some fifteen thousand men, mostly from Shandong, were now wandering this part of the country desperate for work or for any other way to make money. They were known as the 'navigators' and were to the north what the Canton pirates were to the south, described at the time as prowling about like savage bloodhounds.

While the missionaries were involved in giving out tracts, several of these navigators came up behind them, pushing and shoving, trying to get a larger number of books, and when they were unsuccessful, they started to throw stones. William Lockhart proposed that the other two should go on ahead and he would try and keep the crowd back so that they could converse with some local shopkeepers. At this point, one of the navigators struck Lockhart on the head. Walter turned around and faced the mob, asking them what they wanted and demanded to know who the ringleader was, suggesting that he should be reported to the magistrate. With this, the crowd became quiet and parted to allow them passage through the east gate and their return home.

They had not gone more than half a mile from the city, however, before a fresh set of grain men came after them, hooting and threatening to beat them, apparently inflamed by exaggerated reports of what had taken place earlier in the city. They were armed with poles, bars, swords, and other weapons, which they demonstrated with aggressive and violent gestures. The missionaries attempted to reason with the mob and find out what they wanted but it was impossible to make any progress and, seeing an opportunity to escape, they started to run for their lives. Lockhart was grabbed by the mob and thrown to the ground, and the other two returned to rescue their companion. Walter tried in vain to ward off blows but he was struck from behind and fell stunned to the ground. The assailants then struck him several times with clubs as he curled up and covered his face. The other missionaries were equally mistreated, resulting in Muirhead being beaten with a bamboo club so hard that he was hardly able to walk and Lockhart receiving a severe wound to the back of the neck, which bled profusely. One of his attackers held a short broadsword and Lockhart later recalled, 'I thought at this time he was going to cut off my head and I mentally bade farewell to my family.'

Once they were beaten into submission and effectively disabled, the navigators proceeded to strip them of some of their clothes and any valuables that they were carrying. Thankful that they were not murdered, the missionaries struggled to their feet and were prodded and pushed back towards the city. As they were led along, the missionaries appealed to any respectable onlooker to assist them, for which they received additional blows, and if any stranger responded, they too received the same treatment. Discussions broke out about what should be done with the prisoners. One said they should be taken to the bridge by the temple and killed. Others said they should be taken to the grain junks where they could be held for a ransom of $5,000 per head. As they approached the grain junks, some of the men became less ferocious, especially when one person claimed that Lockhart was a surgeon who had healed several of their crewmembers without payment. The discussions continued and others joined the crowd, including some who called for the magistrate. By the time they had reached the bridge over the moat, the junk men had one by one slunk away and the missionaries found themselves in the hands of the police.

The missionaries were conducted to the magistrate's office, and he asked them to sit down and make a report of the whole affair. He promised that the stolen articles would be returned and the men who committed the assault punished. He provided sedan chairs and a boat to take them back to their boat and gave them an escort of two military officers and two civil officers to protect them from further harm. They finally reached their homes in safety, thankful to be alive, but suffering from their wounds and bruises. In his report, Walter described the chain with which he was beaten. 'This instrument, when wielded by a strong arm, inflicted a very powerful blow and my back and shoulders are still very sore from repeated strokes of this chain.' Walter was by now fifty-two and he took some time to recuperate from this attack.

When they returned to Shanghai, the affair was taken up by the British Consul who insisted on an apology, compensation and punishment of the culprits. It was a matter of principle to the British Consul for the Chinese to know that a foreigner was

sacred and to insist on mutual personal security. The treaties
provided for this and right and equity demanded it. Balfour had
moved on by 1848 and the consul was now Rutherford Alcock.
Walter Medhurst junior was on leave in England and the acting
interpreter to the consul was another young man connected to the
missionaries, Harry Parkes, the brother of Catherine Lockhart.
Parkes travelled to Qingpu to interview the magistrate and any
witnesses to the affair that he could find, as well as to ascertain the
position and number of grain junks in the area.

By 13 March, the consul issued a demand to the Taotai giving
the Chinese forty-eight hours to produce ten of the ringleaders in
the attack, failing which, other steps would be taken. Two naval
ships, the *Childers* sixteen guns and the *Espiegle* twelve guns, were
brought up and anchored in the Huangpu River to blockade the
sea-going junks. The Taotai was informed that until the matter was
resolved, no payment of duties would be made for British ships, nor
would grain junks be permitted to leave the port. Having put his
views to the Taotai, Mr Alcock then informed the representatives
of the other foreign powers of his actions, requesting them to
support the British position. By 5 p.m., the French, American and
Belgian consuls assured the Taotai that they fully concurred with
the course adopted by the British Consul.

Wednesday 11 a.m. was the deadline for the demand and at that
time the parties met to review the situation. The Chinese requested
an extension of time, having received no information from Qingpu,
an indication of how difficult it was to seize criminals in China.
Mr Alcock informed the Taotai that he had received a letter from
the magistrate of Shanghai that threatened the consul with danger
from the people. He had returned no answer, but wished to assure
the Taotai that he, his family and his countrymen would remain in
the city without fear, and that any violence, from whatever quarter
it might come, would be promptly resisted. As follow-up to the
meeting and by way of precaution, a notification was issued to

all merchant vessels under the British flag, calling on them to be prepared to be requisitioned to protect British interests in the port.

On Friday, a notification in Chinese was published and Mr Parkes took it aboard the grain junks, explaining the reasons for the blockade and warning them of the consequences of ignoring the warning. 'If you should offer any opposition, the vessel of war, of my nation, now in the river, will open her great guns and you will be involved in misery of your own seeking.'

The standoff went on for more than a week after the deadline, but the Chinese eventually brought the criminals in from Qingpu. The offenders in custody were taken to the magistrate's office. With chains around their necks, the ten offenders were led into the court where they instantly fell on their knees before the neihtai (judge), a middle-aged Mandarin wearing the peacock of the third grade on the breast of his robe. Medhurst, Lockhart and Muirhead were requested to step forward and identify the attackers. This being in the affirmative, the chains were taken from their necks and replaced by heavy wooden collars, called the cangue (a kind of pillory).

The following day a notification went out from the British Consul to the foreign community to say that the provincial judge of the province had produced the ten ringleaders. These offenders had been sentenced to one month in the cangue prior to any further proceedings against them. They would be exposed every day during that period in the public thoroughfare as a warning to all who were in a like manner disposed. A further notice in Chinese went out to all the grain junks informing them of the satisfactory outcome to the affair and the lifting of the blockade.

The next day, the consul met with the neihtai, taking him and his entourage on a tour of the *Childers*, followed by a visit to the home of the missionaries at the mission compound. At Dr Medhurst's, the consul took special care to explain to the neihtai the working of the power-press, which was then in full operation under bullock power. Mr Alcock was very pleased to introduce this high-ranking officer to the families of the men who were the victims of the attacks. The judge was much pleased with the European ladies and not least with Miss Augusta, the youngest daughter of Dr Medhurst, a child of seven years. No doubt Betty would have dressed Augusta in her best clothes and told her to be on her best behaviour. 'Don't forget to curtsy like an English lady when you are presented to the British Consul and the Chinese Mandarin.' This was probably one of the first times that Augusta had stolen the limelight from her older sisters.

28

THE MISSION FAMILY AND THE MEDHURST FAMILY

As was evident when the Ultra Ganges Mission commenced operations in Malacca, the independent personalities of most missionaries and the tyranny of distance made it necessary for them to operate on their own initiative. This sometimes resulted in disunity among them. For the first five years of its operation, the Shanghai Mission had experienced remarkably harmonious relationships among the missionaries, both in Shanghai and with their colleagues in the other stations in China. That harmony was not to last, however, as was indicated in the letter Alexander Wylie wrote to the directors in September 1849.

By that time, the society had seven missionaries in Shanghai with Medhurst, Milne and Stronach working full time on the Delegates' translation of the Bible, Lockhart running the hospital, Muirhead and Edkins looking after the chapels, and Wylie working in the printing office. In addition, they had Chinese assistants working in the hospital, on the translation project and in the press. Alexander Wylie, the superintendent of the printing press, supervised a group of printers who mostly knew more about printing than he did. Nevertheless, for his first year in Shanghai as a single man, he accepted his position without complaint. In 1848, he married Mary Hanson, a former missionary from South Africa, and from that point on he declined to get involved in evangelical activities and began to complain that he was not being treated as a social or professional equal with his colleagues. His dissatisfaction culminated in the following letter to the directors:

Shanghai 7 September 1849
My dear Sir
You will probably feel surprised that my communications to you have not been of a more frequent occurrence and indeed it would have been a source of gratification to me, could I have felt encouraged often to lay my thoughts open to you, but I fear, what I have now to say, while it will in some degree explain my previous silence, will not be calculated to awaken very pleasant feelings: however, such as it is, I deem it most important that it should be laid before you without farther delay...My position here with respect to my Brethren is such, as I think it would not be wise, even were it possible to continue...I was sent out with instructions as Superintendent of the Press: that Office has never been committed to my trust; I am constantly submitted to annoyances and vexations, nor do I see any hope of such a state of things improving; under such circumstances I lay my case before you. I shall wait a sufficient time to receive a replay from you on which if it does not accord with the above request, by removing me to some other station, I must further request that my connexion with the London Missionary Society be at an end. I have not taken this step rashly; but you must see the difficulty of my position; I have endeavoured to the utmost of my power to endure it, but I find it sacrificing happiness to remain under such circumstances. I look to you for advice and trust you will not disappoint me in this and that the God of all wisdom may

give me grace to keep the path he has marked out for me is
the fervent prayer of
Yours ever respectfully
A Wylie[1]

Although Wylie had not singled out any particular member of the
mission as being responsible for his situation, the implication was
that the autocratic and demanding management style of Walter
Medhurst was a likely factor. William Milne arranged to discuss the
situation with Wylie and letters were exchanged documenting those
meetings. Milne's recommendation was that Wylie should withdraw
the charges against his fellow missionaries, especially the charge
that they constantly submitted Wylie to annoyances and vexations.
Milne and his colleagues considered this untrue. A meeting of the
committee of the mission was called to discuss the matter, to which
Wylie was invited, but he declined to attend. All the missionaries
attended and the opinions expressed showed that, while Walter's
management style might have been a factor, Wylie had no support
from his colleagues. In fact, they all considered his work so
incompetent that at the end of the meeting, a resolution was passed
and documented and forwarded to the directors. It read as follows:

That this Committee unanimously beg the Directors to accede
to the request of Mr Wylie and hope that, when they send out
a substitute, they will select a thoroughly practical man'
   With cordial Christian regards, we remain, dear Brothers,
yours very truly,
W. H. Medhurst
John Stronach
W. Lockhart
William C. Milne
W. Muirhead
J. Edkins.[2]

This crisis came to a head when Mary Wylie was dangerously ill in the late stages of pregnancy. She gave birth to a daughter on 1 October and died six days later. Her death was enough for everyone to put aside their disagreements and restore peace in the mission. Just as she had in 1819, Betty Medhurst took on the role of mother to the baby, also named Mary, while Alexander Wylie returned to his role managing the press, this time with more support and encouragement from his colleagues. The result was that Wylie withdrew his request for a transfer and continued to work with the LMS in Shanghai for another ten years.

The years 1847 to 1850 occupied Medhurst, Milne and Stronach in the translation of the New Testament, with assistance from Bridgman of the American Board and a Chinese scholar, Wang T'ao. The tall wide windows of the house on Shantung Road, which in July attracted the elusive summer breezes, in winter hardly lit the gloom of the big room set aside for the missionaries to work in. Wall-mounted oil lamps, complemented by white tapers in candelabra, lighted the dark rosewood desks where they worked with their quill pens. A coal fire took the edge off the chill in the room and added a pungent odour to the space. At one end of the room, Walter's library included hundreds of books in Chinese, Greek, Hebrew, and English, constantly being accessed by the missionaries. Refreshed by frequent calls to the houseboy to bring tea, which he poured from a large pewter teapot into china cups lined up along the sideboard, the missionaries worked twelve-hour days.

As each chapter of each book of the New Testament was completed and reviewed by the group, the handwritten texts were passed to Alexander Wylie in the mission press office where his team of printers set the type for printing. In July 1850, Walter announced the completion of the translation. By means of the metal type produced by their colleagues in Hong Kong, the entire New Testament would now go to press and be put into circulation at a cost of about three pence sterling per copy.

By 1851, the operation of the LMS had grown, along with the entire foreign settlement in Shanghai. There were now a hundred and sixty foreign residents in Shanghai, not including wives and families. There were five foreign consular offices, forty trading companies and more than twenty Protestant missionaries, seven of whom were with the LMS. The LMS missionary compound included Dr Lockhart's hospital, the original chapel, which now doubled as a dispensary, the mission press, and several houses. In the walled city itself, the LMS now had two chapels where services were held in Mandarin and the local Shanghai dialect, and a boarding school for boys run by William Muirhead. Two of the missionaries also lived within the walled city.

The Shanghai Mission also supported a school for Chinese girls in Ningbo, run by an Englishwoman, Miss Mary Ann Aldersey. Miss Aldersey was the first female Christian missionary to serve in China and, like Walter, had previously worked in Batavia and moved to China after the Treaty of Nanking. She had studied Chinese in London under Robert Morrison in 1824–26. When she moved to Ningbo and opened her school, she took three young women from Surabaya in Batavia as teachers. She continued to run the school until 1861, when she handed the operation over to the Church Missionary Society and retired to McLaren Vale in South Australia.

When the vice consul for Amoy returned from leave in England at the end of 1849, Walter junior returned to Shanghai to resume his old job as interpreter at the British Consul. This had been a lonely time for young Walter after the loss of his wife and he had immersed himself in his duties at the consulate to take his mind off his personal situation. Now he would be able to enjoy being a father for the first time. His son, who was now twelve months old, had been living with his grandparents Walter and Betty.

Martha's husband Powell Saul's business was not going well and he was looking around for a new position. Charles and Eliza tried to persuade Powell to move to Hong Kong where they believed he would find plenty of opportunities, but the possibility of joining a family business at home was the deciding factor. Powell and Martha Saul returned to England, sailing from Shanghai for Hong Kong on 15 February 1851 in the *Race Horse* – time for one last visit with Charles and Eliza and an opportunity for Martha to meet her nephews and to show off Eliza's namesake niece. The timing of the visit was awkward, however, as on the day that Powell and Martha left Shanghai, Eliza gave birth to her third son, Harry Mason Hillier, leaving her feeling unwell for the reunion. After the visit, Eliza wrote to Martha and asked her what she thought of Emily. It seems she was referring to a possible new wife for Walter junior. She also advised that she had sent a book to her father, which discussed the question of a marriage with a wife's sister, and stated her opinion that this would be a most undesirable union. Walter's late wife had a younger sister called Emily. Marrying a partner's sibling after widowhood was not uncommon in those days.

Meanwhile, Walter Medhurst broke the news that the Shanghai Mission had been instrumental in procuring documents establishing the existence of a Chinese Jewish community in Khae-fung-foo (Kaifeng) in Henan Province. This discovery came about after a visit to Shanghai by the Revd Dr George Smith, Bishop of Victoria, Hong Kong, who had long held an interest in the possibility of finding the rumoured colony of Jews in China. As a result, the mission persuaded two of its Chinese members to undertake a journey to Kaifeng, armed with letters of introduction drawn up in Hebrew, obtained from some Jewish Baghdad merchants in Shanghai. The travellers were successful in meeting up with a small and declining community that had existed for hundreds of years in that part of China. Their rabbi had died fifty years previously, the synagogue was falling into ruin and not one of the community could still read Hebrew. They recognised the Hebrew writing of the letters of introduction and understood the missionaries' shared stories from the Old Testament. The Christians left after a short stay and returned with eight small books containing each one of the Sabbath sections of the law in Hebrew. Walter sent the documents back to the directors, suggesting that they be lodged with the British Museum so that all sections of the community could access their contents. Later study of the documents showed that the Chinese Jews followed rituals from about three hundred years previously that had probably come by way of Persia.

One sense of satisfaction that Walter achieved from reading the Jewish/Chinese documents was to see that they had used the same term for 'God' that he had insisted on during the translation of the New Testament. In the same letter to the directors, Walter laid to rest the dispute with Bishop Boone. He attached a copy of a letter from Boone stating that he had been misquoted by magazines in England and America and admitted that due to ill-health, he had taken no part in the translation of the Delegates Version of the Bible. That left Medhurst, Milne, Stronach, and Bridgman, assisted by the Chinese scholar Wang T'ao, as the true translators of the Bible.

In August 1851 came the news that Walter's long-term friend Charles Gutzlaff had died in Hong Kong, aged forty-eight. In some ways, they had similar personalities, both being independent and determined to do things their way. Walter had received the support of a much larger and more supportive organisation in the LMS and he returned that support with a loyalty that Gutzlaff lacked. Like Walter, Charles Gutzlaff was motivated by a love of adventure and of China, and his travel experiences in China were useful to Walter in his first journeys up the coast to Shandong and Shanghai. Gutzlaff did not share the concern that Walter had about advancing his missionary activities by linking up with opium traders and the East India Company, and this was one aspect that tarnished Gutzlaff's reputation. A much more flamboyant character than Medhurst, he coined for himself the Chinese name of Gaihan, meaning 'lover of the Chinese'. He lacked the organisational skills that Walter excelled in, which often led to problems when working with others. This became apparent when Gutzlaff formed the Chinese Union, a group of local Chinese preachers, which he intended should evangelise the unexplored interior of China. He was duped by the members, who embezzled the union's funds and sold his Bibles back to the printer to be sold to the Chinese Union a second time. This was a huge public embarrassment to Gutzlaff, one from which he never fully recovered.

At the time of his death, Charles Gutzlaff had been fulfilling the role of the Chinese Secretary to the British Government in Hong Kong. His demise provided an opportunity for Walter Medhurst junior. The governor asked him to fill the role, subject to approval from London, which meant that Walter junior would have to wait at least until Christmas before receiving confirmation.

Charles and Eliza Hillier meanwhile had both suffered sickness in Hong Kong and the doctors advised them to take a sea voyage, possibly to a cooler climate. It had been five years since Eliza had left Shanghai, and now, with three children who had never met their grandparents, Charles and Eliza decided to borrow the cost of their passage and visit her parents. Charles was restricted by the amount of leave he could take from his position as magistrate but it was decided that he would make a quick trip to Shanghai, leaving his wife and children there until the end of the year. They sailed from Hong Kong on 26 August in the *Nestoriah*, which due to rough weather and running aground took twenty-two days to reach Shanghai, leaving poor Charles with very little time before he had to return to Hong Kong. The report of the voyage and her reunion with her parents was recorded in Eliza's letter to her sister Martha in England.[3] She said she was so glad to see dear old Papa and Walter junior, who had both come to meet the ship, but she was shocked to see how much Papa had changed and aged.

By comparison, dear Walter looked so stout and well she could not help but laugh at his abundant red whiskers.

When she arrived home, Eliza ran upstairs to find poor Mama in the parlour crying dreadfully. Eliza confided to Martha about her concern for poor Mama and said that she and her brother Walter had discussed their shared concerns for her, but each talk ended in their being more anxious and uncomfortable about her future. In her expressive outspoken way, Eliza wrote that she considered her mother to be naturally of such a morbid disposition that it only rendered matters worse. Perhaps Betty was suffering from some form of depression; or perhaps the effects of old age were catching up with someone who supported a houseful of missionaries and acted as mother for her grandson and Alexander Wylie's daughter. The mission compound would have been like a nursery that year, for in addition to the four Medhurst grandchildren aged three and under there were Dr Lockhart's son and daughter, both under three, William Milne's four-year-old son and one-year-old daughter, and Wylie's daughter aged one.

Eliza's reunion with Augusta had Augusta crying in excitement, but she soon recovered and fussed over her nephews, who called her Aunt Busta. The Lockharts, the Milnes and other members of the mission were all keen to come and see Eliza and her family and she gave Martha her opinions on each of them. She was 'only grieved to see that man Stronach have such an influence over our father and alas! – not for good'. Without any other opinions recorded of John Stronach, this leaves one to assume that Eliza was a very expressive person who did not hold back on her opinions.

Walter junior was required to spend much of December, including Christmas, in Ningbo, leaving Eliza to bear the brunt of what she called Mama's exacting and fault-finding disposition, claiming she treated her like a ten-year-old child while holding her absent children on a pedestal. She wrote to Martha, 'You are the Cherubim now, I assure you – you never did anything wrong in the whole course of your life and were only surpassed in excellence by dear Sarah. I often pity poor Dustie (Augusta), when she will have the virtues of her three sisters showered upon her devoted head.' She described Dustie as a fine intelligent girl growing strikingly pretty.

A common topic of conversation among the adults that Christmas was the rebellion occurring around Canton. An uprising against the Qing Dynasty had been brewing for several years and around 1849, when famine broke out in Guanxi province, a leader emerged who was able to gather twenty thousand followers and organise them into an armed force that could challenge the imperial troops. The leader's name was Hong Xiuquan and he proclaimed his uprising on 11 January 1851, declaring the formation of the Taiping Heavenly Kingdom. Hong Xiuquan was a thirty-seven-year-old who had received some Christian teaching from Liang Fa, William Milne's assistant in 1814 and ordained by Morrison in 1821. During his travels inland from Canton, Liang Fa had met with Hong and was responsible for converting him to Christianity, even though Hong believed his own variation of the faith. Hong claimed to have received a vision from God and believed he was the brother of Jesus Christ who was sent to rid China of the Manchu rulers and the teachings of Confucius. Apart from following Hong's interpretation of Christianity, the Taipings held strong egalitarian ideas, opposed opium smoking, banned foot binding, and cut off their queues to spite what they saw as a sign of subjugation to the Qing emperors, whom they considered to be foreigners from the old country of Manchuria in China's north. In spite of holding egalitarian ideas, the Taiping rebels were ruthless in their treatment of anyone considered to be on the side of the imperialists, and the loss of life from their conquest and subsequent defeat was staggering. More than twenty million deaths have been estimated over the fifteen-year period of the conflict.

The Europeans in the well-defended island colony of Hong Kong were confident that they were not threatened by the revolt, but they held concerns about the spread of the conflict, which could endanger the mainland trading ports including Fuchow, Amoy and Shanghai. So far, the foreigners in Canton had been left well alone, but the lives and businesses of their Chinese colleagues had been disrupted and many people had disappeared without trace.

Walter junior, his son, his sister Eliza, and her children left for Hong Kong on 1 February 1852, sailing on the *Island Queen*, Walter to take up his new position as Chinese secretary and Eliza to return to her husband Charles, now the chief magistrate. The *Island Queen* was anchored down river at Woosung but since it was blowing a heavy gale and snowing, no boat would take them, so they were forced to go overland by sedan chairs. Walter and William Milne went with them and each adult carried a child on their laps as they set out on what was normally no more than an hour's journey. Two hours later, they arrived at the dock, exhausted and nearly frozen, for the crossing to the ship's anchorage. Eventually they boarded and were delighted to find a bright fire burning in the cabin and the crew preparing a hot dinner. Eliza confessed what a great trial it was parting from her father, saying that she could not bear to think about it. Fortunately, the wind dropped and a boat was found to return Walter senior and William Milne to Shanghai. The *Island Queen* set sail the following morning and soon left the cold weather behind, reaching Hong Kong in seven days.

No sooner had Eliza settled back in Hong Kong than word came that Powell had taken a position with a trading company in Batavia and he and Martha were leaving England again. The British papers announced that the partnership between George Saul and Robert Powell Saul of Saint Helens, coal proprietors, had been dissolved as of 1 April.[4] Eliza wrote a letter to Martha, to be delivered via their Aunt Sophia in Singapore, sharing happy childhood memories of Batavia, expressing the hope that they might be able to see each other soon. She also revealed that her doctor strongly recommended that she return to England for the good of her health and that Charles was trying to obtain leave so that the whole family might make the trip. Just one month later, she again wrote to Singapore to announce that they were going to England via Singapore and begged Martha to wait there so that they could meet again. Unfortunately, the delays in communicating over such distances meant that the messages passed each other at sea and, in July, when the Hilliers reached Singapore, the Sauls had already left for Batavia.

The Hilliers arrived in England in September, going to stay with Charles's brother Edward in Bury St Edmonds. Charles had just one month before he had to return to Hong Kong, but Eliza and the children would end up spending almost three years in England before she returned to the East.

29

THE TAIPING REBELLION

During these years, the living conditions of the missionaries improved considerably from what they had experienced in 1843. They now lived in European style homes rather than the native houses. Shanghai was served with regular steamer services from Hong Kong via which they could source almost every product and service available in the West. Their diet and hygiene had improved and even though they faced greater risks to their health than would be the case in nineteenth-century England, life was much more secure than it had been.

The same could not be said for the rest of China, however. The country had always suffered from natural disasters such as floods, famine and earthquakes but as the population expanded, the governing political and economic order could not keep pace with the population growth. Peasant farms were divided into smaller and smaller lots each generation, such that in a poor season, a family could not produce enough to survive. The overcrowding of farms and villages led to a decline in the supply of clean water, creating health problems and increasing the spread of infectious diseases. The machinery of government had not kept pace with the population and by the mid-nineteenth century, it was estimated that a magistrate, the lowest level official responsible for all local administration, might be responsible for as many as two hundred and fifty thousand people. Small wonder that when real crises came, officials in government were powerless to avoid them, and people had nothing to fall back on except for meagre donations and national and international relief efforts, which reached few people. Added to this was the scourge of opium addiction, which affected a huge percentage of the population at all levels, especially in urban areas. Besides being a drain on the country's financial resources, the distribution of opium attracted crime and corruption, leading to a breakdown of law and order.

The situation gave rise to the formation of numerous rebel groups, which called for a revolution of the political and economic organisation in the country. This had happened before but never had such a rebellion led to the people's deliverance from oppression and misrule.

The advance of the rebels in the general direction of Shanghai led to panic in the city. The provincial governor, Wu Taotai, appealed to the foreign consuls for naval support, which was declined in an effort by the foreigners to remain neutral in any internal conflict. The British Government had made little provision for a rebel attack and the solitary British gunboat was about to be recalled south. A message was sent to Hong Kong, the order to withdraw the gunboat was countermanded, and Sir George Bonham, the plenipotentiary, was despatched in the sloop *Hermes* with all available force.

On reaching Shanghai, Sir George Bonham determined to maintain the position of neutrality, although he had to take steps to protect the foreign settlement from the possibility of an invading horde of savages bent on pillage and devastation. He had no wish to support the cause of the imperialists, which to all appearances he considered doomed. There was a level of support for the rebels from the foreign community, including from Walter and his colleagues, but protection of their own interests was paramount.

In order to ascertain the foreign policy position of the rebels, Sir George Bonham sailed to Nanjing in the *Hermes,* along with the Americans in the *Susquehanna,* where the Taipings had set up their capital. Neither the British nor the Americans received a welcoming reception and little was resolved concerning building a relationship with the rebels. The Americans reported that the rebels became so defiant that they executed the Nanjing governor, who had so far been spared, and displayed his head on the city ramparts as a trophy.

When the *Hermes* returned to Shanghai from Nanjing, the interpreter, Mr Meadows, handed Walter a series of documents he had received from the rebels, which described the religious beliefs of the Taipings. These were translated by Walter and published in the *North China Herald,* and newspapers around the world reprinted sections of it. What the documents clearly showed was that the basis of the religion professed by the Taipings was borrowed Christianity. Walter's views were clearly stated in the London newspaper.

The remarks of the Revd Dr Medhurst upon this subject seem to be entirely to the point. 'Questionable though it be,' he observes, 'the form of Christianity which the insurgents profess is far better than the stupid idolatry hitherto practiced by the Chinese. Should the Imperialists, prevail over the insurgents (of which there seems little probability); they will become much more exclusive and insolent than before. They will remember our neutrality, our intercourse with the insurgents and above all, the apparent similarity between our religion and theirs. 'On the other hand,' Mr. Medhurst remarks, 'should the insurrection succeed we may at least expect a perfect toleration for Christian missionaries.' The reverend writer adds truly that this would prove the forerunner of commercial enterprise and scientific improvement throughout the empire. *It is very evident, indeed, from the whole tenor of these despatches that the sympathies of our countrymen in China are in favour of the insurgents.*[1]

This was just one example of the reports that appeared throughout the British and American newspapers in 1853 and 1854. Walter was becoming a household name throughout Britain and the world, and it seemed that the sympathies of the foreign residents in Shanghai were with the rebels.

The fall of Shanghai did not occur as the result of an invasion or a battle, and it was not even taken directly by the Taiping rebels. An insurgent horde, under the banner of the Small Sword Society, an offshoot of the Triads, entered Shanghai on 7 September 1853, killed the few guards on duty and the district magistrate, and took over the city. Wu Taotai escaped over the wall and sheltered in the settlement with some American friends. Any of the city's residents who could leave did so, reducing the population by two-thirds, while the foreign settlement began to fill with refugees. The insurgents consisted mainly of men from the southern provinces and included some foreign mercenaries, deserters from ships and Straits-born Chinese who spoke English fluently. Their leaders now proclaimed the revival of the Ming Dynasty and adherence to the Taipings. Although this was all very confusing to the residents in the settlement, the rebels promised immunity to the foreigners. Since the LMS had two chapels within the walled city at which regular services were held and William Muirhead was resident in the walls, the missionaries had many reasons to continue visiting the city. For this reason, Walter and his colleagues were the first foreigners to enter into discussions with the rebel leaders and they were pleased to find that no objection was made to their passing through the gates.

Back in the British settlement, public meetings were held during the first weeks of April 1853 under the auspices of Consul Alcock, who pointed out that there should be no divided national interest; British, American and French should work together as a single defence force. A defence committee was elected and defence embankments were built around the perimeter of the foreign settlement. On capturing the city, the insurgents compelled all able-bodied men to enlist in their service, but some managed to escape into the foreign settlement. The imperialist troops set up a camp along Soochow Creek and kept a close watch over the native partisans, capturing and decapitating any they caught outside the city walls or in the foreign settlement. Henceforth, the Chinese were in constant terror of being seen on the wrong side of either the insurgents or the imperialists. The accumulation of refugees in squalid shanties added to the dangers of everyday life in the foreign settlement, a place without a police force and patrolled only by the small naval forces of the foreigners.

The missionaries carried on their daily routine as much as they could, but their normal preaching engagements within the city walls were often disrupted. On one of these visits to preach at the chapel, a follower of the Taiping movement stood up to support Dr Medhurst's sermon and exhort the truth and excellence of the Christian religion. Walter's subsequent letter to the *North China Herald*[2] describing this encounter, which was reprinted in newspapers around the world, expressed admiration for the man and his message, even though his description of the Christian faith differed to most established beliefs.

30

SHANGHAI UNDER SIEGE

Having taken over control of Shanghai in September 1853, the insurgents were by the following year under siege by the imperialist forces, making life difficult for those living in the international settlement. Throughout this time, the residents of Shanghai were under constant threat of falling victim to the warring factions of the Taipings and the imperialists. Battles and skirmishes occurred almost daily and occasionally large fires broke out in the city, caused by bombardment from the imperial war junks. Despite the stated position of the foreigners to maintain neutrality between insurgents and imperialists, this was difficult since the foreign settlement was squeezed between the warring factions, described in the *North China Herald* as 'an Imperial rabble on the one side–an Insurgent mob on the other and on the water-face, by a Pirate fleet in Imperial Pay'.[1] The situation was aggravated by the friendly disposition of the foreigners towards the insurgents and the violation of neutrality exhibited by the supply of arms and ammunition by the trading companies. This activity was a source of resentment to the imperialists, who on one occasion crept into the settlement to seize guns and ammunition. A naval group, along with some volunteers, drove them back.

The encampment of around ten thousand imperialist troops stretched along Soochow Creek behind the racetrack to the city walls, encroaching on the foreign settlement, thereby representing a threat to the residents. On 5 April 1854, Dr Medhurst was one of several foreigners against whom the imperialist soldiers made attacks. Joseph Edkins reported the incident to the LMS directors in his letter dated 11 April.

Dr Medhurst was one of those who were wantonly and carelessly attacked by the Mandarin soldiers. He was near the new road recently constructed within the limits assigned to the foreign settlement. It was on the same afternoon (5 April) that numerous attacks were made on other foreigners. Fortunately Dr M was on horseback and escaped with ease from his assailants, ten or twelve in number who tried ineffectively to seize his bridle. The intentions of the soldiers may be known from the fact that one gentleman received seven sword and spear wounds and that he thus suffered in parrying the thrusts aimed at an English lady with whom he was walking. You will join with us with gratitude to God that Dr M was uninjured and that the ruffians were hindered from taking a life so valuable.[2]

Because of these attacks, the whole foreign community was faced with the alternative of retreating to the ships and abandoning Shanghai, or standing and defending the settlement at their own peril against all assailants. The foreigners were clearly of the view that peace in China was too often only achieved by war, and consequently, Consul Alcock issued a demand to the Chinese to remove the camp from within the confines of the foreign settlement, failing which, at 4 p.m. the following afternoon, steps would be taken to enforce this measure. The British and American consuls and naval commanders met the following morning and approved the action of Consul Alcock and an hour before the appointed time, the naval forces, the volunteers and all able-bodied men, including merchant seamen, mustered before the cathedral. At 3.30, the force marched up Nanking Road with drums beating and colours flying. Field guns were brought from the HMS *Encounter*, the HMS *Grecian* and the USS *Plymouth*, to back up two howitzers and a total force of about three hundred men. By the appointed time, the foreign force was ready to attack.

The Chinese sent a despatch saying that the camp was on Chinese soil and promised to prevent any recurrence of the attacks on foreigners. For a reply, the force was ordered to advance and precisely at 4 o'clock, the action began. The British and American forces failed to coordinate their actions but gained position where they could shell the Chinese camp. Eager to reach the camp first, the American commander ordered a charge but came to a sudden halt when they reached a creek too wide to cross. Meanwhile the British found a bridge to cross, successfully flanking the enemy, who were now starting to retreat. By this time, another force was observed advancing from the old city and their red turbans identified them as the insurgent Small Sword rebels, joining the battle in support of the foreigners. The main British naval force, along with the volunteers, took the camp, which encroached on the foreign settlement, setting a fire that quickly spread in the fresh breeze and forced the imperialists to retreat towards Soochow Creek.

The battle was soon over once the imperialist force retreated to what was definitely Chinese territory and they were given to understand that no re-occupation by them would be allowed. The British and American commanders stopped the fighting and the Small Sword soldiers followed suit, ending the encounter. Two foreigners were killed and fifteen wounded, with many Chinese casualties in what was to become known as the Battle of Muddy Flat, a misnomer in view of the fact that the action took place on dry ground. This battle was over, but the war between the Mandarins and the Taipings would continue for several years yet, resulting in a continued threat to Shanghai.

At the beginning of 1854, Walter junior announced that he was to be married on 15 February in Macao to Ann Isabel Rawle, granddaughter of the American Consul. The beautiful nineteen-year-old with a Peruvian mother would have been accustomed to life in a diplomat's family, but she was very young to take over as mother to Walter's son who was now five years old. It was a busy time for Walter junior, who in April gained a new boss when Sir John Bowring was appointed as Governor of Hong Kong. In reaction to the Battle of Muddy Flat, one of the governor's first decisions was to visit Shanghai, along with his Secretary, Walter Medhurst, sailing aboard the HMS *Styx*, which together with HMS *Rattler*, was being sent to replace the *Hermes*. Seeing an opportunity to visit his parents and introduce his new wife to them, Walter arranged for Ann to sail on the *Lady Mary Wood*, which left Hong Kong on 19 May, arriving in Shanghai on 25 May. While staying with the Medhursts, Ann was able to give them the happy news that she was expecting a child in November. Walter was not able to spend much time in Shanghai during the visit as he was ordered to take the *Rattler* on to Nanjing, where it was hoped he might have discussions with the Taiping leadership.

The visit to Nanjing did not bring the success hoped for, with Walter failing to make contact with any of the senior Taipings, and the *Rattler* returned to Shanghai in July 1854. He managed, however, to return with an interesting document entitled 'Important Observations Regarding Celestial Principles', which described the existence and nature of God. The document had a ring of familiarity about it, which prompted the young diplomat to ask his father to translate it and determine the origin of its ideas. When translated, the document extended to over seven thousand English words, but a cursory look by his father was enough for him to proclaim its origin. 'I composed this pamphlet in Batavia, some twenty years ago,' Walter told his son. 'It was republished in Shanghai ten years ago in the form which has been imitated here by the Taipings. Thank you for bringing this to me as it will be of great value in understanding what they know of the Christian doctrine.' The next few weeks were taken up with a translation of the document from which Walter added a list of omissions, additions and changes from his original composition. He speculated about the reasons for the changes, which helped to create a picture of how the Taipings' ideas differed from accepted Christian beliefs. An obvious omission that 'God is immaterial and invisible' was very significant since if it were included, it would question the claim that Hong Xiuquan had actually met with God. After publishing the translation of the document, along with his remarks about the changes, Walter concluded, 'If this be the doctrine of thieves, it is a very good doctrine and were all thieves to circulate such opinions, we should have little reason to regret their ascendancy.'[3]

With the governor in Shanghai, discussions took place regarding the future of Shanghai. The foreign settlement had survived its first major test, which only proved what a long way they had to go to achieve anything more than an illusion of security. They needed improved administration for the settlement, including a police force, better defence and a common voice for all the residents, British, American and French. Walter Medhurst had been involved in the process of government of the foreign settlement for many years, working with Rutherford Alcock, the British Consul, and sitting on committees for roads, jetties and parks and the committee to manage the Shanghai Cemetery. Now, after the troubles emanating from the civil war, the three consuls met and agreed to the formation of a new municipal council with a range of powers and expectations. At a public meeting on 11 July at the British Consulate, under the auspices of the three consuls, an election was held and the first meeting of the Shanghai Municipal Council was held on 17 July 1854. The first elected councillors were:[4]

William Kay, Chairman
The Revd Dr Medhurst
D.O. King
C.A. Fearon

J. Skinner

W.S. Brown

E. Cunningham

At that first meeting, J. Skinner was appointed Chairman of the Roads, Jetties and Police Committee and Dr Medhurst was appointed to chair the Taxation and Finance Committee. The first municipal budget amounted to $25,000, of which $14,000 was to be expended on the police, leaving little for the construction of roads and municipal improvements. The service of Mr S. Clifton, an ex-army man who had served as inspector of police in Hong Kong, was secured as Superintendent of Police at a salary of $150 per month. The estimate for lighting the streets with oil lamps was $12 a month and a similar amount was appropriated for sanitation. In October, a special land renters' meeting was held to obtain permission for borrowing $12,500 for the erection of police barracks. The land renters were generally opposed to raising loans or increasing taxation but a small majority, eighteen votes in favour and fifteen against, supported this sanction.

It is interesting to compare that first meeting of seven councillors with the meeting a hundred and two years later, starting on the same day in July 1956, of the First CPC Shanghai Municipal Congress. This was held for over seven hundred official delegates, eighty alternate delegates and almost two hundred observers on behalf of a hundred and fifty thousand party members in the city, with the meetings extending over fifteen days. The annual budget was not disclosed.

Throughout the time that the walled city of Shanghai was under siege, the missionaries carried on their daily routine as much as they could. In a letter dated October 1854, Walter Medhurst wrote how they visited the city almost every day to conduct religious services at the two chapels belonging to the society. 'On visiting the city for these purposes, cannon balls frequently passed over our heads in very dangerous and alarming proximity, while some have been lodged in both our chapels; yet we have been mercifully preserved.'[5] In accordance with the doctrines of the Taipings, the rebel leaders issued proclamations to remove idols and to worship only the one true God. The second in command, with his followers, became regular visitors to the services held in Fukien at the LMS chapel. Of greater attention to the missionaries was the opportunity to minister to the distressed poor of the city, of whom there were many. Thanks to a few benevolent foreigners, the missionaries were able to supply hundreds with a pittance of rice three times a week and to distribute a few pence weekly to help keep these people alive. Three women were admitted into the Church by baptism on 17 September while the bombardment of the city went on around them. About the same time, back at the mission centre, a group of graduates from Mr Muirhead's boys' school, and Walter's Chinese teacher Wang T'ao, were also baptised. Both Wang and his father had worked with Walter on the Delegates' translation of the Bible. Wang senior had fallen ill and died soon after the translation was completed, firmly attached to his Confucian beliefs. As his son assisted Walter in his translations, the subject of the material he was translating aroused his interest. Wang T'ao spent many years working with the missionaries of the LMS and his later career as journalist and publisher influenced the reform of China during the late nineteenth century.[6]

Ann Medhurst spent two months in Shanghai with the Medhursts, occasionally managing to see her husband for brief periods between his government duties. Although Augusta was only fourteen, she was mature for her age and she and Ann became friends. By the end of July, the governor and his secretary had left Shanghai so Ann returned to Hong Kong, looking forward to the birth of their first child in November. Unfortunately, a familiar tragedy, which appeared to stalk poor Walter, struck again, when his young wife gave birth on 8 November to a daughter who died the next day on Ann's twenty-first birthday. On the same day, the foreign office made an announcement about her husband, which read as follows:

FOREIGN OFFICE. NOVEMBER 9TH 1854
THE QUEEN HAS BEEN GRACIOUSLY PLEASED TO
APPOINT WALTER H. MEDHURST, ESQ., TO BE HER
MAJESTY'S CONSUL TO FOO-CHOW-FOO.[7]

This announcement would normally be the excuse for much celebration, but the loss of another Medhurst baby placed an enormous cloud over their lives. The birth took place at Ann's parents' home in Macao and the baby's headstone can still be found today in the Old Protestant Cemetery in Macao. Walter took up his appointment in Fuzhou, leaving his wife with her parents, where her health continued to decline. In an attempt to improve her recovery, they took her on a sea voyage to Singapore, but to no avail as she died there on the 13 February 1855. Walter, once more a widower, immersed himself in his work in an attempt to overcome his loneliness.

As Walter was leaving Macao for Fuzhou, his sister Eliza was about to return from England, along with her daughter Maude, having left her three sons with the family in England so that they could continue their schooling. This time, she had arranged in advance with Martha to rendezvous in Singapore and although their meeting was short, they filled every minute catching up on all that had happened over the past four years. Afterwards, Eliza wrote that it seemed like a dream that they met. Although she was disappointed that Walter had left by the time she reached Hong Kong, Eliza was overjoyed to be reunited with Charles and he was so keen that he scrambled on board before the ship's anchor was down. Their reunion was to have the happy consequence that she was expecting another child the following January. No sooner had she discovered she was pregnant, Martha wrote to say that she was expecting a fourth child in the same month.

·31

TRIUMPH AND TRAGEDY

After striving in vain to defeat the rebels holding Shanghai, the imperial forces finally found an ally in the French. The British and the Americans were determined to remain neutral in the conflict and the position of the British and American residents had generally been favourable towards the Taipings. The Taiping doctrines covered a mixture of traditional Chinese beliefs, basic socialism and Protestant Christianity. They were absolutely opposed to idolatry and in this, they included the Catholic Church, placing them in opposition to the French. Success for the Heavenly Kingdom would strike a great blow against the Catholic Church, so the French Consul determined that it was very much in France's interest to see that the imperial forces came out on top. A deal was struck for the French to increase their territory in the foreign settlement if assistance from France resulted in an imperialist victory. Accordingly, the French forces, although small and unable to make an assault on the city, staged attacks and effectively blockaded the city.

On 31 January 1855, Walter wrote the following report of their perilous situation to the directors:

The war, which has so long carried on around us, has now approached to our very doors. Ever since the commencement of the siege of Shanghai, the Imperialists were not permitted to come within the precincts of the foreign ground to carry on their military operations, but now they have been allowed to erect a battery between our houses and the rebel city, so close that if the rebels fired upon them the shots must necessarily fall among our own dwellings. A week ago a shell was thrown directly into Dr Lockhart's hospital, where it burst and filled the whole building with smoke. Providentially no one was hurt, though there were about 50 people in the hospital at the time. Since then a bullet has been fired into Mr Edkins's room and we are in continual danger of being struck by these winged messengers of death. The only thing that prevents the rebels from firing more frequently (which would make our residences absolutely untenable) is that they are short of powder and cannot afford to throw away a single shot. The city is now so besieged very closely so that no one can go out or come in; famine now threatens the inhabitants of the city and they must either submit or starve. A few days more will perhaps bring matters to a crisis, when we anticipate a dreadful carnage among the poor and principally unoffending inhabitants of the city. We pray daily for our personal preservation and that the calamities we see about to come upon others may be averted.[1]

On the evening of 17 February 1855, in spite of the war going on all around them, the people of Shanghai, including the rebels, the imperialists and the refugees in the foreign settlements, were determined to farewell the calamitous year of the Tiger and with an optimistic hope for a new start, they welcomed in the year of the Rabbit. Augusta was allowed to stay up late and go up to the roof at the back of their house to join her amah and the houseboys watching the salvos of fireworks, which resounded throughout the city. The Chinese servants added to the cacophony by setting off their own fireworks on the roof, including Catherine wheels, fiery fountains, waterfalls, and jumping crackers. A smoky haze veiled the walled city, but Augusta could still see fireworks and rockets erupting from the area of the Garden of Ease, the headquarters of the Small Swords. Concerned about the possibility of shellfire continuing in spite of the celebrations, Walter joined his daughter on the roof, being ready to bring her back into the house at the slightest sign of danger. All looked peaceful, however, as the flashing lights of firecrackers came from almost every direction, including within the imperialist camp. From within the foreign settlement, flashes from long strings of firecrackers illuminated the shacks of the refugees with their crackling sounds echoing off the buildings to the squeals of laughter from children and adults alike. It seemed like any other Chinese New Year.

The sounds of the celebrations continued until well after midnight and the whole city glowed with incandescence under clouds of coloured smoke. Revellers who stayed up until the small hours would have wondered why the glow from the walled city continued and towards dawn seemed to increase. When dawn arrived, the alarm was raised; the walled city was on fire. Residents in the foreign settlement arose to see thick black smoke coming from the timber buildings of the old city, under which crimson flames soared up into the clouds. Added to the sounds of the crackling firestorm came the unmistakable reports of gunfire and the cries of men. The Small Sword rebels, knowing that they could no longer survive the blockade and the cannon of the French, had put the torch to the eastern district and staged a break-out from the city. Catching the imperial troops unawares, the Small Swords attacked through their ranks in an attempt to break out southward and disperse into the countryside to join up with the Taipings. Close-quarter fighting saw the flashing of steel and the orange flares of muskets as two thousand rebels attempted to hack their way to freedom. Belatedly, the French naval batteries came into action, firing on the former hideout of the rebels. When the imperial troops entered the walled city and drove back the remaining rebels, they were shown no mercy. Every rebel soldier was dragged into the square, where an executioner wielded a two-handed scimitar to behead the poor victim. No one was spared and the square was reported to be full of severed heads, the flagstones greasy with blood. When a rebel soldier was reported to have hidden in a coffin, the imperial commander ordered all coffins to be opened and everybody beheaded.

The emperor's troops killed more people and destroyed more property than the Small Swords rebels had done in a year and a half. More than a thousand civilians were accused of supporting the rebels and summarily executed in the square, and but for the presence of the French Admiral Laguerre, the imperialist soldiers would have plundered what was left of the city. The stench and detritus of the slaughter and the ruins of the Eastern buildings presented a grim scene for the survivors, who only wanted to live a peaceful life. Dr Lockhart's hospital at the mission centre was overwhelmed with wounded from both sides. It was reported that during 1854, the hospital treated over twelve thousand patients, resulting in respect by both sides for the mission centre and the missionaries.

In spite of all the terrible carnage and destruction around them, Walter remained optimistic about the prospects for the Shanghai Mission. On 28 May 1855, he wrote, 'We believe that the prospects for the conversion of China were never more bright.'[2] He claimed that the Chinese had an increased respect for foreigners, resulting in a decline in the restrictions previously placed on their travel. He and Joseph Edkins had travelled a hundred miles west of Shanghai in April, distributing tracts and publicly preaching in cities never before visited by Europeans. At least one or two of the missionaries were now regularly absent on these tours. Hundreds now attended the chapels daily and sometimes twice daily. Sunday had ceased to be a special day for services and continual preaching had become their business. Baptisms were increasing and those converted were preaching to their countrymen with zeal and energy.

Meanwhile, Walter junior wrote to his father to persuade him to take some time off and bring his mother and sister Augusta down to Fuzhou for a holiday. The word 'holiday' was not in Walter Medhurst's vocabulary but he was persuaded to make the trip with his family. This would be the first time Betty had left Shanghai in the twelve years they had lived there. As a fourteen-year-old, Augusta was excited to be going on a sea voyage and looking forward to staying with her brother at Government House. No doubt Walter relaxed and enjoyed his visit with his son in Fuzhou but that is not apparent from the letter he wrote to the directors. He outlined the size and character of the city and the local dialect spoken, and explained the difficulties a new missionary might have in establishing himself in Fuzhou, recommending ways in which that could best be achieved. He said he had many opportunities to speak with the people and had distributed a large number of testaments and tracts.

To return home, the Medhursts were booked to travel in the *Ranee,* when another ship, the *Winton,* arrived in port, also bound for Shanghai. Some friends persuaded them to transfer from the *Ranee* to the *Winton,* which the captain of the former vessel readily agreed to. Both ships left within days of each other but three days out, a severe typhoon occurred and the *Ranee* was wrecked on a reef. Two sailors managed to reach the shore but all other crew and passengers were drowned. After six days, the *Winton* arrived in Shanghai, with the passengers feeling exhausted but thankful to God for preserving their lives.

In his letter informing the directors of their narrow escape, Walter also wrote that the printing of a hundred and fifteen thousand copies of the Chinese Bible was complete. He promised to send copies for the directors to produce at the next annual meeting as the work of the society's missionaries. This really marked the completion of the work that Morrison had started some forty-eight years previously. Walter confessed his satisfaction at being able to say, 'This is done' and 'That is done'. It must surely mark the triumph of his career as a missionary to China.

Unknown to Walter, his son was writing to the secretary of the LMS at the same time:

23 August 1855
Reverend and Dear Sir
I take the liberty of addressing you to beseech your kind services in placing before the Board my request that they should permit my father, Dr Medhurst to return to England for the benefit of his health and to recruit himself after his long residence in this country...

   With every sentiment of respect and esteem both for yourself and the other Members of the Society, believe me, to remain,
Yours faithfully and Sincerely
W.H. Medhurst
Consul[3]

Back in Shanghai, the affairs of the mission centre continued to demand Walter's attention, with two more missionaries, Alexander Williamson and Griffith John, arriving with their wives in September. At this time, a twenty-one-year-old British man, James Hudson Taylor, had also arrived from England and although he was not sent out on behalf of the LMS, he initially lived at the mission centre, from where he commenced a fifty-one-year career as a missionary to China. He went on to take over the remnants of Charles Gutzlaff's organisation, turning it into the China Inland Mission, which established over three hundred mission centres in all the provinces of China and brought eight hundred missionaries to China, resulting in eighteen thousand Christian converts. It was the Shanghai Mission Centre and the young missionaries who passed through it that gave Walter the optimism and enthusiasm for the future of Christianity in China. In addition to the affairs of the mission, Walter's role as a councillor on the Shanghai Municipal Council placed demands on his time.

One overriding passion that Walter had held ever since his arrival in China was the elimination of the opium trade. The trade was officially illegal in China but the authorities ignored infractions, partly because many of the officials were users of the drug themselves. To stimulate discussion and support ending the business, Walter compiled an analysis of the opium trade into China covering the preceding fifty-five years and identified the stakeholders in the trade. He showed how profits had declined due to lower prices resulting from increased supply, and that the Indian Government, the East India Company and others had grown dependent on the revenue from the trade. He described how opium was used, estimated the numbers of Chinese addicted to opium, and presented expert opinion on the effects the drug had on long-term users. He also described the many distressing scenes of victims dying on the streets in China from the effects of the drug. It was a detailed and comprehensive report from which any reader would find it hard not to support the abolition of the trade. By identifying and quantifying the stakeholders in the trade, however, it illustrated the difficulties of imposing any such abolition.

A summary of the report was printed in the *North China Herald* and the full report was added to parliamentary papers, which were presented to the House of Commons in 1857. Unfortunately, the British Government, a second opium war and the end of the Qing dynasty were not enough to terminate the trade in opium and by the twentieth century the import of opium ceased, only to be replaced by Chinese-grown product.

While Walter was trying to solve the opium situation, further problems were brewing for the family in Hong Kong and Batavia.

Charles and Eliza had been invited down to Canton in November to attend a grand ball, held on a chartered steamer. Friends had offered them a place to stay and they were encouraged to take two-year-old Maude with them, which they did. They had a wonderful time with friends and acquaintances at the ball but when they returned to Hong Kong, Maude came down with a severe fever and the doctor was called. The diagnosis was smallpox and for four days, Charles and Eliza took turns at her bedside expecting at any moment that she would be taken from them. She rallied and was soon on the road to recovery, with the doctor saying that he had never met with such a surprising recovery as hers had been. With Eliza being eight months pregnant and Charles frequently in poor health, this was a stressful time for them both.

In Batavia, where such diseases were endemic, Powell had come down with a fever and the infection was severe and fast acting. He succumbed and died on 21 October 1855, leaving Martha seven months pregnant and with three young children to look after. Having no family members to assist her and her husband's business affairs to attend to, she soon realised that she would have to remain in Batavia until after the baby was born. Fortunately, she had many friends to help her and within weeks, messages of support were coming from Hong Kong, Shanghai and Fuzhou. With the likely return of the Medhursts from Shanghai to England, Martha told them that as soon as possible, she would go to Shanghai to return home with them, calling in on the way in Hong Kong. The baby arrived without complication in January, a little girl named Dora Ellen. Martha arranged to leave Batavia by the end of February and left for Shanghai, via Singapore and Hong Kong. She looked forward to seeing her mother and father after an absence of five years and especially to catching up briefly with Charles and Eliza in Hong Kong.

Another sad story awaited Martha in Hong Kong. Eliza had given birth to a son on 22 January, whom they named Hugh, and all had seemed well at first. Eliza and Charles both wrote home excitedly to tell their boys in England that they now had a new brother. Eliza recounted how Maude would sing to 'Tiny Hugh' as she called him and they looked forward to taking him home to England. That was not to be, however, because three weeks later, Hugh became sick and died. Once more, the family took comfort from the belief that Hugh had gone to a better place where they hoped to meet him when their time came. Charles had been put forward for a new position as British Consul to Bangkok. Nothing would be confirmed until royal assent but they nevertheless relied on a possible new beginning to overcome their sadness.

Martha and her four children arrived in Shanghai on 9 April aboard the *Formosa*, which was bringing in a cargo of opium.[4] Walter and Augusta were on the dock waiting to meet Martha and the four children, three of them for the first time. Just as Eliza had observed, Martha was shocked to see how much her father had aged. Aunt Busta was again tearful at the excitement of seeing her sister, nieces and nephew. One month after Martha arrived in Shanghai, she received a letter from Eliza in Hong Kong confirming that Charles had been appointed British Consul in Bangkok. 'Having two brother Consuls,' she wrote, 'you ought to be a very proud little woman.'[5] Walter and Betty would share this pride in seeing their children succeed, having gone through so many trials and tribulations.

The return of Martha with their four grandchildren would have been small comfort to Walter and Betty, considering the reason she was there. They would soon all be travelling to England together, as soon as arrangements were made.

32

HOMEWARD BOUND

Early in 1856, the Medhursts were requested to arrange to hand over the affairs of the Shanghai Mission and return to London. Walter's health had deteriorated significantly, as evidenced by his handwriting in the letter to the directors of 5 April 1856. He still managed a nine-page report of handwritten text covering the activities of the previous six months of the mission's operations, including a description of the latest converts for baptism, but his penmanship was heavy and uneven compared to his previous letters.

Walter enclosed with his report the copy of a letter from the Roman Catholic Bishop of Peking to the Emperor of China in which he pleaded on behalf of a messenger sent by him to Peking in 1854. The messenger had been apprehended by the military and subjected to torture. A section of the letter, which Walter said should be of more serious concern to the directors, was the report that the bishop had travelled in China to within fifty miles of Peking and had met with the magistrate and viceroy of that city. This showed that the French Roman Catholics were permitted to visit Peking with impunity and under the terms of the treaty, Protestants and Englishmen should be entitled to the same rights of ingress. He outlined the case of an English missionary who had been ejected from the island of Changxingxaian, whereas two Roman Catholics were residing there. Walter suggested that they bring these documents to the attention of Lord Clarendon, Britain's Foreign Secretary, so that the matter might be taken up with the Chinese Government.

In May, the Medhursts heard from Eliza in Singapore where she was staying with their Aunt Sophia and her family. Since Charles was establishing a new consulate in Bangkok and servants were almost impossible to hire there, they recruited their domestic staff in Singapore. A follow-up letter from Eliza in June told them that they had to wait six days with the ship at anchor in the mouth of the river that led to Bangkok before a boat was sent to fetch them. By 1 August, they were settled in to their home in Bangkok where they had become reacquainted with the Montigny family, Monsieur Montigny now being the French Ambassador. The Montignys formerly lived in Shanghai and their daughters, Blanche and Mina, were friends of Augusta. They passed on birthday wishes to Augusta, who on that day was turning sixteen. Eliza confessed to feeling down, since poor Charles was unwell and out of sorts.

Walter passed several busy months gradually handing over the affairs of the mission centre and his obligations with the Shanghai Council. Passage was arranged for the whole family to leave Shanghai on the *Anglo-Saxon*, which would take the clipper route around the Cape of Good Hope to London. On the Sunday before leaving, Walter was asked to preach at the Union church in Shanghai, where he spoke to a packed congregation of colleagues and friends. The *North China Herald* published an article praising his achievements, summing up, 'As a Man, as a Scholar, as a Christian Missionary, Dr Medhurst deserves the regard and respect of all men and whether he return to this scene of his labours, or spend the evening of his days in his native country, we trust he will reap that rich harvest of peace, happiness and honour.'[1]

The *Anglo-Saxon* sailed under Captain Laird from Shanghai on 12 September 1856 with Walter, Betty, Augusta, Martha, and

Martha's four children, bound for London. Walter and Betty knew this marked the end of their quest to make a difference in the most populous country of the world. Had they made a difference, or would China continue as if they had never been there? Only time would tell. Walter and Betty had to farewell their many good friends and colleagues, knowing that they would probably not meet again in this life. For Augusta it would be the start of a new and exciting chapter in her life and for the grandchildren, it would be just another adventure. The ship's journey around the Cape was very dependent on favourable winds, the fastest ships completing the journey in around a hundred days. The *Anglo-Saxon* was not one of the faster ships, however, and the winds were not favourable, resulting in the Medhursts being confined to the wooden walls of their cabins for a hundred and thirty-one days.

At the time of their sailing, Charles Hillier had fallen ill with a bout of dysentery in Bangkok. For several days, he struggled with his work, dictating dispatches to Eliza, his health rapidly deteriorating. Without any response to the medical treatment and feeling that he might never recover, Charles felt sure that his only hope was to leave the oppressive heat of Bangkok and take a voyage out to sea. A large American clipper was found to be at anchorage off the coast and arrangements were made to take Charles back down the river and out to the ship, a transfer that took nine hours. The results were positive and after a week on board the ship, his health improved. On 27 September, his doctor returned, along with dispatches requesting that, if possible, the consul return to Bangkok. Charles became concerned that he should be back at the consulate and sought his doctor's permission to return, to which the doctor objected strongly. Eventually the doctor agreed to allow Charles to return to work for a few days and the transfer was made on the next available tide at three in the morning.

The return to work resulted in another attack of dysentery and a week later the doctor advised that Charles should be immediately removed to the ship. Again, they travelled down the river and Eliza confessed that she felt that Charles was far weaker now than on the previous trip. The next day Charles appeared to be suffering even more but on the second day, he passed what appeared to be tumour, which may have formed in his stomach. The doctor was very anxious about his health and insisted that Charles return to England as soon as he could bear the journey to Singapore. The very thought of returning home seemed to revive Charles, even though he felt disappointment at leaving a career which had only just started for him. Another week passed during which Charles showed signs of improvement, but his strength did not come back and he continued to control the pain with morphine. Eliza became his constant nurse, trying to encourage him to eat and dispensing medicines as instructed by the doctor, but he just seemed to be wasting away. On 18 October, he finally succumbed and passed away. For the third time in two years, one of the Medhurst children had experienced widowhood.

Eliza had no option but to sell everything and return to England. She spent two weeks with her aunt in Singapore and left by the overland route in late November, travelling by hybrid steam and sailing ship via Egypt and the Mediterranean. She arrived in London a few days before her parents were scheduled to arrive. Only then would they receive the sad news about Charles.

On board the *Anglo-Saxon*, Walter's health was also deteriorating. He tried to continue with his work of writing and translating until Betty insisted that he should restrict his time to rest and the occasional walk on deck. As they approached the English coast, his spirits lifted and he longed to step ashore in his homeland once more.

They landed at Southend on the evening of 21 January and the following day Walter took his first train journey on the new railway line to London. Lodgings had been arranged at 17 Cambridge Street in Pimlico where Walter arrived in a state of exhaustion. Adding to the physical problems Walter faced, he received the dreadful news that Charles had died and that Eliza had returned to England and was now staying with her sister-in-law in Cambridge. A doctor was called to the house on Friday and he came again on the Saturday, but to no avail. Walter fell into a coma on Saturday afternoon and at 8.30 p.m. on 24 January, he quietly passed away.

The LMS arranged a public funeral and he was buried at the Abney Park Cemetery in North London on 30 January 1857, where his epitaph reads, 'Forty Years a Missionary to the Chinese'. By coincidence, the first missionary of the LMS, Dr Morrison, embarked for China on 31 January 1807 and Dr Medhurst was buried on 30 January 1857. Thus was completed the cycle of the first fifty years of the Protestant Mission to China.

EPILOGUE

Walter Medhurst had never placed any emphasis on financial security for his family and it appeared that the LMS required some prompting to provide security for his widow and Augusta. A report in the British newspapers quoted a letter from the Bishop of Victoria (Hong Kong) to the secretary of the LMS in which he says:

It is scarcely necessary that I should remind you that our lamented friend might, if he had chosen, have left his widow in circumstances of affluence. He declined the offer of the British Government to fill a situation, with nearly £1,000 a year, as interpreter and preferred labouring as a missionary on the limited stipend furnished by your society. A few friends, who hold in the highest honour and esteem his character and labours and who feel the forcible claims of his widow and bereaved daughter, have determined to use their influence in raising a sufficient amount to insure an annuity adequate for the comfortable support of Mrs Medhurst.[1]

The directors of the LMS decided to contribute the sum of 200 guineas, the committee of the British and Foreign Bible Society generously made a grant of £200 and the committee of the Religious Tract Society donated £100. Several friends who managed trading companies in China and who had valued Walter's labours likewise made generous contributions.

According to the 1861 census, Betty and Augusta were living with Martha and her children in Bedford and Eliza and her five children were living close by. Eliza had given birth to a son in March 1857. Another tragedy had hit the family only two months after Walter's death when Walter junior's eight-year-old son died of whooping cough in Cambridge. In 1862, Eliza was given an opportunity to send her boys to Blundell's School and she moved to Tiverton in Devon. In 1864, she married Charles Marshall-Hole, a local solicitor with whom she had two more children. By the 1871 census, we see that Betty, Augusta and Martha had all moved to Devon. Betty would remain there for the rest of her life, dying in Newton Abbott at the age of seventy-nine.

Walter junior returned to England in 1858 and married Juliana Burningham, with whom he had three children. He retired from consular service in 1877 and was knighted by Queen Victoria for his services. In 1881, he took part in the foundation of the British North Borneo Company, which he ran from Hong Kong until 1884, when he and his wife retired to Torquay, where he died in 1885, aged sixty-three. Martha remained single and lived on in Devon until 1890.

Augusta travelled extensively through Europe as a lady's companion until she met and married the Revd Jonathan Bates in 1875 and moved to Kirstead in Norfolk. She and Jonathan had two children, Jonathan and Violet, but unfortunately, what seemed to be the curse of the Medhurst children struck again. The Revd Bates died when his children were both under three years of age. Augusta did not remarry and lived to the grand age of eighty-five, living in the home of her son and grandchildren until 1926.

What of Walter's legacy in China? Had he made any difference? There was not a lot to show for his efforts by the time he left China but he laid the foundations for significant success for the future. According to the 2010 Chinese Spiritual Life Survey conducted by Dr Yang Fenggang, of Purdue University's Center on Religion and Chinese Society, there were forty million Protestants in China. The Chinese hospital, which he and William Lockhart started, went on to become the Renji Hospital, with a thousand six hundred beds, two thousand six hundred and fifty employees, treating over two million emergency and outpatients per year. The City of Shanghai is now one of the largest cities in the world and its modern city centre started from the international settlement of which Walter was one of its first councillors. The printing works, which the Shanghai Mission set up, was the first time that typography was used in China, compared to the thousand-year-old technology of printing blocks used at that time. The introduction of the first font of Chinese type proved to be an important factor in transforming Chinese society. The Delegates' translation of the Bible was widely used by most of the Protestant churches from 1853 until the publication of the Union Bible in 1919.

Had he made a difference? Yes, he had.

NOTES

2 Ross-on-Wye

1. *The Hereford Journal* 11 July 1804
2. Pat Hughes & Heather Hurley, *The Story of Ross* (Herefordshire: Logaston Press, 1999), p. 118
3. G. Medhurst, *A New System of Inland Conveyance* (London, 1826)

3 St Paul's School

1. A. H. Mead, *A Miraculous Draught of Fishes* (London: James & James, 1990), p. 53

4 South India

1. House of Commons parliamentary papers: nineteenth century, 1801–1900. Tanjore debts. The ninth report of the commissioners appointed under an agreement, concluded on the 11th February 1824, between the East India Company and the private creditors of His Late Highness Ameer Sing, formerly Rajah of Tanjore. 1833 (104) XVII, p. 34
2. W. J. Wilson, *History of the Madras Army, Vol. 2* (Madras Govt. Press, 1882), p. 350
3. W. J. Wilson, *History of the Madras Army, Vol. 3* (Madras Govt. Press, 1883), p. 100

5 Trouble in Madras

1. S. Taylor, *Storm and Conquest* (Faber & Faber, 2007), p. 140
2. No fewer than fifteen ships were lost: seven disappeared in the hurricanes which swept the Indian Ocean that year, two went aground and six were captured by French frigates.
3. S. Taylor, *Storm and Conquest*, p. 268

6 The Mission Chapel, Blacktown

1. C. M. Birrell, The Life of the Revd Richrd Knill (London: James Nisbet & Co., 1860), p. 65

7 Gloucester

1. J. A. Benwell, *Sunday Home Magazine 1857*, Memorial on p. 325
2. *Memoir of the Late Revd Dr Medhurst* (Cornell University Library, Wason Pamphlet Collection), p. 163
3. *Ibid.*
4. *Cheltenham Chronicle*, 15 February 1816

8 London Missionary Society

1. CWM/LMS Archives, SOAS University of London, Letter dated 29 August 1816
2. B. Harrison, *Waiting for China* (Hong Kong University Press, 1979), p. 31
3. CWM/LMS Archives, SOAS University of London
4. *Ibid.*
5. *Ibid.*
6. SOAS Archives. Ref. CWM/LMS/South India. Tamil/Incoming correspondence/ Box 1

9 Journey to Malacca

1. B. Harrison, *Waiting for China* (Hong Kong University Press, 1979), p. 9
2. *Ibid.*, p. 12
3. *Ibid.*, p. 15
4. *Ibid.*, p. 16
5. *Ibid.*, p. 21

10 Malacca

1. B. Harrison, *Waiting for China* (Hong Kong University Press, 1979), p. 12
2. W. Milne, *A Retrospect of the First 10 years of the Protestant Mission, Malacca 1820*, (Anglo-Chinese Press), p. 195
3. W. H. Medhurst, *China: Its State and Prospects* (London: John Snow, 1838), p. 311
4. Milne, *A Retrospect of the First 10 Years of the Protestant Mission*, p. 213
5. Harrison, *Waiting for China*, p. 39
6. *Ibid.*, p. 42

11 Anglo-Chinese College

1. CWM/LMS Archives, SOAS University of London
2. CWM/LMS Archives, SOAS University of London, Letter to Col. Bannerman 4 April 1819

3. Milne, *A Retrospect of the First 10 Years*, p. 221
4. CWM/LMS Archives, SOAS University of London
5. Medhurst, *China: Its State and Prospects*, p. 314
6. B. Harrison, *Waiting for China*, p. 63
7. 'The Chinese Name for Australia', Canberra 2013

12 Penang

1. CWM/LMS Archives, Penang Journal, SOAS University of London
2. *Ibid.*
3. *Ibid.*

13 Arrival in Batavia

1. CWM/LMS Archives, SOAS University of London
2. W. H. Medhurst, *China: Its State and Prospects* (London: John Snow, 1838), p. 332

14 Tyerman and Bennet

1. CWM/LMS Archives, SOAS University of London Letter dated 8/9/1825
2. J. Montgomery, *Voyages and Travels Round the World* (London: John Snow, 1841), pp. 197–210

15 Java, Siam and Borneo

1. Mary Morrison, *Memoirs of Robert Morrison DD*, Vol. II (London: Longmans, 1839), p. 351
2. W. H. Medhurst, *China: Its State and Prospects* (London: John Snow, 1838)
3. Reisverhaal van Zendeling Gutzlaff, 11 Sept 1826–12 Feb 1827, NZG Archives, Kast, 19 No.1, Doss.G.
4. *Evangelical Magazine* 1829, pp. 512–14
5. *The Chinese Repository* (Canton, 1833), p. 227
6. WHM Journal, SOAS

16 Built to Last

1. CWM/LMS Archives, SOAS University of London, Letter dated 5 August 1830
2. G. R. Williamson, *Memoir of the Revd David Abeel, DD* (New York, 1849), p. 86
3. CWM/LMS Archives, First Annual Report of the Committee and AGM held at the English Chapel, Parapattan, 13 March 1834

17 Finally to China

1. *The Chinese Repository* (Canton, 1835–36), pp. 310–11
2. W. H. Medhurst, *China: Its State and Prospects* (London: John Snow, 1838), p. 451

18 Home and Home Again
1. *The Hobart Town Courier*, 3 February 1837
2. Gloucestershire Archives

19 England
1. *The Bristol Mercury* 24 September 1836
2. British Library UK Web Archive. Search Booty Meteorological.

20 Tours of Britain
1. *Missionary Magazine* June 1837, P. 293
2. *Wiltshire Independent* 5 October 1837
3. *Royal Cornwall Gazette* 22 September 1837
4. *Morning Post* 24 November 1837
5. *Morning Chronicle* 1 August 1838
6. *Essex Standard* 27 July 1838

21 Return to Batavia
1. *The Chinese Repository*, Vol. VIII, p. 9
2. R. Bickers, *The Scramble for China* (Allen Lane, 2011), p. 82
3. *Ibid.*, p. 87

22 The First Opium War
1. SOAS Archives, Letter to the Directors from Manila, Milne and Medhurst 21 October 1843
2. From the Library of Congress
3. Now known as New York University
4. SOAS Archives

24 Shanghai
1. R. Bickers, *The Scramble for China* (Allen Lane, 2011), p. 98
2. A. P. Hughes, *Dr William Lockhart, a Short Biography* (SOAS, 1995)

25 Travels within China
1. W. H. Medhurst, *A Glance at the Interior of China* (London: John Snow, 1850)

26 Growth of the Shanghai Mission
1. *Liverpool Mercury*, 7 November 1845
2. SOAS Archives, Hillier family papers
3. *Memoirs of Walter M. Lowrie, Missionary to China* (New York: Carter Brothers, 1849), p. 457
4. *The Evening Mail* 26 February 1847
5. *Gloucester Journal* 23 October 1847

28 *The Mission Family and the Medhurst Family*
1. SOAS Archives
2. SOAS Archives
3. Hillier family archives
4. *Perry's Bankrupt Gazette* 17 April 1852

29 *The Taiping Rebellion*
1. *The Morning Post* Tuesday 30 August 1853
2. *North China Herald* 26 November 1853

30 *Shanghai under Siege*
1. *North China Herald* 8 April 1854
2. SOAS Archives
3. Shanghae Almanac, *North China Herald* (Shanghae, 1856)
4. Minutes of Shanghai Municipal Council Volume 1 (Shanghai Classic Publishing House)
5. *Missionary Magazine* March 1855, p. 162
6. P. A. Cohen, *Between Tradition and Modernity* (Harvard University Press, 1974)
7. *The London Standard* 24 November 1854

31 *Triumph and Tragedy*
1. SOAS Archives
2. *Missionary Magazine* September 1855, p. 552
3. SOAS Archives
4. *North China Herald* 12 April 1856
5. Hillier family archives

32 *Homeward Bound*
1. *North China Herald* 6 September 1856

Epilogue
1. *Bradford Observer* Thursday 21 May 1857

BIBLIOGRAPHY

Books

Bickers, R., *The Scramble for China* (London: Allen Lane, 2011)

Birrell, C. M., *The Life of the Revd Richard Knill* (London: James Nisbet & Co, 1860)

Cohen, P. A., *Between Tradition and Modernity, Wang T'ao and Reform in Late Ch'ing China* (Harvard University Press, 1974)

Dodwell & Miles, *The Officers of the Madras Army* (London: Longman, Orme, Brown & Co., 1838)

Edwards, B. B., *The Missionary Gazetteer* (Boston: William Hyde & Co., 1832)

Harrison, B., *Waiting for China* (Hong Kong University Press, 1979)

Hughes, A. P., *Dr William Lockhart, a Short Biography* (London: SOAS, 1995)

Hughes, P. and H. Hurley, *The Story of Ross* (Herefordshire: Logaston Press, 1999)

Jackson R. P., *Historical Records of the 13th Madras Infantry* (The Naval & Military Press Ltd, 2006)

Lake, A., *Changes and Chances* (Jakarta: All Saints Church, 2004)

Lovett, R., *The History of the London Missionary Society Volume 2* (London: Henry Frowde, 1899)

Lowrie, W., *Memoirs of the Revd Walter M Lowrie* (Philadelphia: Presbyterian Board of Publishers, 1854)

Mead, A. H., *A Miraculous Draught of Fishes* (London: James & James, 1990)

Medhurst, G. A., *New System of Inland Conveyance* (T. Brettell, 1827)

Medhurst, W. H., *China: Its State and Prospects* (London: John Snow, 1838)

Medhurst, W. H., *An Inquiry onto the Proper Mode of Rendering the Word God into the Chinese Language* (Shanghai Mission Press, 1848)

Medhurst, W. H., *A Glance at the Interior of China* (London: John Snow, 1850)

Medhurst, W. H., *Geographical Catechism in Chinese* (Malacca: Anglo-Chinese Press 1819)

Merrillees, S., *Batavia* (Singapore: Archipelago Press, 2000)

Milne, W., *A Retrospect of the First 10 Years of the Protestant Mission* (Malacca: Anglo-Chinese Press, 1820)

Montalto, C. A., *Historic Shanghai* (The Shanghai Mercury Limited, 1909)

Montgomery, J., *Voyages and Travels Around the World* (London: John Snow, 1841)

Morrison, M., *Memoirs of Robert Morrison DD Volume 2* (London: Longmans 1839)

Philo-Sinensis (pseudonym for Medhurst, W. H.), *Notices on Chinese Grammar* (Batavia Mission Press, 1842)

Taylor, S., *Storm and Conquest* (London: Faber & Faber, 2007)

Williamson, G. R., *Memoir of the Revd David Abeel DD* (New York, 1849)

Wilson, W. J., *History of the Madras Army, Volume 2* (Madras Government Press, 1882)

Wilson, W. J., *History of the Madras Army, Volume 3* (Madras Government Press, 1883)

Wylie, A., *Memorials of Protestant Missionaries to the Chinese* (Shanghai: American Presbyterian Mission Press, 1867)

Articles, Essays and Dissertations

Bickers, R., [Various articles in the *Oxford Dictionary of National Biography*] (Oxford University Press, 2004–14)

Chang, E. H., 'Converting Chinese Eyes: Revd W. H. Medhurst, "Passing" and the Victorian Vision of China', *A Century of Travel in China, Critical essays on travel writing* (Hong Kong University Press, 2007)

Ching Su, 'The Printing Presses of the London Missionary Society among the Chinese', The School of Library, Archive and Information Studies (University College London, 1996)

Gosling, A., 'Religion and Rebellion in China', *National Library of Australia News* (July 1998)

Jupp, D. L. B., 'The Chinese name for Australia' (2015)

Periodicals

The Chinese Repository. Published in Canton between May 1832 and 1851, initially by the Revd Elijah Bridgman, the first American Protestant missionary in China.

The Evangelical Magazine and Missionary Chronicle. Published monthly by Ward and Co., London.

Bibliography

The Missionary Herald. The publication of the American Board of Commissioners
for Foreign Missions. Crocker and Brewster, Boston.

The Foreign Missionary Chronicle. A publication of the Presbyterian Church and
similar institutions. Robert Carter, New York.

The North China Herald. A weekly newspaper, first published in Shanghai on
3 August 1850.

Other Sources

The Council for World Mission/London Missionary Society Archive. School of
Oriental and African Studies, University of London.

Gloucestershire Archives. Gloucestershire Count Council, Gloucester.

Dr Williams's Library. Research library of English Protestant nonconformity.
Gordon Square, London.

Shanghai Municipal Archives. Shanghai, China.

Andrew Hillier. Hillier family archives.

Panti Asuhan Parapattan. The Parapattan Orphanage in Jakarta, Indonesia.

Revd Andrew Lake. Former Vicar of All Saints, Jakarta.

CSI William Charles Memorial Church. George Town, Chennai, India.

INDEX